For Lisa and Holly

Stephanie Alexander

A Cook's Life

LANTERN

an imprint of

PENGUIN BOOKS

LANTERN

Published by the Penguin Group
Penguin Group (Australia)
250 Camberwell Road, Camberwell, Victoria 3124, Australia
(a division of Pearson Australia Group Pty Ltd)
Penguin Group (USA) Inc.
375 Hudson Street, New York, New York 10014, USA
Penguin Group (Canada)
90 Eglinton Avenue East, Suite 700, Toronto, Canada ON M4P 2Y3
(a division of Pearson Penguin Canada Inc.)
Penguin Books Ltd
80 Strand, London WC2R 0RL England
Penguin Ireland
25 St Stephen's Green, Dublin 2, Ireland
(a division of Penguin Books Ltd)
Penguin Books India Pvt Ltd
11 Community Centre, Panchsheel Park, New Delhi – 110 017, India
Penguin Group (NZ)
67 Apollo Drive, Rosedale, North Shore 0632, New Zealand
(a division of Pearson New Zealand Ltd)
Penguin Books (South Africa) (Pty) Ltd
24 Sturdee Avenue, Rosebank, Johannesburg 2196, South Africa

Penguin Books Ltd, Registered Offices: 80 Strand, London, WC2R 0RL, England

First published by Penguin Books Australia Ltd, 2012

1 3 5 7 9 10 8 6 4 2

Cover design by Daniel New and Evi Oetomo © Penguin Group (Australia)
Text design by Evi Oetomo © Penguin Group (Australia)
Front cover photograph © Anson Smart
Back cover photograph courtesy of Vogue

Excerpt from *Changing* by Liv Ullmann (Weidenfeld & Nicolson, London, 1997) used by permission of Orion.
Foreword by Claudia Roden, originally written for *Stephanie's Seasons* by Stephanie Alexander (Allen & Unwin,
Sydney, 1993), used by permission of Claudia Roden.
Excerpt from *Birds of America* by Mary McCarthy. Copyright © 1971 by Mary McCarthy. Reprinted by permission
of Houghton Mifflin Harcourt Publishing Company and the Mary McCarthy Literary Trust. All rights reserved.
Excerpt from *Friendship: Being ourselves with others* by Graham Little (Scribe Publications, Melbourne, 2000)
used by permission of Scribe Publications.
Extracts from *The Whole Beast: Nose to Tail Eating* © Fergus Henderson, 2004, used by permission of
Bloomsbury Publishing Plc and HarperCollins Publishers.
Excerpt from the Proceedings of the Fourteenth Symposium of Gastronomy (2003) used by permission of
Stefano Manfredi.
Lyrics to 'Everybody's Got to Eat' by Eddie Perfect reproduced by permission of Eddie Perfect.
Every attempt has been made to contact and acknowledge copyright holders; the author and publishers would
be grateful to be notified of any unintentional omissions.

Typeset in Fairfield by Post Pre-press Group, Brisbane, Queensland
Printed and bound in Australia by McPherson's Printing Group, Maryborough, Victoria

National Library of Australia
Cataloguing-in-Publication data:

Alexander, Stephanie, 1940–
A cook's life/Stephanie Alexander.
9781921382789 (hbk.)
Includes index.

641.5092

penguin.com.au

Contents

Introduction .... *page 1*

1 **RICE PUDDING & RAINBOW CAKE**
   Essendon to 1949 .... *page 9*

2 **MUM'S RABBIT PIE**
   Rosebud West 1950–8 .... *page 25*

3 **STRINGY ROASTS & TOO MUCH CHOCOLATE**
   Student Years 1958–60 .... *page 58*

4 **SALADE TAHITIENNE & PAIN POILÂNE**
   Foreign Adventures 1962 .... *page 69*

5 **ACKEE & SALTFISH**
   Monty 1962–4 .... *page 86*

6 **SOLOMON GUNDY**
   Lisa and Jamaica House 1965–8 .... *page 106*

7 **CLANKING MILK BOTTLES & A JAM DOUGHNUT**
   Getting on with Life 1968–71 .... *page 120*

8 **GRILLED TROUT & WILFRED'S POT-AU-FEU**
   Maurice and a New Home 1971–5 .... *page 126*

9 **RADISHES WITH BUTTER**
   The First Stephanie's 1976–8 .... *page 139*

10 **SAUMON À L'OSEILLE**
Inspiration from France's Grand Restaurants 1978–9 .. *page 165*

11 **BEEF ON A STRING**
The Second Stephanie's 1980 .... *page 174*

12 **DUCK GIZZARDS & SOME HEROES**
Eye-opening Experiences of the Eighties .... *page 189*

13 **SNIPS, SNAILS & TAILS**
The Symposium of Gastronomy and Meeting Maggie .. *page 207*

14 **A SPODE TEA SET & A LOAF OF BREAD**
Loss and Starting to Write 1980–7 .... *page 213*

15 **NEW SEASON'S OLIVE OIL**
Family Life, Travel and the Road
to Recession 1987–9 .... *page 224*

16 **CRABAPPLE TART & A SQUEEZE OF CALAMANSI**
High Expectations in the Nineties .... *page 243*

17 **A IS FOR APPLE**
The Cook's Companion 1992–6 .... *page 267*

18 **ELDERFLOWER FRITTERS**
Tuscany, Richmond Hill and the Last Big Bash .... *page 277*

19 **JERK PORK & DUCK FAT**
Family and the New Millennium .... *page 292*

20 **SILVERBEET & SALAD LEAVES**
The Kitchen Garden Project 2001– .... *page 301*

21 **PINNED FISH AND YABBIE & YALKA WONTONS**
Brain Food, Bush Food and the New Gastronomy ... *page 316*

22 **CUPCAKE MEMORIES**
My Seventieth Year & What Comes Next .... *page 333*

Acknowledgements .... *page 353*

Index .... *page 354*

Introduction

I opened the first page of my mother's unpublished autobiography, 'The Other Half', and read the first few lines.

> As I approach the age of seventy I think it is perhaps time for me to set down the story of my life, making it my project for 1982. But at what point do I begin? I remember the advice that the King of Hearts gave to Alice who asked the same question. 'Begin at the beginning . . . and go on till you come to the end: then stop.' It sounds so succinct and simple, but is it?

What is uncanny is that my own instincts to do something similar have become impossible to resist. At the time of writing these first few lines I have just turned sixty-nine. My mother died at seventy-two. Could it be a fear that my time is about to run out?

I am very disturbed by my loss of short-term memory. I imagine a bowl of melting savoury jelly that I scoop into another container. Bits of it slip between my fingers, in blobs of different sizes, some slipping slowly and others falling quickly with no hope of capture. My memory slips and slides and melts away just like this.

I have kept a collection of notebooks over the years, and in among the shopping lists and the to-do lists are detailed travel notes, and now and then a deeper thought. I wish that I had kept a diary, or been better at keeping letters from friends or lovers. Without them it is the notebooks I rely on to jog my memory. When I reread them the briefest note can take me back to my first glimpse of that tiny square in Paris, or I can see again the whirling dancers at a party on the sand in Tunisia. I can immediately remember the controversy around some important decision, the issues that were important at the time, or the finest details of a memorable dish. But without this written record it would all be a blank.

I also have my souvenirs, which are tangible reminders of some important times in my life and wonderful places I have visited. I can serve cheese on a carved wooden platter I bought in Tahiti, or serve soup in some salt-glazed grès stoneware bowls bought in Paris in the early sixties. I can turn salad leaves in the bowl made from beautifully grained olive wood that was given to me by a disapproving relative on the occasion of my first marriage. Or I can merely admire eggshell-fine teacups from Vietnam and a basket made from corn husks bought in Sonoma County in the United States.

Apart from my notebooks it is a great help to be able to read the unpublished memoirs of both my mother and my father. And I am assisted by memories from my daughters, my sister and brothers, and from the friends who were around at different times when I was younger.

My father was a meticulous archivist and almost every experience in his life is documented. In his autobiography he describes himself as a 'compulsive keeper of records' and I have had many occasions to thank him for it. I can read the scripts of radio broadcasts he gave in the thirties in Ballarat, book reviews he penned at the same time, a political and social history pamphlet entitled

Nehru of India, again written sometime in the thirties, as well as day-by-day accounts of his travels. This storehouse of detail is fascinating to my siblings and me but perhaps not to the general reader. He also recorded most of the important family events, along with travelogues of places he and Mum visited, on super 8 film. Later he transferred it all to VHS tapes, believing that the material would be more accessible in this format.

A few years ago I reviewed some of the tapes in preparation for an interview with journalist Peter Thompson for his program *Talking Heads.* The ABC crew wanted family footage. I idly mentioned to the crew that the original super 8 film reels were in an old vinyl bag at the back of the wardrobe. Their eyes lit up. The super 8 film was found to be in pristine condition and, according to Peter Thompson, provided the best home movies they had ever seen. This precious material has now been transferred to DVD and the original reels kept safe.

Similarly my mother was an early chronicler of her own experiences. She writes that her first published piece appeared in June 1951 in *Australian House & Garden,* entitled 'I had a little nut tree . . .' and relating her excitement at harvesting and using the first crop from her almond tree, and that she contributed food pieces to one of Australia's earliest food journals, *Australian Gourmet.* I am struck by how similar my writing style is to hers. Her discursive approach includes a bit of history, a bit of personal anecdote, a bit of travel colour and then rather haphazard instructions. I like to think that my recipe writing is more reliable, but I cannot fault her ability to engage the reader.

I find it fascinating to identify connections between my parents and me. I examine my behaviour or mannerisms and even my health against what seems to have been derived either by nature or nurture from my parents. I keep a running tally and add a certain action or motive or physical failing to one pile or the other. On the Dad pile is my ability to persuade with rhetoric – usually. And a powerful drive to move any project forward. My introversion and introspection fall on the Mum pile, together with a tendency to see the negative side of a proposal before its possibilities. And although I can be melancholy, fortunately I have never been clinically depressed as my father was.

I was dumbstruck by a passage in Mum's memoirs. Before leaving for Japan in 1937 and while still an art student, my mother became convinced that she had discovered an innovative way of teaching art to children that was in direct contradiction to the way it was taught at the time. She needed to find a school that would permit her to try out her theories. Seventy years later I now believe that I have put into practice an innovative way of teaching children all about good, fresh food, and at the start I needed to find a school to put it into practice.

Mum arranged to start her art teaching as soon as she returned from Japan. She did this for a year until she was married. Her central theory was to allow children to express themselves freely using huge sheets of paper, big brushes and pots of bold tempura colour, rather than trying to teach young children adult techniques. 'Just let yourself go' was to be the catch-cry. This idea, while universally followed today, sits oddly with another aspect of my mother's personality. In later years she frequently expressed her suspicion of any behaviour that she regarded as being 'out of control'. And there were occasions when she levelled that criticism at my behaviour.

I can portion up my life by saying I did ten years in libraries for Dad, thirty-plus years of restaurants for Mum, and more than twenty-five years' writing for both of them, and now ten years of giving back to the community, which would have greatly pleased my father.

From Mum I absorbed an awareness and appreciation of culinary diversity and cultural richness. From her also I understand that for a shy person who finds it difficult to shine in a large group, the intimacy of the meal table offers a more comfortable and delicious way of gaining approval and affection and of showing what one could achieve. Slaving away in a restaurant kitchen for more than thirty years does seem a rather extreme way of proving the same thing, however.

I discovered how much enjoyment she received from pattern and shape, landscape and gardens, colour and texture. She often arranged a small still life of a certain vase and a sprig of something from the garden with something surprising – perhaps a treasured souvenir. These little creations were a private pleasure. I know that she was very annoyed when one day, aged about twelve or thirteen, I altered something. She sharply told me, 'When you have your own house, you can arrange your own things.' I was surprised at the time but now understand perfectly. In my bedroom on a small table I arrange and rearrange a clay figure from Mexico with a tiny teacup from Vietnam, a dramatic seed pod from Alice Springs, a smooth bowl from a Japanese potter and many other treasures.

With Dad it was his love of books that influenced me from a very early age. We always had a house full of books, not just a significant collection of early Australian literature but art books, biographies, travel sagas, collections of essays and poetry, and reference books. 'Look it up in the index, Stephanie,' he must have said to me a thousand times. 'What are you reading?' was probably his favourite way to begin a conversation with his children or friends.

Music was my father's other great love and in this area I let him down. Once television arrived, Dad found he had to build a retreat where he could play classical music. We had just one living room, and with four children transfixed by this new medium, he hadn't a hope. It meant that I grew up without music enveloping me each day as it did him and I regret this. The music room was his sanctuary and classical music was such a pleasure to him right up to the end of his life.

I have always felt that an understanding of what has gone before is an essential starting point for those wishing to forge new ground. One of the motives for writing this book is to record the culinary changes I have lived through, hoping that my account may be of interest to the up-and-coming food practitioners of the new millennium.

I have experienced the full flowering of Australia's food culture. In the early fifties, thanks to the culinary curiosity of my mother, my attention was drawn to the 'new' foods introduced by post-war immigrants. Olive oil and sauerkraut, poppy seeds and broccoli, sausage containing squares of fat and blood, real coffee rather than coffee and chicory essence, sheets of seaweed and smelly cheeses all found their way to the family table before I was in my teens. Only when school friends came to visit and to share a meal and expressed wonder and suspicion at what was on offer did I understand how different our nightly fare was from what they were used to.

As a university student I discovered Melbourne's Queen Victoria Market and saw the high-quality and exciting produce sold by the Chinese stallholders. By the late fifties significant numbers of immigrants from Greece and Italy had transformed Carlton and Brunswick and the wholesale and retail markets. Interested shoppers discovered calamari, octopus and mussels, taramasalata and globe artichokes, fresh ricotta, dried salted codfish and tins of olive oil. Small cafés sprang up and wine was served in coffee cups. The civilising of our liquor laws was in the future. Those who were students or grew up in the late fifties or early sixties learnt to appreciate this colourful and delicious food more or less depending on where they lived and how adventurous they were.

By the mid-sixties the flavours of the Mediterranean had become mainstream. And then in 1975, with the fall of Saigon, Melbourne was again transformed. This time it was mountains of green vegetables that astounded and excited, bundles of lemongrass, chillies and coriander, and a seemingly infinite variety of noodles. The young loved this food – its immediacy, its freshness, its relatively low cost – and it too became mainstream, at least in our cities. There have been other waves of migration from the Middle East, from Africa, from India. With every new influx of migrants the food scene has expanded. Now, at the beginning of a new millennium, the food-loving population in Australian cities and regional centres has the world's flavours to choose from.

Not surprisingly, many professional cooks have borrowed and blended, sometimes brilliantly, sometimes less successfully, until the present day where anything goes. You can eat classic French food, you can eat a Greek, Spanish, Lebanese or Italian meal, you can grab a *pho* or a roasted duck, you can eat a subtle Indian curry or an Afghani meal. Or you can visit one of the current exponents of the new gastronomy and have food that has been prepared in fantastic ways using amazing techniques and revolutionary equipment, and be served dishes where the basic ingredients are hardly recognisable or have been totally transformed. In my opinion, some of these dishes are brilliant, some are unconvincing.

We have come a long way from chops on Monday, sausages on Tuesday, steak on Wednesday, cold cuts on Thursday, fish on Friday, pies on Saturday and a roast on Sunday.

As someone with a public profile, I have been interviewed hundreds of times and I am regularly asked 'What is Australian cuisine?'. The expectation is that this can be summed up in a sentence or two. Of course, the answer is far more complicated, and whole books have been written on the topic. Rarely have commentators

7

wanted to discuss what I believe to be the really special thing about Australian cuisine: the diversity of produce, techniques and traditions available to every cook and derived from our cultural diversity. With almost fifty per cent of the Australian population born elsewhere or having a parent born elsewhere, there are many who have generations of traditional culinary knowledge to influence them. Young professional cooks without such a background have to choose a path to tread and must decide to what extent they will follow, copy, mix or blend.

My friend Helen Murray once described my writing as 'impressionistic' and at the time I wondered if I should take this as a negative comment. I have come to realise that this is indeed an apt description. Despite the melting jelly, with the help of friends and my precious notebooks, I find I can still capture the flavour of the most memorable or significant times, and looked at together they will make some sort of pattern, maybe even offer improved self-knowledge if I dare to be truthful and frank. Writing this memoir has sometimes been uncomfortable as I touch on incidents that are still raw. Sometimes I fear the truth is too painful to expose even to myself. Where necessary I have disguised identities and omitted bits that would hurt others.

Here, then, are my fragments – my memory splashes.

1
Rice Pudding & Rainbow Cake

Essendon to 1949

My mother, born Mary Elizabeth Bell, was the only child of elderly parents. She was born and raised in Henley Beach, a suburb of Adelaide. My maternal grandmother, Emily, was forty-one when Mum was born; there had been two stillborn children beforehand. Mum describes her parents as 'doting'. Her mother was brisk in manner and highly organised. Her father, John, was a shy, silent man, interested only in cricket and in raising prize flowers – carnations at first, moving on to dahlias. His year was dictated by the life cycle of his dahlias. Mum had no knowledge of how the family income was earned, although she had a vague notion that her mother had inherited some money. Her father retired aged fifty and Mum had only a hazy memory of him ever going to work. What did he retire from?

Mum tells of receiving a toy stove for her fourth birthday, which had a tiny firebox she was forbidden to stoke and light. As soon as she was able, she started to make 'treats' (she gives no details of what they were) for the family. For her sixth birthday she received tubes of paints and remembers the tube of Crimson Lake oozing the colour of rich velvet. In fact she admits to loving the raw materials almost as much as she enjoyed their application.

She describes a solitary, lonely childhood and herself as being pathologically shy. She was a voracious reader and hated all sport. Her enthusiasms were poetry, elocution and English literature. Other than these subjects her concentration at school had been minimal. Convinced of her unattractiveness, by eighteen my mother believed that she did not need other people in order to feel content and was certain she was destined to remain a spinster. She found it nearly impossible to relate to most of her contemporaries. For her twenty-first birthday her parents gave her (at her own suggestion) a cottage in the Adelaide Hills named 'The Tryst'. With one or two of her few friends she would spend weekends in the cottage, inventing and experimenting in the kitchen.

In 1934, at the age of twenty-two, encouraged by an acquaintance, she decided to enrol at the School of Fine Arts in North Adelaide, under the direction of F. Millward Grey. This was a seminal moment in her life, marking the first time she found herself with young people with whom she could communicate easily, and she found the experience stimulating. Years later she would refer with fondness to her teacher 'Freddie' who had been central to her discovery of art.

An important London exhibition of art from the Far East was attracting much attention, even as far as Adelaide, and Mum and her fellow students became very interested in this work. Mum started to study and create Japanese-style woodblocks. An undated press cutting from a student exhibition singles out *Blue Crabs* by Mary Bell as showing distinct promise. I have a framed print of *Blue Crabs* hanging in my kitchen and it is a lovely work, with a distinctly Japanese feeling, perhaps due to its soft hazy blue.

Many Chinese masterpieces had been removed to Japan after Japan invaded Manchuria in 1931. Mum plotted with her cousin Betty how to persuade her elderly parents to permit her to travel to

Japan to see some of these treasures for herself. Her successful tactic was to convince her parents they could enjoy a sea voyage to Japan, have a few days in Tokyo, then return home, leaving Mum and Betty to explore Japan at their leisure. Cousin Betty was a lifelong friend of my mother. They had grown up more like sisters in Adelaide and their friendship endured right to the end of Mum's life.

And so the trip took place just as she had planned. It was typical of the unworldliness of my mother and her parents that none of them saw any reason to be wary of visiting Japan in 1937. They knew nothing of world politics. The Anti-Comintern Pact between Japan and Germany was signed in late 1936 and Shanghai was captured by the Japanese as Mum and Cousin Betty were admiring a bronze Boddhisattva stored in a nunnery not far from Nara.

Mum was very impressed with much that she saw in Japan: the landscape, the Zen gardens, the bronze Buddhas, the appointments and meal service in a traditional inn, the exquisite porcelain and the food. On the boat trip to Japan she started experimenting with chopsticks and describes the difficulty of using them with cold buckwheat noodles. But she persisted and became adept. Her souvenirs were dishes and utensils as well as a beautiful kimono. She returned to Japan years later, in 1964, still enchanted with the country.

My father's childhood was spent on a small dairy farm in Poowong, which he described so vividly in his memoirs that one can 'see' the rivers of mud and manure. The family then moved to Ballarat, where he attended school and discovered the works of Mark Twain, H. G. Wells's *The Outline of History* and Hendrik Willem Van Loon's *The Story of Mankind*, all of which had a powerful influence on him. He was fascinated by the big questions. (In 1996, when he was eighty-eight years old, we discussed the development of the

Internet. Dad was excited and saw it as the mechanism for the long-awaited universalisation of knowledge, available to all without restriction of colour, class or creed. He viewed it as the realisation of a far-off dream that his hero, H. G. Wells, had spoken of in the thirties.)

Dad left school at thirteen to help support the family, his first job cleaning in a shoe shop. He always regretted the sudden end to his formal education and throughout his long life took every opportunity to find out more about the world and deepen his understanding of important issues. He worked with his father and older brother Clive as a builder and later in a plaster-sheet factory. The Depression forced Dad's father back to Poowong and Dad took the factory apart piece by piece, successfully selling the pieces and realising enough to begin a new venture. He started a small commercial library in Ballarat, thus reinforcing his lifelong love affair with books. His library included a section for children (unheard of at the time) and I have a copy of a flier he wrote to entice young borrowers:

> Dear Boys and Girls,
> I'm opening a 'Bookworm Library' for you. It is only for children under sixteen years of age. No grown-ups are allowed to belong to it.
>
> I've got books all about my pals Mickey Mouse and Flip the Frog. Then there are Fairy Stories, School Stories, Pirate, Cowboy and Indian yarns, books about wireless and aeroplanes and everything.
>
> It only costs a shilling to be a bookworm and this shilling makes you a member until your sixteenth birthday. You get a Bookworm Badge too.
>
> When you're a member I'll lend you any of my books for a fortnight for threepence each.

Ask Mum and Dad if you can join up straightaway!
Bertie the Bookworm

He also regularly reviewed books on Radio 3BA. Dad often made the point that for so many the Depression meant nothing but misery and hardship and yet he found release from drudgery in a world of ideas.

Dad was a man ahead of his time – by his thirties, at a time when much of Australia adopted a narrow view of the world and looked to England and the church for guidance, he rejected dogma and insisted that the only tenable view was that of the internationalist. He was a lapsed Methodist who could not accept the Christian faith, aghast at what he saw as its hypocrisy and what had been done in its name. As a teenager in Ballarat his social and religious life were intertwined. It was not until he queried a teacher of his Bible class regarding some point of fundamentalist belief and the teacher told him that 'much learning hath made thee mad' that he began to question the teachings of the church. He similarly rejected the view that communism could save the world and instead was inspired by the writings of H. G. Wells, George Bernard Shaw and Tom Paine. 'Having freed myself from acceptance of the Bible, I was in no mood to accept as infallible the writings of Karl Marx,' my father wrote in his memoirs, adding:

> I believe that for a mind to clamp on a dogma and close to all alternative views is a major tragedy, and that the closed mind has caused mankind more suffering that any other human failing.

He believed in a democratic society in which one had an obligation to participate and contribute. He joined the Australian Labor Party (ALP) in the late 1930s and became very politically active. He had no time for those on the left who sneered from the sidelines, rather he believed in working towards solutions. He was equally appalled with the far right of the ALP, which after 1955 was represented by the Democratic Labor Party with its Catholic dominance.

He was a passionate Australian and proud of his pioneer family's achievements, both past and present. My great-great grandparents James and Maria Burchett arrived in Victoria in 1854 just three years after the fledgling state had separated from New South Wales. My great-grandfather Caleb Burchett selected land in Poowong in the foothills of the Strzelecki Ranges in 1876. The family interest in social justice goes back a long way. In 1891 the Women's Petition was presented to the Victorian Parliament with thirty thousand signatures requesting the vote for women. It includes the signatures of two women named Burchett of Poowong.

Every family has its stock of stories that are told over and over again. As a small child I never tired of hearing how my father Winston and his brother Wilfred set out from Poowong in 1936 to see the world. They left Australia on a French cargo boat of the Messageries Maritimes line and the family photo album has an astonishing shot of my father wearing a grass skirt and standing in the doorway of a hut in Tahiti. Wilfred, we were told, was so seasick that the captain of the ship refused to take him any further than Tahiti. This used to be retold with huge guffaws, and later in life I wondered just what had transpired in Tahiti.

After Dad had his own amazing adventures in Europe and India, he headed home, and while onboard the ship *Kamo Maru*, he met my mother, who was returning home from Japan. My mother's reminiscences are of a charming young man with whom she could talk easily. Right away they started discussing books, and to her delight they had read and enjoyed many of the same works. He told her that he was engaged to be married. And she, already smitten and completely inexperienced, made a decision that as she was never likely to fall in love again, she might as well enjoy a full-blown affair.

Of course they fell in love, and soon conversations included thoughts of what might happen 'when we are married'. My father had no idea how he would make this happen, nor did my mother, but they were both determined to be together. Mum returned to Adelaide, and they wrote to each other every day until they could arrange their shared future.

In reminiscing many years later, Dad told me that when the ship docked at Port Melbourne, he was met by both his parents and by Beryl, his fiancée. He pulled his father to one side and announced that he was not going to marry Beryl after all, and that Mum was his bride-to-be. On his father's advice he waited until they returned home before announcing his change of heart to Beryl. Poor Beryl! He did say his conscience was eased a few years later, however, when he heard that Beryl was happily married.

Mum's mother was horrified to learn that her daughter wanted to marry a Victorian. Winston was more or less summoned to Adelaide to be inspected. My mother and father agreed to wait for a year to marry. In the meantime Mum worked as an art teacher and Dad set about opening another subscription library, this time in Ascot Vale, Melbourne. On a trip to Melbourne Mum and her mother bought exquisite brocaded satin for her wedding dress. This dress has since been worn by both my sister and my sister-in-law at their own weddings.

Mum writes compellingly of their early married life spent in two rooms behind the library in Ascot Vale and of how adept she was at creating a two-course meal cooked on a gas ring, with one saucepan holding three containers, which could variously provide soup, steak and kidney pudding and a vegetable.

Within a year a house was being built in Essendon and Mum was pregnant with me. I was born in November 1940. The cream brick-veneer house was designed and built by my father and his brother Clive. My parents moved into the as-yet-uncompleted house when I was still a baby in a pram. They told stories of builders hammering and of me screaming with fear. No-one picked me up to cuddle or soothe me as it was the era of Truby King, a paediatrician from New Zealand whose influential book *Feeding and Care of Baby* was the accepted authority. It counselled all progressive mothers to quickly establish feeding at regimented four-hour intervals and never to lift or comfort a crying baby between feeds. There should be no 'sentimental nonsense' and a baby should be disciplined from birth. It must sleep in its own room with lots of fresh air and all daytime sleeping must be in the open air. In her memoirs my mother writes that she breezily discussed how life would continue 'after the baby is born', assuming that it was just a passing event to be got over and that life would resume as before. (Here I have an uncomfortable flash of recognition as I remember having the same attitude in my firstborn's early months.)

In her memoirs Mum speaks of how in 1943 it was common to speculate on what to do 'when the Japanese reached Melbourne'. Her private fear was that she and Dad might be killed and that I, as their only child at the time, would be a war orphan. She says that she deliberately set about making me as self-sufficient as possible, pressing me to do things for myself, to grow up quickly. She made a little canvas haversack for me, in which some essentials might be carried, in case I was abandoned! On a trip to Darwin a few years ago I read at the memorial to those who died in the Japanese raids that more bombs fell on Darwin than at Pearl Harbor. It must have been a very frightening time.

Diana was born on Boxing Day, 1943. One of the earliest memories I have is staring into a cot in which lay a small baby. This baby girl had her hands wrapped in calico mittens to prevent her tearing at her eczema. I felt a welling of rage. This was my new sister and I was just over three years old. I did not want a sister – or anyone else really.

Diana was a delicate child. She had asthma as well as eczema, later contracted rheumatic fever, wore leg irons to correct a tendency to knock knees, and to cap it all was an adorable and angelic child with golden hair and golden skin. I had pale freckled skin and straight brown hair. I made her life as difficult as possible. Dad built a playhouse for us to enjoy. When I was about six years old I used to run there with my friends and lock out Diana, who was struggling down the path to join in. I still feel sick when I recall this cruelty. Has she ever forgiven me? Can she actually remember it? I am scared to ask her.

At about this age my mother writes that I had a constant imaginary friend by the name of Ballas, with whom I had many conversations. I have no memory of Ballas but apparently we had great adventures together. I suppose I have always wanted a soulmate I could confide in.

Margaret Reid from next door was my constant playmate from the time we were toddlers until I was nine. Dad made a gap in the paling fence between the houses so that we could come and go. From time to time it was boarded up by one or other of us during a short-lived feud. Mostly we played happily and our mothers took us on enjoyable excursions to puppet theatres, to the beach or on picnics. My imagination always worked overtime and I persuaded Margaret to join me in many escapades and adventures. I loved the stories of Milly-Molly-Mandy and, in my mind, Margaret was little-friend-Susan, and Geoffrey over the other fence was Billy Blunt. We walked to school together in the charge of Margaret's older brother Robert.

Schooldays at Essendon North Primary School are largely a blank. I don't remember learning anything at all. These are just a handful of small incidents that come to mind like a collection of snapshots. One is a humiliating one from my first year. Playing with other children, we were crouching down on the asphalt and I felt a drop or two of wee escape. Surprised that there was no evidence, I decided to relax my bladder and can still recall the shame at the spreading puddle. Another memory is of stealing one of the new ballpoint pens from a newsagent and refusing to own up when the shopkeeper came to the classroom to announce the theft and offer an opportunity for the thief to confess. I also remember lining up pennies on the chalked outlines of a basketball court – something to do with the war effort. But what war? It would have been 1947. And I was impressed with the announcement by a teacher that the mother of my friend Jan had just had twins. I don't think I had ever heard of twins before. Finally, I have a memory snapshot of Robert Reid and his friends catching yabbies after school in a nearby quarry and his mum cooking them in a large pot and spreading them on newspaper for all of us to eat. Strangely I cannot remember whether I did or did not eat these scarlet creatures.

Our home in Essendon included a sunny room that became Mum's painting studio. She introduced sewing and painting classes on a Saturday morning for her own and various neighbours' children. We sat around making potato prints, dragging sheets of paper through a bath of oil and colour and marvelling at the swirling patterns, learning to embroider brightly coloured daisy-stitch patterns on hessian squares, and making table mats on a handloom. I don't think I was particularly skilled at any of these crafts, but my memory is that they were happy times. Margaret joined in these classes too.

After just a few years in Essendon my paternal grandfather George returned to Australia, newly widowed. He and my grandmother had been in London visiting Wilfred, who was starting his career as a war correspondent. My grandmother had fallen ill and died suddenly – probably from cancer, but no definite diagnosis was ever revealed. Grandpa moved into Mum's studio and became part of the household for the next twenty-five years. Mum never had another studio to call her own and did not resume painting for another fifteen years. I believe that the kitchen took the place of the studio as a daily outlet for her creativity.

The Reids remained good friends with my parents throughout their lives. Together they formed a club known as The Wayfarers, and once a month a group would gather to read poetry or plays, discuss current affairs or read from a selected book. A forerunner to the currently popular book clubs perhaps? Mum writes in her memoirs of a series of meetings when the reading was *Van Loon's Lives*, which detailed imaginary dinner parties given by the ghosts of famous people. The ingredients for these imaginary meals were set out in detail and Mum would interpret the menu and serve it for supper. After my family moved to the Mornington Peninsula, the four adults sometimes went on holidays together. Margaret and I continued our friendship throughout our student days, then as young mothers, through domestic upheavals up to the present day.

Where some families had fierce loyalties to football teams, we were fierce with our politics. Margaret Reid and I could not credit that any reasonable person would vote for the Liberal Party of Australia. Elections were very exciting times. I am not sure if we actually handed out how-to-vote cards (surely not – we were about eight years old), maybe we just helped arrange the stacks of cards for older helpers, but we were definitely involved from the early days. We both remember the generous supper tables on election night as the faithful gathered to wait for the scrutineers to deliver the verdict. Results took hours and hours to come in in those days.

Dad accepted the position of Parliamentary Secretary to the Honourable Arthur Drakeford, who later became Minister for Air and Civil Aviation, in the Chifley Government after 1945. This meant he spent Monday to Friday in Canberra, travelling to and fro by car. My mother was left to cope, not just with a fierce and uncooperative elder daughter but with sickly, put-upon Diana.

Mum had many theories and strove to be a 'modern' parent. As the firstborn I was her testing ground. She decided that my birthday party would feature food guaranteed to be 'healthy'. I must have been six or seven. I remember her serving small rice puddings with a dollop of plum jam. I also remember nobody eating them. Another birthday party memory from this era was when I went to a party for a schoolmate whose parents were recently arrived Maltese migrants. The broadmindedness and tolerance that my parents extended to all groups was not matched by me at eight years old. To my mind, the party was all wrong. The room was dark and hung with thick curtains. The furniture was dark and highly polished. There were lots of adults around the table and few games. The food was all wrong too. My memory is of a wet syrup-soaked fruit-filled cake that was far removed from the cream sponge or rainbow cake more usual at the birthday parties I was used to attending. I cannot remember more but I know that when an invitation came for another party at this house, for the little girl's brother, I made excuses and stayed away. I was later told that the family had got the message and at this party, 'proper' food such as fairy bread (bread and butter with hundreds and thousands) and cocktail sausages were served.

Mum also needed to help her mother care for her father. Her parents had moved in next door on the other side from the Reids, and Grandpa John had developed dementia. He had taken to wandering and Margaret and I found his aimless escapades very amusing. On one occasion we watched him dressed in his pyjamas and banging saucepan lids together as he marched down the centre of the road. Not surprisingly my mother dealt very severely with our ill-placed humour. I made several plans to run away but each time decided to return home once it became dark.

This was also about the time that my mother had a near-fatal ectopic pregnancy. She writes that there was subtle propaganda to 'populate or perish' and she decided to have another baby in about 1946. From the start she felt that something was not right but the doctor pooh-poohed her concerns. One weekend the pain was excruciating and she ordered me to go and get her mother from next door. Fortunately cousin Betty was staying for the weekend and, as a qualified nurse, recognised that Mum's condition was serious. An ambulance was called and it must have been at this stage that I saw Mum being carried out on a stretcher. Somehow this memory is linked in my mind to that of the subsequent death of my dog. Strange, because the two events must have been at least a year apart, but the horror of seeing my mother being carried out of the house on a stretcher was matched by the horror of coming home from school to find my dead dog laid out in the kennel for me to farewell.

My brother John was born in June 1948, and he also suffered from eczema and asthma as a newborn. Grandpa John's senility was getting more and more difficult to manage and Grandma Emily's blood pressure was dangerously high. A few months later she had a major stroke and died. I do not think I had seen my mother cry before that day. It was shocking. And as well as being shocked I felt guilty that my tears were really still for the loss of Judy the dog, rather than for my grandmother. Mum's father died three weeks after his wife.

I became a real problem child, especially after John arrived when I was seven-and-a-half. I stole money from my parents on a regular basis and spent it on sweets. I roamed the neighbourhood late after school, causing much anxiety. Search parties were sent out to look for me. I enlisted a school friend as an accomplice to assist with all my looting, spending and gorging. I even picked flowers from local gardens, tied them into posies and sold them to the same people from whose gardens I'd pinched them. When he discovered this, my father insisted that I donate all of this money to the Red Cross, as well as apologise to the neighbours.

One day I spied a brown paper parcel in the basket of someone's bicycle, which was resting against the front gate of a nearby suburban house. I whisked the parcel away and can still recall my shiver of excitement as I imagined the surprise and disbelief that would accompany the realisation by the owner that it was gone. I thought that the parcel would contain something wonderful and was disgusted to discover the contents consisted only of a pair of nylon stockings. I cajoled my partner in crime to offer these stockings to a shop where I had noticed a painted sign 'We buy anything'. The shopkeeper refused, not surprisingly. His trade was in selling feed for animals! I stuffed the useless stockings into a small conifer growing outside our house. Many, many years later a fragment of rotted nylon was still there. I never owned up.

Diana was such a happy little girl with a sunny personality, who endeared herself to her grandparents and everyone really. Of course I resented this. I bullied her and then sneered at her crying. I wanted her to fight back but she never did. After one nasty physical attack Diana's yells brought Mum running. Mum slipped and fell heavily on our brick path, breaking her arm. I was very frightened (I was also punished for my behaviour, I am sure). Contrite and wanting to help, the next week I volunteered to put the clothes through the electric wringer as one-armed Mum could not manage. She had already called in family help to care for baby John while she was incapacitated. I was eight years old. My own hand became entangled in the wringer and this time my yells had Mum running again. She activated the emergency release and I too had a broken arm. We really did look like the walking wounded.

It seems likely in hindsight that this behaviour was all attention-seeking. I felt that the sick ones in the family got the lion's share of care and concern. Even at the age of eight, as the eldest, I think it was expected that I help domestically and carry a bit of responsibility. I also missed my Dad. I was his special friend, or that was what I believed. Holiday snaps of family camping holidays show me wearing boyish overalls, helping with the tent, climbing alongside Dad as he explored, being the capable, strong one. I wonder whether I thought that boys had all the fun. I do remember experimenting with trying to urinate standing up as boys did. It was messy. I only tried this once.

I absolutely hated my pale skin and wanted above all else to have smooth brown legs like my best friend Margaret did. Diana's were brown, even if they were crooked! My childhood and early teenage years were punctuated with some spectacular sunburns.

Once I was taken to the beach as a treat with some other children and their parents. I stood out with my pale freckled skin among all of the other olive-skinned children. Long before the days of 'Slip, Slop, Slap' no-one used sunscreen lotion. After a few hours someone noticed my burning shoulders and gave me a cotton shirt to put on. By the time I returned home my shoulders and back were agonising and the shirt was stuck to oozing blisters rising like poached eggs. I was put in a shallow bath and Margaret's father came (my own father being, of course, in Canberra) and cut the shirt from my back. I can still remember the pain.

Another time, when I was a teenager I was convinced I could make my own bikini. It turned out to be far skimpier than I had intended – a result of poor workmanship – and I then spent an afternoon on the totally shade-free beach at Portsea. Memory tells me that for at least one night after that day at the beach I could not lie down and I wandered the house all night weeping, draped in a cotton sheet like some sad ghost.

In the late forties there was a developing crisis in the ALP. The anti-communist atmosphere of the early Cold War years began to erode Labor's support and in 1949 the Chifley Government was swept from office by the Liberal Party led by Robert Menzies. My father had been frustrated in his efforts to progress to a permanent position in the public service, which he attributed to suspicion of the family's left-wing sympathies. My parents believed that dire events lay ahead. In fact I can remember being told at breakfast, presumably the morning after the election, that it was a 'terrible day for the nation'.

Feelings certainly ran high, and not just because of the political situation. Diana was in hospital with rheumatic fever, John was still suffering from asthma and eczema, Mum was six months pregnant with Christopher and I was being my usual difficult self. Things at home were almost out of control and my father wisely decided he should let the ALP sort out its problems without him. He and Mum took a short holiday and did some thinking. They holidayed in a caravan park at Lakes Entrance and it was here that they developed the Big Idea. Shortly after Christopher was born, in October 1949, Dad borrowed a sum of money from the family solicitor, bought some farming land abutting a piece of natural bushland and the decision was made to move to Rosebud West and build a caravan park, in the hope of a new and better life.

2

Mum's Rabbit Pie

Rosebud West 1950–8

Dad and Grandpa moved first of all and built a large storage barn on the property. I remember it housing terrifying rabbit traps (Grandpa was a great rabbit trapper), bins of feed for the cow, chickens and ducks, lots of tools and the family van. We must have had a pig at some stage as my sister and I discovered a bin filled with broken Peek Frean cream-filled wafer biscuits intended as pig food. We were never permitted to have 'shop-bought' biscuits, so this discovery was thrilling and we helped ourselves as often as we liked.

For the first few months Dad and Grandpa rented a room from a neighbour and set about building the new family home. So soon after the war, building materials were scarce, so they decided on what was at the time a novel method of construction, making the best use of what they were able to find. Much of the framing was put together using timbers salvaged from the crates that transported cars to Australia. Dad purchased these crates from the docks and deconstructed them to retrieve usable timber. Wire mesh was stretched over the framing, held away from the timber by a regular pattern of nailed-on crown seals, presumably purchased from a brewery, given the number required. Stucco was then trowelled over this and left a bit rough. It was very attractive. The effect was similar to the adobe houses that I saw many years later in New Mexico. (This same method of plastering over a wire frame is used in some of the school gardens I work with these days, as a simple and speedy way of defining garden beds.)

At that time in Rosebud West it was seen as avant-garde and attracted much comment from the locals. This was not the first time my grandfather had got right into the spirit of an unusual construction method. A few years before my father died I took him for a weekend to revisit Ballarat, where he had spent happy years as a young man. He directed me to one of the several bizarre houses designed and constructed by his father, more than sixty years before, all made from reinforced concrete. Grandpa had apparently been fascinated by the sculptural possibilities of this material and had included flowing alcoves, curved window seats and even flower-boxes moulded into the concrete shell. I did fleetingly wonder whether Grandpa had ever heard of Antoni Gaudí.

Dad befriended a local stonemason who constructed a hand-some terrace connecting the two wings of the house, and inside, a stone wall to frame the open fireplace. The family house was to be called 'Greenslopes'. (Forty years later the wooden container frame was found to be infested with white ants and the house was demolished. There had been several owners since our happy days and I did not feel any special pang, having moved on from that part of my life.)

Dad was faced with seemingly endless challenges in obtaining materials to finish the house. It was a cold, wet winter, the family was a long way away and communication was not easy from his rented room. He slid into his first depression. Mum decided that even though nothing was finished we would all have to be together to help Dad recover.

I am not sure whether any treatment for Dad's depression was suggested at the time. I think we all did what we could to jolly him along. Grandpa was a tower of strength and helped wherever he could.

First the family moved into extremely basic rented accommodation down the road from the new house. The shack was draughty and cold, there was just one hot tap and a concrete outside trough, and the only place to dry the washing, including nappies from two babies, was a string between two tea trees in almost total shade. Mum used to put the wet washing into a laundry basket, balance it on top of the pram with the two babies inside, and precariously push the lot up the road to where Grandpa had constructed a clothesline in full sun.

I am not sure if my behaviour improved during this time. I know that I was pretty good at changing nappies and spooning pureed vegetables into one brother while reading stories to another. And I do remember trailing after Grandpa, 'helping' him to plant potatoes.

We moved into the new house long before it was finished so that the wind whistled through and we dashed across the unfinished section from the completed kitchen wing to the completed bedroom wing. The windowless living room allowed easy entry for various bugs, birds and, most memorably, snakes. Grandpa saw one slip behind a newly built bookcase and sat in wait, offering a saucer of milk. When the creature emerged, he was there with a knife and carving fork to despatch it.

Mum set about slowly creating a beautiful garden, her plantings winding in and around the local tea trees and banksias. She was never interested in geometric beds, preferring a garden to be full of surprises, and loved patterns of branch and leaf. There was an abelia bush outside the kitchen window that she never clipped, preferring to allow its lovely foliage to arch so that the morning sunshine would catch the pink-bronze bracts. In every garden I have created or lived among I have planted at least one abelia. I now wonder whether Mum knew the work of Edna Walling. I insulted her once by enquiring why she didn't grow 'real flowers' – I meant roses. She was never into roses, preferring the opulence of crimson and purple fuschias, or the innocence of the blue agathea daisy, or subtle patterns of bronze ajuga and silver foliage. A stone bird bath was built to attract kookaburras and the wattlebirds that loved to swing and suck the banksia flowers. A dry creek bed remained grassy all year round – a perfect spot for a badminton court.

Grandpa and Mum were always getting 'good ideas', but not all their farming experiments were successful. Two cows were milked, which provided far more milk than we could use, so Grandpa suggested raising ducks as he believed they would eat milk mixed with cereal, which they did more or less. Then we got some geese, supposedly to keep the grass down, but the geese preferred to eat the duck feed. Then there were two lambs, also for their potential as lawnmowers, but they preferred to eat Mum's shrubs and flowers.

Mum was in her element with a beautifully designed kitchen and she cooked lovely food for us all every day. There was no gas at Rosebud so she decided on an Aga slow-combustion stove. Ours was wood-fired, designed to provide the family's hot water as well. I can close my eyes today and hear the exact sound of the raddling of the grate that was part of the morning routine. You raddled until all the ash fell into the lower grate and then stoked and lit a new fire for the day. The ashes were carried to the compost pile. The stove stayed warm all through the night. It also left a film of dust over everything.

One memorable night a possum fell through the chimney and landed on the still-warm hotplate. The poor creature was terrified as well as burnt and went crazy trying to escape. The entire family was woken by the crashing of chairs overturning. We all thought it was a burglar until probably Grandpa investigated and opened a door and the possum fled. In the sixties the kitchen had a makeover and the Aga disappeared.

Grandpa was a great help to both my parents. He helped pull out trees on the newly acquired property to clear the site for the house. He hammered and sawed along with Dad and used his considerable strength to assist in lifting the formed framework for the house. He dug a vegetable garden for us all and planted the first crop of potatoes. He built structures to house the ducks. He did most of the milking in the first year. He dug out blackberries and burnt patches of bracken fern and generally used all the skills he had acquired earlier in his life as a farmer in Gippsland. He also killed the snakes. And he could always be relied upon to read us stories or tell stories of his own childhood.

But Grandpa could be fierce when it came to a discussion of international politics. He was completely obsessed with the doings of Dad's younger brother and my uncle, Wilfred Burchett.

My first memory of meeting Uncle Wilfred was just before we all moved to the new family home at Rosebud West. I have a memory of sitting next to this mysterious but interesting relative in North Essendon and being introduced to my first oyster. My recollection is a positive one, of being shown how to slip this delicacy down my throat. It was the first of many: freshly opened oysters, swimming in their own briny juices, remain a treat to this day.

My next memory is of Wilfred with various female 'friends' all living with us in the half-built house at Rosebud West. In my mother's memoir she betrays great anxiety at the impact of all these strangers when money was so tight and the weather apparently so hot. She writes that she fed them all on jugs and jugs of milky iced coffee and Grandpa's potatoes. My memory as a ten-year-old is of two of Wilfred's female friends, Kath and Kate, sunbaking to an astonishing chocolate brown.

Wilfred was sponsored to visit Australia by the Peace Council to give a series of lectures on the developments in post-war Europe, with a special interest in the Eastern European socialist world. He had recently attended the trial of the Hungarian Cardinal József Mindszenty and reported on it for the London *Daily Express*. He had also written a play about the trial, which had its one and only performance at 'Greenslopes'. All I remember from being part of the audience is Grandpa leading a pony across the 'stage' – our stone terrace – and actors entering and leaving the 'stage' via Dad's study on one side of the terrace and the kitchen on the other. In Australia in the 1950s many conservative bodies and individuals, including the Catholic Church, were fearful of the rise of democratic socialism. Wilfred, who had been an outspoken critic of fascism, now championed the rise of left-leaning governments all over Eastern Europe. There were some spirited exchanges in the press and at some of his lectures. There is much to be ashamed of as an Australian after reading the sloppy and inaccurate ASIO investigations of my father and other members of the family obtained under Freedom of Information laws.

Over the years Grandpa made sure we heard about Wilfred's whereabouts – be it Germany, Japan, Korea, Russia, Cambodia, China or Vietnam. Grandpa often held forth with his own views – always fiery, sometimes outrageous – about US imperialism and foreign policy, and the dominance of sex in American popular culture. He relived each and every adventure and incident that Wilfred was involved in and had total belief in every word Wilfred wrote. If my father sought to suggest that there might be a more moderate point of view, or asked what the evidence was for Wilfred's conviction, Grandpa would fly into an amazing rage, thump the table, become puce in the face and generally alarm us all. Sadly this sort of confrontation between my father and grandfather was a frequent occurrence. I think Dad would have allowed Grandpa to believe what he liked except that my father held an equally passionate belief in the need for democratic discussion and deep suspicion of anyone or any dogma claiming infallibility. As the whole family was gathered at the table each evening, he wanted us to know that there was often another side to an argument or, at the very least, that there were questions to ask, or possibly another interpretation of an action or event.

We grew up knowing that our politics were of the left, but more than a bit concerned at the heat, controversy and distress that seemed to surround political discussion. Both my sister and I, and to a certain extent my mother, withdrew from these discussions whenever we could. This has had an effect on Diana and me to the present day that is maybe not surprising. Back then, I often repaired to the kitchen to cook something delicious, and I still do the same today. If there is no kitchen handy, I retreat from the fury as quickly as possible – either physically or mentally. And if the discussion is accompanied by shouting, I become absolutely incapable of replying.

I remember Grandpa chasing me around our house trying to force me to look at an official publication with horrific colour images of victims of Hiroshima. I also remember him waving pages and pages of closely typed onion-skin airmail paper under our noses and wanting to read us every word that Wilfred wrote – and he was a regular correspondent.

As a family we were proud of Wilfred and what he stood for. We understood that Wilfred was out there at the barricades in the midst of important and often confusing conflicts, risking his life and reporting the truth as he saw it unfold, always convinced that people should have the right to decide their own destiny rather than have a regime imposed upon them. We know that there were various plots and attempts to prevent this side of many conflicts being known. As onlookers from the distant vantage point of a very safe Australia it was sometimes difficult to believe in the evil abroad.

Years later, in 1985, just two years after Wilfred died, my elder daughter Lisa made a short documentary about him as part of a university assignment. My father appears in it, setting the record straight and displaying an amazing recall. There is footage of a letter from Wilfred describing the atrocities he observed in Germany in 1938, seized presumably by ASIO and suppressed at the time and only seen by my father under Freedom of Information legislation months before the film was made. It was chilling to see an extract from the Melbourne *Argus* denying that there was any ill-treatment of Jews in Germany. And yet Wilfred knew this to be untrue. This flying in the face of the popular or preferred interpretation of political facts would be the hallmark of Wilfred's journalism for the rest of his life.

By Christmas 1950 our caravan park was open for business. The grand plan was to start with camp and caravan sites, which would provide the family income, and then to subdivide some more of the land to sell as residential blocks. Finances were stretched very thin. While construction proceeded Grandpa set out to catch eels in the local creek, trap rabbits, and grow potatoes and other vegetables as well as help with the milking of the two cows. I have an indelible memory of Mum and Grandpa wrangling eels in the kitchen sink. I don't know whether they were beheaded or not at the time but I was transfixed with horror as these slimy creatures sprang from the sink and slithered across the floor. Then I fled.

With Grandpa and Mum taking care of domestic life, Dad concentrated on activities that included septic tank installation, clearing campsites using his small tractor, building toilet blocks, pursuing permits for this and that, chasing materials to complete infrastructure and assisting with the grading of the roads through the caravan park. Both Mum and Dad wanted to retain as much of the beautiful natural bushland as possible, and they did. It meant that many campsites were tricky to back a caravan into, but the bonus was that, apart from shade, the trees also provided convenient boughs to attach canvas annexes or even clotheslines. Perhaps because of all this activity, and certainly because of the companionship of the family, Dad's anxieties receded and he found a degree of equilibrium that lasted for several years.

In his rare spare time my father went fishing and brought home flathead in large quantities. As my brothers grew older they loved to accompany Dad on these expeditions. Every time I buy a flathead I think of my father. Mum tried to insist that the fish should be scaled and gutted in the boat on the way back into shore. Sometimes the quantities caught did not make that possible and they arrived back home with a hessian bag of fish in rigor. I helped, rinsing the fish and scaling them under a stream of hand-pumped bore water, and then picked fish scales from my clothes and hair for hours afterwards. But we loved eating the fish.

They must have been very worrying times for the adults but my memories of being ten, eleven and twelve are mostly blissful. Rules were relaxed in the country. We were allowed to roam where we pleased. A friend, Judith, who lived nearby, and I would ride our bikes to the beach, around the curving tea tree through the dense foreshore, admiring the lovely native orchids. Or we went mushrooming, finding plenty of them pushing up through the fallen tea tree leaves. We cooked and ate all the mushrooms we gathered.

(We had never heard of the poisonous 'yellow-staining' *Agaricus xanthodermus*. Did it not exist in those days? Nowadays almost every wild-growing mushroom I see in a park or along the river bank turns yellow as soon as I scratch the skin and has a distinctive unpleasant smell, quite different from the woodsy smell of a true field mushroom, *Agaricus campestris*, the kind Judith and I collected many times.)

At other times we picked blackberries. There was wild bushland to build treehouses and bush camps. And it was fun to accompany Grandpa or Dad to the daily milking and to watch the milk being separated into skim milk and rich cream. I had my own small garden and in the long summer holidays I attempted rather unsuccessfully to grow lettuces with a view to selling them to the campers now installed in the brand-new caravan park. Grandpa certainly sold his excess potatoes that way. And Mum developed a wide repertoire of rabbit and flathead recipes. Her paints and pastels were firmly packed away.

Every night Mum sat on either Diana's or my bed in our shared bedroom and read to us. Early favourites were *The Way of the Whirlwind* by Mary and Elizabeth Durack and *The Complete Adventures of Snugglepot and Cuddlepie* by May Gibbs, with special emphasis on the wicked banksia men. We had plenty of our own banksia trees and I did sometimes let my imagination run wild when eyeing the fallen cones. I also remember with affection *The Story of Shy the Platypus* by Leslie Rees and others in the series, as well as *The Magic Pudding* by Norman Lindsay and many more Australian stories. I have vivid memories also of *The Chinese Children Next Door* by Pearl S. Buck, originally published in 1942. I pored over the illustrations of the children wearing soft cloth shoes, playing an unknown game called shuttlecock, and their father wearing what looked like a dressing gown. Winnie-the-Pooh and the poetry of

A. A. Milne in *Now We Are Six* and *When We Were Very Young* were great favourites too. This reading time with our mother was a very special half-hour and continued long after we could read well for ourselves. By now I was a voracious reader and a special favourite was *The Family From One End Street* by Eve Garnett. I loved the stories of the Ruggles family and remembering the stories now I can smell the aroma of wet washing that permeated the house where Mrs Ruggles washed and ironed for others. I identified with the skinny smart daughter Kate, although my life was actually more like that of the eldest Ruggles daughter, Lily Rose, who did a lot of 'minding' of the younger ones.

Another highlight of my week was collecting my copies of *The School Friend* and *Girls' Crystal* magazines from the post office. These 'story papers' contained exciting short stories of British schoolgirls who captured villains, found smugglers' treasure, invaded haunted houses, and had many other implausible but riveting adventures that apparently happened if you went to boarding school. Eventually the stories became comic strips and I lost interest, or maybe I had graduated to the school library by then. But the stories certainly inspired elaborate fantasy games between Judith and me. We made treasure maps with scorched paper and watery ink and convinced each other that these maps were genuine, and set out to follow the clues.

My father saw sport as a waste of time. And although I think he was reacting against the popular obsession with spectator sports, it did mean that none of us was taught to swim, or encouraged to participate in anything physical. As the bayside beaches were so shallow there was little chance of us drowning as we splashed in water that barely reached our knees.

My brothers caught up when they went to boarding school and not only learned to swim but became interested in rowing, athletics, cricket and so on. Diana and I remained lounge lizards for most of our lives, other than riding our bicycles and playing the occasional game of tennis.

Despite the stresses of establishing a new business there was plenty of quality family time. Before 1956, without television, family evenings were spent with music, either gramophone records or the radio, and of course with books. There was no local library at this stage so as a family we all selected books from a long list provided by the State Library of Victoria and once a month a book box arrived. And of course the bookshelves at home were full too. My father's special favourites included a complete set of the novels of Charles Dickens, and he owned almost every novel written by Australian authors that had been published since the thirties and even earlier. My early interest in art was helped along by two volumes of reproductions of masterpieces held in collections of major galleries of the world. These books were folio-sized and every colour plate was protected by a stiff sheet of translucent tissue that had to be carefully lifted before the beautiful image was revealed. I loved these books and yet so many years later have no recall of any specific work, just a hazy memory of pink naked flesh and of sun-touched cloudscapes. But not all interests were shared. I retired to my bedroom with a small radio once a week to listen to *The Goon Show*, a masterpiece of surrealist comedy that did not appeal to my parents.

There were also family treasures to examine – souvenirs of long-ago travel, sometimes with stories attached. The stories took on legendary status and were told over and over again. Mum had a Japanese umbrella that we found fascinating. It was very heavy with its lacquered bamboo ribs and we were not permitted to play with it outside. But if we were well behaved and if Mum was in a good mood (to get both together was rare), she would open the umbrella so that we could admire the beautiful scene painted on its underside. She also occasionally modelled her kimono. It had a pattern of flowers and butterflies against a background of smoky grey shading to black and was lined with coral-pink silk. We pored over the snaps in the family album showing our youthful and beautiful mother wrapped in the folds of this gown onboard the *Kamo Maru*, sitting on cushions and holding chopsticks over an array of small bowls on a nearby low table. I kept this kimono for a long time, but didn't care for it properly, and years later discovered it had been attacked by moths and was disintegrating.

One time Grandpa gave me a small nugget, about the size of a quail egg; the greenish stone sparkled with fragments of gold. I kept this stone in a special box with my other treasures and would take it out to examine it, along with a gold sovereign given to me by my mother's cousin. Grandpa told me of how he had tried his hand as a young man at fossicking for gold at Kalgoorlie and had returned after a year even poorer than when he had set out, with only a few of these gold-flecked stones. I couldn't resist taking the special stone to school for a 'show and tell' session. Somehow I lost it, along with the gold sovereign.

I have so few other memories of my one year at Rosebud Primary School. Just this other painful one. One day, probably in 1950, sitting at the regulation desk, I reached under to draw out my wooden pencil box and yelped with sudden pain. A razor blade stored in one of the slide-out compartments, for use in sharpening pencils, had worked its way half out and as I pulled, it sliced. There was lots of blood and tears and I refused for some reason to allow a doctor to stitch the thumb. To this day if I hit my thumb against a bench or table I see the proverbial stars.

By primary school age Diana had outgrown all her ailments but the boys were both serious asthmatics and for years my mother could anticipate disturbed sleep as one or other of my brothers regularly had asthma attacks in the middle of the night. Her blue dressing gown was always draped at the ready at the end of the bed for when she would need to attend to a cry of distress. I distinctly remember Christopher sitting bolt upright in bed, with huge, terrified eyes, tearing at the buttons on his pyjamas because he was desperate for air. Often without any warning he would vomit trails of mucus. I found this traumatic and whenever we went on an outing with Christopher I kept an anxious eye on him, scared he would vomit again. And he often did. I am still traumatised by vomiting. John overcame his asthma by the time he was about five; Christopher's continued until he was about twelve.

Christopher was Grandpa's favourite and Grandpa often carried him around on his back. He was so often ill and weak and painfully thin. He struggled to keep up with other children and could not take part in any boisterous play. He missed a lot of school due to asthma attacks. John, once his asthma had disappeared, was a very robust little boy, full of energy, although he would still gasp for air if he was near freshly cut grass, or had inadvertently eaten a lightly cooked egg or a nut.

Grandpa would defend Christopher from any verbal attack. Sometimes we all got tired of this favouritism towards the permanent invalid and made nasty remarks – especially John, who objected to Christopher's special status. Grandpa was intolerant of John's normal noisy boy play and often reprimanded him unfairly. Christopher loved lighting fires and on one occasion one of his little fires was located underneath the house. It required attention from wet hessian bags and the fire brigade. So he was not a complete angel and not always an invalid!

Mum and Dad tried to get away for short breaks when possible. 'Taking a holiday', long or short, was seen as a panacea for

stress throughout my parents' life together. The usual arrangements were that a local woman came in to clean; Grandpa, in his
vigorous early eighties, was responsible for security; and I did the
cooking. We were left with pretty detailed instructions and Mum
pre-prepared much of the food. But I also recall on one occasion
being the one to clean up Christopher's vomit and ring the doctor in a panic. The doctor soothed me, saying, 'Give him half a
phenobarb, Stephanie. They're in a labelled bottle behind the egg
cups.' I was about twelve.

By the mid-fifties Banksia Park at Rosebud West was very popular, a combined caravan and camping park that ensured relentless
labour for the adults and magical summers for us four kids. What
could be better than to be reunited every December with friends,
and to have games, dances and competitions available every day?
I imagine each of us children has special memories of that charmed
period in our lives. Those summers seemed to go on forever.

As Banksia Park grew in size and reputation it became a seriously demanding business. My father's older brother Clive came
to live nearby and the brothers worked together. Clive and Aunty
Molly had three daughters, with whom Diana and my brothers
were very close. John and cousin Helen spent most of their days
together until he and Christopher left for boarding school in 1961.
In the winter months, maintenance and new projects filled Dad
and Uncle Clive's days; in the summer months, the caravan park
population swelled to include more than a hundred families, all
needing attention, and more and more services were provided. The
same families returned year after year.

The original campers came with one car and a tent per family.
As the years rolled by they branched out to a caravan with a canvas

annexe. As family finances improved, the following year they might also have a boat and a boat trailer. Too soon the children were old enough to drive and the same single campsite was now expected to accommodate all of the above and a second car. It was increasingly stressful. Cabins were built. An outdoor entertainment stage was constructed. A tennis court and a shop were built. Dances were arranged, and competitions of various sorts – dress-up evenings, sandcastle building for the little kids, bingo for the oldies and concerts. For us children it was paradise. We had new friends who had all the time in the world to play. There was a different activity every day and every evening. There was a camp committee that managed much of all of this.

After writing about my childhood and the caravan park a few years ago for a magazine, I received a letter from one of the happy campers, who remembered the table tennis and the outdoor movies and the lime spiders from the camp shop. He told the story of meeting a woman at an office whose face was familiar and discovering that her family had camped alongside his own at Banksia Park for many years when both were children.

But it was at about this time, maybe six or seven years after Banksia Park first opened, that my father had his next serious bout of depression. He just could not cope with so many people requiring him to be jolly at all times of the day and night, as well as the frequent emergencies of bogged caravans, blocked septic tanks, disputes over campsite boundaries, lost property and a million other details. He took to sitting, all crumpled, in a chair in the kitchen and suggesting it might be a good idea if he took fifty pounds and just walked away. I was very frightened, dimly understanding that the rock our family depended upon was crumbling.

Many years later when I needed to be the rock my father could rely on, and feeling my own equilibrium threatened by the weight of the responsibility, I marvelled at how Mum had coped with his collapse as well as with four demanding children, a business, and a willing but not always helpful father-in-law.

My mother, one of the most introverted and socially inept people I have known, rose to the crisis. Dad had to go to hospital. She would run the camp shop. She would co-opt Aunt Molly to keep the books. She would contribute to the camp entertainment by reading stories at sunset to a growing group of rapt small children. She would try to keep a handle on everything while Dad was away. Clive became more and more involved with the management.

My memory is vague as to how we kids coped during this period. I suspect there was a bit of 'out of sight, out of mind'. I remember visiting my father once at Larundel Psychiatric Hospital. I know that he had electroconvulsive therapy and if he ever mentioned it later in life it was always with a shudder. He must have improved because he returned home after about four weeks and life seemed to proceed as before.

During the year outside of 'The Season', as the local community called the summer months, my parents led a full life. They had made good friends locally and they formed a music group and a play-reading group that met regularly at our house. My mother was also a member of a local dressmaking club.

Like mine, Mum's social awkwardness was to do with interacting with many people at once. Being part of a crowd was something she hated and I still hate. But with a small group of trusted friends, or a small group pursuing a shared interest, once we've broken through the shyness barrier, we relax and enjoy the interaction.

By 1954 my mother had discovered Elizabeth David and had a copy of the first edition of *French Country Cooking* and of *A Book of Mediterranean Food* on a shelf in the kitchen. *French Provincial Cooking* came a few years later. These books were read from cover to cover by my mother (and less thoroughly by me at that time), and Elizabeth David was the authority referred to in our kitchen. Other favourites, and often consulted, were the Australian classics *Oh, for a French Wife!* by Ted Maloney and Deke Coleman and *The Garrulous Gourmet* by William Wallace Irwin.

We all had regular chores and responsibilities that were non-negotiable. For years Diana and my particular responsibility at home was the washing-up. Diana had a lovely singing voice and was involved in school productions of Gilbert and Sullivan operettas, and we used to sing our way through many an operetta or popular musical as we rinsed and dried the plates. *Oklahoma* and *Carousel* were favourites.

Mum encouraged her children to help in the kitchen if they felt so inclined. I loved it and had many a session leafing through Mum's small collection of illustrated cookery books and deciding to try something special. I loved the step-by-step illustrations in her *Good Housekeeping's Picture Cookery*, published in 1950. The crumbs scattered beside the close-up of the slice of fruit cake looked so real!

From time to time in interviews over the years, when I have been asked to comment on the influence of food writer and *dame extraordinaire* Margaret Fulton on my cooking, I have always been embarrassed and flustered. The truth is that my mother outlawed women's magazines in our house, considering them a waste of time and probably money. (Tabloid newspapers and comics were also banned in our household.) Margaret Fulton established her reputation as a food authority by contributing to several women's magazines and she remained unknown to me for at least two decades. I am ashamed to admit this as Margaret is such an icon in the world of Australian food. Her own memoir, *I Sang for My Supper*, shows such good humour, commonsense and knowledge that I am doubly ashamed of this bizarre snobbery on the part of my mother.

My mother loved to cook. She loved to make bread. She loved to sit at the table with friends and was at her most relaxed at this time. Favourite recipes were shared. This is exactly as I am, which reinforces my belief in the power of family modelling on behaviour and values. She planned meals days in advance. And wrote herself little notes that could be found stuck under jars on windowsills. She searched and found shopkeepers who cared about their produce and made friends with them: the man in the delicatessen who knew about caring for cheddar cheeses and turned them regularly as they matured; the Italian family who grew their own globe artichokes and sold them in the shop in Rosebud; the local butcher who knew Mum liked to order a corner cut of topside beef each week to turn into several simple but delicious family meals. She was not yet painting again but she did join a group that made baskets and took up embroidery.

Our dining table was round, made of silky oak by my father. It had a circle of frosted glass in the centre that could be illuminated by a low-wattage globe. Often my mother would arrange a wreath of flowers around this circle, which looked very beautiful. On more regular weekday meals we had a wooden lazy Susan that sat over this circle so that condiments, salt and the pepper mill could all easily be shared between the seven of us. Mum collected lovely plates that were not expensive but she took care to decide which would be used for a special occasion. If the meal was celebrating the cuisine of a particular country she would try to reflect that in the tablemats she used, or the colours of the plates. She would place a whole hand of bananas on the table to cool a fiery Sri Lankan curry, or serve chopsticks if she had prepared a small starter of raw fish. Her interests were very wide. Anything to do with culinary traditions, special equipment or specific flavour combinations she found fascinating and sooner or later she would attempt her own version. She was an early student at classes in Chinese cookery given by Melbourne authority Elizabeth Chong in the early sixties.

But not all my mother's food was exotic. I remember rabbits soaking overnight in a green enamel bowl, presumably to remove any strong flavour. She would then simmer the pallid creature with onions, celery, carrot and a bundle of herbs until it was tender. Then all the meat was stripped from the bones. This was a satisfying shared activity and one could sneak a little bit of tender rabbit at the same time. The pieces of rabbit were finally folded into a thick curried velouté (made with Keen's curry powder) and served with rice. Best of all, a collection of extra bits would be set out on the lazy Susan to add extra piquancy to this favourite family dish. I remember toasted coconut, sultanas, pickled watermelon rind, fried almonds and maybe sliced banana.

Mum tried her hand at many things. She made simple bag cheeses. She made clotted cream, by slow-cooking the milk on top of the Aga stove overnight. She briefly took up beekeeping. I can still see the chunks of honeycomb dripping into a white enamel bucket and recall my fascination with the few bees still imprisoned in their wax cells. She experimented with cooking wild greens, she made her own sauerkraut, she made pot pourri from her herbs and dried lavender, she hung spirals of orange peel to dry alongside the bay leaves, she pickled chicken feet and she experimented with new dishes all the time. One day I was horrified to find a calf's head on a platter in the cool pantry. She was planning to make some sort of potted meat, maybe *fromage de tête*. She was so far ahead of her time.

My father loved red wine and would regularly visit wine merchant Jimmy Watson's in Carlton's Lygon Street for supplies. Most nights my parents enjoyed a pre-dinner sherry or a dry vermouth and Dad would enquire what was for dinner before selecting a suitable bottle. In 1955 few Anglo-Celtic Australian families had table wine with their meals as a matter of course. Grandpa, who had once been a lay Methodist preacher and had at that time railed against the demon drink, had been converted and now enjoyed a glass of wine 'for his health'. I do not remember my first taste of wine but it was probably around the family table just before I set out for university. The drinking of wine with meals was just a part of our family life, unremarkable until a guest or school friend expressed amazement.

In her rare spare moments my mother taught herself to type (badly) and worked on her own cookbook, *Through My Kitchen Door*, illustrated with woodcuts by one of her student friends from art school days, Christine Aldor, which was eventually published in 1960 by Georgian House. In her memoir Mum dismisses this book as 'a complete failure'. Apparently it did not sell well. She felt that her publisher had been enthusiastic during the production process but had lost interest by the time the book appeared and there was no promotion. The truth may well have been that Georgian House was about to close down. And this little book, with its stylish woodcut illustrations and little essays to introduce each chapter, was very different from the straightforward recipes that could be clipped from the women's pages in the newspaper. It remains a collector's item today and is a true picture of the culinary scene as it was then.

It was republished in 1997 with original text intact and my annotations under the title *Recipes My Mother Gave Me*. I think all four of us children still refer to this little book from time to time. I still make several of the biscuit recipes. It was fun to prompt my brothers and sister to revisit the text and I think it caused fond reminiscences of the family table during the fifties. The annotations help the contemporary reader realise the distance that we have travelled since then in terms of food availability and culinary understanding of other cultures.

The population of the Mornington Peninsula was growing but there was no secondary school available by the time I was ready to move on from primary school. So all children needing a secondary school from Portsea to Red Hill went by bus to a temporary location in a rough-and-ready church hall at Red Hill. Suffice to say it was mayhem and very little learning took place until the appearance mid-year of an effective teacher, Mary Turner, a newly arrived Englishwoman who introduced strict discipline. In later years she confessed to me how aghast she was to arrive in this new country, to be sent to this ramshackle building and be confronted by children running wild.

(Mary Turner became good friends with my parents and joined their play-reading and classical music groups. Her daughter Hilary became very friendly with Diana as they were very similar in age. Mary and I remained in touch for many years, almost to the end of Mary's life. We often laughed when we remembered the diabolical behaviour of that class of 1952. When I was struggling with Statistics in Psychology I at Melbourne University in 1959, Mary Turner successfully coached me to a pass.)

The following year there was still no school so this time the same students were bundled off to Frankston High School. Some spent nearly four hours a day on a bus but for me it was more like three hours. In the winter we left home in the dark and returned in the dark. Again, the teaching was minimal. My only memory of any actual schooling was a French-speaking teacher instructing the class in repetitive drills in order to master the music of the French language. I enjoyed this and contorted my cheeks and tongue to make the nasal sounds. The results are a lovely French accent and considerable gaps in grammatical knowledge. My parents were

concerned about this haphazard education and there were mur-
murings of boarding school. I was ecstatic at the thought, having
devoured many, many English books describing the thrills of life in
the 'fourth', complete with midnight feasts and mysterious adventures. However, it was not to be as by the next year, 1954, Rosebud
High School was built and my proper schooling was established.

I was in Year 9 – third form, as it was known then. I was happy
there but it had significant drawbacks. As yet there were no Years
10, 11 or 12, and I continued to be in the most senior year of the
school as my education continued. Inevitably this led to increased
responsibility. I was school captain. I was reasonably intelligent but
probably seemed brighter than I was – a big fish in a very small
pond. Until I went to university I had few close friends due to the
size and location of my high school. The few kindred spirits I had
found had dropped out of school at the end of Year 10. My special
friend Judith lived just down the road and we shared many adventures until her family moved away from the Mornington Peninsula
and after a while we lost touch. I did reconnect with my friend
Jan Patrick, whom I had met originally at Essendon North Primary
many years before. Her family had moved to Point Leo and she was
now one of the bussed commuters to Rosebud High. Whenever
there was a school social or a party, Jan would stay at my place.
I would 'dink' her home on my bike and we would wobble through
the lovely foreshore, before a lengthy and enjoyable primping session preparing ourselves for the exciting occasion.

In the mid-fifties party wear for most girls was a starched petti-
coat under a gathered cotton skirt and most likely a scooped-neck
white blouse. Otherwise you wore a school uniform or, for 'going
out', clothes that closely resembled your mother's. If churchgoing
was part of your tradition you would wear a hat and gloves. The
phenomenon of the teenager as an important commercial niche

market was still to hit. In Year 10 I saw my first copy of the American *Seventeen* magazine. It was an absolute revelation. I pored over the images and desperately wanted clothes like that, and to look like one of those carefree, perfectly groomed American girls. My mother secretly made me a very special dress copied from a *Seventeen* pattern for my fifteenth birthday. It was a waisted dress in sky-blue fine wool with a huge skirt, a neatly buttoned bodice, a round Peter Pan collar and a thin cherry-red belt. Just like Debbie Reynolds, I thought.

Just before the Debbie Reynolds birthday dress I experienced my second brush with Christianity. The first had happened many years before. As a very young child when we lived in Essendon my maternal grandmother, apparently concerned by my lack of spiritual education, bribed me to go to Sunday school with the promise of a new dress. I was about seven years old. It seemed like a good deal, so off I went. At the Sunday school we were told a well-known Bible story, and handed a large illustration of some part of the story to take home, colour in and to bring back next Sunday with the story written in our own words. My grandmother asked how I had got on. I showed her the picture and she showed me how, by following the text reference at the bottom of the picture, I could find the Biblical text. I promptly copied the text, word for word, coloured in my picture and took it back the following Sunday. The Sunday school teacher solemnly asked me, 'Stephanie, did you copy this work from the Bible?' I vigorously denied doing so and the teacher did not even challenge me. My grandmother made me a new dress and I did not bother going to Sunday school again. I was astonished that the teacher had not confronted me with my lie and I rather despised him for it.

When I was about thirteen I realised my school friends all went to church and thought perhaps I should too. My father and grandfather had made it very clear that they considered organised religion to be responsible for many dreadful happenings in the world and that all religions were intolerant of other groups, so could not claim any omnipotence or authority for directing behaviour. It was obvious I would not be able to get away with an easy conversion. I could expect fierce debate.

Dressed in a very ugly pudding-basin hat and a matronly too-long tweedy coat and gloves, I had to cycle about two kilometres to the Methodist church. Once seated in the pew, my mind just drifted. I remembered absolutely nothing although I probably made an effort to sing the hymns. On my return home my father and grand-father cross-examined me about the text of the day. What had the minister spoken about? What did I think about the sermon? They were both poised to go on the attack but they need not have worried. My lack of recall was total. I think I lasted about three Sundays.

Whenever I have written about my mother and how she inspired my own love of culinary adventure the implication has been that our relationship was one of mutual affection. And so it was; but my goodness, I also found my mother irritating and her emotional responses to life disappointing. Her reaction to any confidential disclosure of a new project was always a negative one. Without fail she would home in on why this latest scheme would not be a suc-cess. I think my daughters might say that I have done this to them too. And what is one supposed to do if the ideas are crazy? But I should admit that some of my own most definitely were.

A special school friend of mine during the Rosebud West years once asked me, 'Why is your mother always so crabby?' And it struck me at the time that it was true and I didn't know why. She had a very low tolerance of noise and until my brothers went to boarding school they yelled and fought and generally thundered through the house. I would hiss and scream at them and Diana would make herself scarce. This drove Mum crazy. All of it.

My father had plenty of disappointments and anxieties to unload regarding all that was happening in Banksia Park. And my grandfather spent a good deal of time at the family table fulminating against American foreign policy and thumping the table. My father would attempt a reasonable counter-proposition, which just made my grandfather even angrier. The boys would leave the table with a loud shoving of chairs and slamming of doors, and my mother would quietly seethe.

Diana and I have pondered our mother's bad moods and we both wonder whether she was suffering from symptoms of menopause. Sometimes she would disappear to bed and lie with the sheet pulled over her head. We will never know.

Mum was reluctant to join in any impromptu fun – and impromptu fun was not a common occurrence in our household, where most interests were taken very seriously. But I can recall dancing around the kitchen, aged twelve or thirteen, and grabbing her hands and wanting her to be part of my moment of joy. She almost angrily pushed me away. I tried to explain that if she shared the moment it would be even more fun. I suppose I was wanting her stamp of approval. I didn't get it.

Sadly I have also been guilty of this unthinking, hurtful behaviour. One incident that comes to mind is a time many years ago, when three-year-old Lisa clung to me, pulling me to her so hard that I thought my neck would break. I firmly disentangled her stranglehold but failed to validate the affection she was offering. If only I could have my time over again.

On another occasion I went to a performance of the Katherine Dunham dancers, a black company from New York. When I showed

Mum the program of these gorgeous bodies scantily clad in their brilliant flouncy costumes, she was dismissive of my enthusiasm, pronouncing them 'primitive'. How extraordinary, compared with her wholehearted acceptance of and affection towards my black husband many years later.

Anyway we all soon understood that riotous laughter, spontaneous leaps or shouts, or unplanned outings were not approved of. It was 'out of control' behaviour. We all learnt this very well – too well. And speaking for myself, without the effect of alcohol I am always tightly, tautly, mindfully in control of my behaviour and emotional responses.

In 1955, when I was in Year 10, among the students who came to our part of the Peninsula to continue their secondary education was Malcolm Good, whose family lived at Red Hill at that time. He was very smart and somehow different, and, some of us thought, seemed supercilious. Annoyingly he excelled at everything. He could draw, he grasped concepts very quickly, he excelled at maths and English, he was tall and dark, and he was also good at cricket. After a year of adolescent false starts, with parties at which we played 'spin the bottle' and school dances where many of us had our first experiences of actually touching someone of the opposite sex, Malcolm and I fell in love. We were both fourteen. We walked back to my home along the beach after a school dance (a distance of two kilometres, which seemed quite safe to everyone, parents included), and I can still remember the touch of the soft scarf he wore as it brushed against my face, and the feeling of belonging in the curve of his arms as we exchanged the first proper kiss of my life.

Life became more complicated as Malcolm's parents decided to return to Melbourne to live, just months after we had connected. We were devastated at first, but the reality was that our love affair progressed in leaps and bounds. The only way to see each other was to spend weekends together either at Malcolm's home in the city or at my home. There was plenty of passionate hugging and kissing but nothing more. The fear of pregnancy was very real and of course we were years away from the contraceptive pill. Away from school we became young people rather than schoolmates. We talked for hours, we went to concerts, and both of us still remember the shock and excitement of hearing 'Rock Around the Clock' for the first time, performed by Bill Haley and His Comets at a packed venue in West Melbourne. We looked at paintings, we went to see art-house movies. It became clear that the manner some perceived to be supercilious was merely a disguise Malcolm assumed when he felt awkward or found his schoolmates gauche, an unease that disappeared when he was with me or with his family. Malcolm's family was arty and bohemian compared with mine. I spent long hours around the table with them discussing art, politics (theirs were even more radically of the left than the views of my grandfather) and philosophy, and I developed a deep and very special lifelong friendship with Malcolm's mother, Joyce.

Joyce and Malcolm Good Senior were friends with many of the significant artists of their day. Joyce's brother-in-law Martin Smith, brother of Gray Smith, framed the works of these artists and Malcolm Senior was an accomplished artist himself. In their young days Joyce and Malcolm painted and socialised with Albert Tucker, members of the Boyd family, John Perceval, Charles Blackman, Neil Douglas, Jean Langley and art patrons and collectors Sunday and John Reed.

When I met Malcolm's parents I was introduced to the fringes of this world. Every weekend we spent together included contact with artists and their works. Malcolm Senior might recite from the work of Dylan Thomas, we would listen to early jazz recordings and there was always plenty of lively discussion.

I gazed at stacked paintings of schoolgirls leaning against a wall and admired landscapes on the walls of Joyce and Malcolm's home, where pots thrown by Merric, David and Arthur Boyd were in daily use. Artistic sensibility was an unselfconscious part of life for them. I think it influenced me a great deal. To be in any one of the homes that Joyce lived in was to be surrounded by beauty – a pot of cottage flowers on a table, a small stool with a smooth patina of age, a hand-crocheted rug on the bed, a gathered shell or stone, an embroidered oven cloth, a basket of dried grasses or pinecones next to the fireplace, a pottery bowl of apples on the table, a garden full of useful and beautiful plants. Simple things, never costly, but adding so much to a life. Somehow the modern interest in contrived 'lifestyle' seems obscene set against this other way of being.

In recent years I visited an exhibition of the extraordinary pottery of Merric Boyd and his son Arthur at the Mornington Gallery. These hefty pots with sculptured three-dimensional gnarled and restless decoration were wonderful to see brought together like this. The colours were those of the bush – all greens, greys, ochre and cloudy blue. Most of the pieces on display were very large but they did take me back to sitting with Joyce around a table at the age of fifteen, drinking my tea from a Merric Boyd mug.

I remember planning a special dinner for one of the nights when Malcolm was arriving for the weekend at Rosebud. My memory tells me that I cooked *pommes dauphine* (mashed potatoes beaten into choux pastry and fried), making a hollow in each ball of dough before frying it that was to be filled with French-style simmered green peas. Steak was the main course with a *sauce Bercy*. The finale was a tart shell filled with *crème patissière* dotted with shaved dark chocolate. I did write out the menu but have no memory of its reception. Positive, I hope, although it was very rich.

Monday to Friday my life continued at Rosebud High School. The principal teenage entertainment in Rosebud was a Saturday-night dance. Nothing as crude as a DJ – we had one of Melbourne's best-known jazz groups, the Frank Traynor's Jazz Preachers, and the music was irresistible. It was at one of these Saturday night dances when I was just sixteen going on seventeen that I met a local boy whom I shall call Peter, who would be very important in my life for the next year or two. I was still in my final year of school. Although I lived for Malcolm's letters they became less frequent as he became more and more taken up by his studies.

It was of course inevitable that the intense relationship between Malcolm and me at such an age would burn out. Nonetheless I nursed a broken heart through much of this final year and remember my tears spilling into my teacup as I sobbed on receiving his final letter. My dedication to study would never be in the same league as Malcolm's.

By the time I was in the final year there were just six students doing their Matriculation. I was the only girl (Jan had already left to go to Teacher's College). I took many subjects by correspond-ence. It was not at all satisfactory and I believe that my education suffered greatly through lack of a strong peer group and through lack of face-to-face teaching (not to mention my broken heart). Assignments were posted to the school: great bulging envelopes with supporting material photocopied in slabs. I tried to respond to the topics and questions and dutifully posted them off. The comments, often quite vague, would take at least two weeks to be returned. It was all so impersonal. I marvel at the success of online study these days when I compare it with the distance education I received that was so very unsuccessful.

At school there was almost no opportunity for peer-to-peer exchanges. The others were involved with mathematics and physics and seemed to have no interest in historical issues or literature, and I was not interested in their conversations about science or sport. I was alone in struggling to grasp the importance of the revolutions of 1848 or the British Corn Laws. We did share a class in English, which was compulsory. Interestingly, this was the only subject in which I did well at the final examinations.

I was certainly ill-prepared for university. I was already awkward with new people and hung back from engaging in discussion. Was this because my mother was very shy and often surprisingly tongue-tied with those she did not know very well? Was it because I was pretty sure I was unable to achieve at the level my parents hoped for? More likely it was because none of my schoolwork engaged me emotionally, unlike all that I had discovered during my time with Malcolm and his family. I knew that my parents, like many others who had lived through the Great Depression, saw a good education as the key to a successful future. I had already seen the flash of disappointment in their eyes when I failed to top the class consistently or to win a Commonwealth scholarship.

In 1956 Melbourne hosted the Olympic Games. As a totally non-sporting family the only immediate impact it had on our lives was that Dad bought one of the first television sets. All the neighbours gathered to hear Bruce Gyngell announce the dawn of television. From then on the circle at our family table had to be broken to allow the reading of the ABC News to intrude into the dinner hour. Another consequence of this date, which would be important in my life, was that a young Swiss chef, Herman Schneider, arrived to cater for the French and Belgian teams. He stayed and eventually opened Melbourne's landmark European restaurant, Two Faces.

Around this time Dad had become more and more involved in the campaign to introduce to Victoria rate-funded libraries modelled on the system operating in the United Kingdom. Rosebud had one of the first such libraries, the Peninsula Regional Library. The first year of its establishment coincided with my final year at school and my father and I volunteered to staff the library on a Saturday evening as council funds did not stretch to pay for a staff member on a Saturday. I suspect this started my interest in library work.

Life at Rosebud West continued for many years for my parents. At some point my father arranged for his brother Clive to take over full management of Banksia Park, so that he could work full-time in the new regional library. He did this happily for some years.

By this time Diana had left home to train as a Home Economics teacher. With the boys at boarding school in Geelong my parents made regular weekend trips to visit them, and there is evocative footage of the family picnics that were an important part of these weekends.

Our parents' decision to send John and Christopher to Geelong Grammar in 1961 is remembered by my brothers with mixed feelings. To this day John resents what he perceives as being pulled from the family, 'rejected' and sent away. The decision to choose the school was made on the advice of a family friend who admired Dr Darling, the then principal, and recommended him as a great educationalist. No-one seems to have given any thought as to how two boys, reared in an atmosphere of social equity, leftist politics and concern for the less fortunate, might feel in the company of the wealthy sons of the Western District. My brothers could not have been more different from their schoolmates, and both often felt miserable and out of place. As adults looking back they acknowledge the good times, but still seem uncomfortable with the decision.

I missed out on contact with my brothers during their years at Geelong Grammar. For their first two years I was in Europe and after that they would briefly appear for end-of-term holidays and longer in the summer. By this time I was starting my restaurant career as well as motherhood and relaxed family gatherings were rare.

Later I brought my first husband, Monty, to our family home and I have some of the loveliest home movies of Monty with our baby daughter, Lisa, taken at 'Greenslopes'. To the sweet sounds of Gershwin's 'Summertime', Dad is filming Mum gently rocking baby Lisa, while her proud father looks on. Whenever I see this footage I have an ache in my throat. We were so happy then.

3

*Stringy Roasts &
Too Much Chocolate*

Student Years 1958–60

During the fifties school students were required to nominate whether they wished to take the 'professional' stream or the 'commercial' stream from Year 10 onwards. Those who chose commercial could look forward to working in an office of some sort or a bank. For women the professional stream led most often to teaching, or maybe to nursing. I was uninterested in either of these professions, and it was my father who suggested librarianship as an alternative. I had no objection, having always enjoyed books. And I had had that fleeting experience of working with my father on Saturday nights in the Peninsula Regional Library at Rosebud. Many of the staff at the newly created rate-funded libraries had no formal qualifications and learnt on the job. The first school of library training was run by the State Library of Victoria, with most students already working in libraries when they were not attending classes. An Arts degree was not a prerequisite for library training, but I certainly wanted to go to university. (It never occurred to me or to my parents that there might be a possible career in food.)

Without question the best thing that happened to me as a young adult was being accepted as a resident of University Women's

College. Here I found the peer group I had never had at secondary school, and I made lifelong friends, girls with whom I could explore ideas, share adventures, develop confidence, reveal myself and just luxuriate in this new experience of having friends.

As a consequence of my lack of interest in becoming a teacher I was not bonded to the Education Department as were many of my new friends. The bonding ensured that they received a fortnightly pay cheque. Because I had failed one subject in the Matriculation (ironically it was French, which became such a strong interest later in my life) I had also missed out on a Commonwealth scholarship. It was a definite disappointment from my parents' perspective, but they agreed to pay the fees and to give me a monthly allowance while I was at university.

I farewelled my father at the Frankston train station early in March 1958 with a big hug and set out for a new life. My stomach was knotted and I felt very, very nervous. I knew absolutely nobody and the future loomed darkly. I cannot recall any feeling of cheerful excitement or anticipation.

I met Helen Pyke within days of unpacking my bags. Helen had come from Methodist Ladies' College, although she had also spent several years at a country high school, unlike most of my fellow students, as I was to discover very soon. Within days she had introduced me to her close school friend Jean Watters. Jean was living in a hostel for young women while she waited for a place to be available at University Women's College, which happened quite quickly. Both girls were welcoming and seemed open to a new friendship, which was very comforting for me.

Helen was a few months younger than Jean and I. With her round, pink-cheeked face she looked younger than her years. (And still does, which is pretty annoying.) She had won a scholarship to University Women's College and it took me a little time to appreciate her very sharp mind. She was never one to push her opinion, but if asked, her analysis and comprehension were impressive. She appeared to do no work at all as far as I could see and was one of those who started an essay the night before it was due. I, on the other hand, hated deadlines and would have to slog away for at least a week to produce anything worthy of submission. Gallingly, she always received the better mark. I have always admired Helen's optimistic nature and love of new experiences. When we travel she reminds me of a bright bird, turning this way and that, eager not to miss a curious sight or interesting person, building or physical feature. She finds it puzzling that the rest of the world does not necessarily share her need for novelty.

When I first met Jean I was attracted by her energy and her openness. Jean was interested in what I had to say, which I found a welcome change after the terrifying anonymity of arriving at Melbourne University from such a small high school. And she had lots of good stories to tell of boarding school. I loved and envied her bouncing, curly hair and wide smile. During our college years, eating dreadful stodge every day, Jean became a bit plump and one of the silly memories I have is of her and a fellow student squashing the lumps out of some disgusting meal-replacement drink instead of eating dinner. Often this self-sacrifice was counterproductive, as their hunger would drive one of us to the nearby shop for chocolate in some form. These days Jean is willow slim and has an incredible willpower. Chocolate rarely passes her lips.

University Women's College was a warren of corridors and different wings. Girls were allotted rooms more or less haphazardly and proximity often encouraged special friendships. Jean and Helen were in adjacent rooms and they soon met science student Kathy Chester, who was in the next room along. Kathy became a special friend to us all. My room was in a separate far-off wing of the college and I often felt left out of the fun and games that happened in their wing.

Kathy was a country girl and, like me, came to University Women's College from a country high school. She offered commonsense opinions about practical matters, and was curious and interested in the lives of her fellow students. She fascinated me because she was one of the small number of girls studying science. We all turned to Kathy then – as we do now – for a no-nonsense opinion. I have often asked her advice on financial matters. She seems to understand the taxation system and the intricacies of superannuation, which makes her a genius in my book. Kathy is genuinely curious, likes to find out more, does not care for humbug, is a shrewd shopper, always responsive to the less fortunate, a sucker for an appealing child, knowledgeable about every plant and tree, and willing to eat almost anything. We have shared some great travel adventures in Malaysia, China, India and the United Kingdom.

Girls from all over the state, many from country areas, were hand-picked by the Head of the College, Englishwoman Myra Roper. She wanted her college to be intellectually impressive, but as importantly, she wanted its student population to reflect a broad cross-section of interests and viewpoints. Myra Roper, although strongly influenced by the traditions embedded in the great British universities, was also interested in what could be seen as 'leaning-to-the-left' causes. A major interest was China. She was an early member of the Australia China Society (now the Australia China Friendship Society) and visited China in the late fifties when what went on in that country was mostly a mystery. I am convinced it was because of my uncle Wilfred Burchett's reporting from 'the other side' that I was given a place by Miss Roper at University Women's College. It certainly was not on the basis of brilliant results.

It was also at University Women's College that I was asked for the first time, 'What school did you go to?' As a complete innocent I gave the name of my school, not realising the question was loaded with meaning, that there was even a hierarchy of private schools. In fact, other than a few very well-known schools, I had never heard the names of most of these privileged places. When someone replied, 'I went to St Catherine's' or whatever the school, my response was blank and clearly not the impressed look I was supposed to give.

It did not take long before I realised with dismay that I was not coping very well at all with the work of university. I was majoring in English and history. I had had absolutely no training whatever in critical analysis. I had never experienced being part of a small tutorial discussion group. I had not had any teachers who were qualified to discuss the detail of my subjects, much less fellow students. I had no understanding of how to read around a subject, and could no more open my mouth in a tutorial than fly to the moon.

I took to sleeping in and deliberately missing early morning lectures, thus missing breakfast. I might attend a mid-morning lecture but would skip a midday lecture because I was starving and concerned that my loud, rumbling stomach would embarrass me. I would then head back to University Women's College for our pitiful lunch and rail against the quality of the food.

I am not sure what would have become of me had I not made friends in my second year with a girl whose room was adjacent to mine, who was two years older and who was already an honours student in history. Katy Richmond helped me by pointing out that studying a particular period in history was really about understanding historical problems, noting the circumstances that gave rise to these problems, and looking at how these issues were resolved. I stopped trying to memorise pages and pages of dates and started to become interested in the issues.

While I still find it difficult to think deeply and critically, especially if the topic seems rather abstract, from this time on I found enough to interest me in my course work to pass most of my exams. I particularly loved Australian history, which gave me the opportunity to read or reread so many early Australian novels that were part of Dad's collection.

A fine arts subject did not go so well. Practically every lecture was held in the dark – all the better to view the slides – but the esteemed lecturer, Franz Phillips, had a strong accent and wrote almost nothing on the board, so that I was left wildly guessing as to the name of the artist, the church where it was to be found and when in fact it had been created. 'Quattrocento' or 'Cinquecento', he would intone, rolling the syllables. I wondered with irritation why he could not say the fourteen or fifteen hundreds. Unsurprisingly I did not pass this subject, thus failing to complete my Arts degree at the same time as my friends.

There was a tradition of a play being jointly presented each year by University Women's College and Ormond College. *The Green Pastures* by Marc Connelly was the play chosen in 1959. I was persuaded to audition for a part as one of the group of Babylonian dancers. I always enjoyed dancing and believed I was quite good at it. This was significant in my life mainly for the fact that I was required to bleach my hair and have my body painted gold. The paint washed off but I kept the blonde hair for several years. Shallow as it may sound, my personal confidence increased while I had blonde hair. (This production was also notable in hindsight for the fact that one of the children's roles was played by a very young Olivia Newton-John.)

Of course I was living another life during these three years. In my final year of school I had become involved with Peter. I imagined myself to be in love again. My parents were disapproving, but being the hospitable and democratic people they were, he was welcomed to the family table despite their conviction that this was a completely unsuitable match. Peter had left school at fifteen and had moved from job to job. But he was a great dancer, handsome, and seemingly so much more worldly than the gangly university boys my friends were going out with. Jean had already met her future husband, John Tinney. Helen had a student boyfriend as did Kathy. My relationship continued and intensified during my first year at university until I announced my engagement at the ripe old age of twenty. Meanwhile I was spending Saturday nights at various town halls, dancing, or returning to the Peninsula, where both our families lived.

We planned to marry and take up various rural pursuits, given Peter's complete lack of qualifications for any professional career. (One of my friends tells me that I spoke about establishing a duck farm! That does seem extreme as neither of us had any idea of how to manage a farm, or of running a business, or of how such a venture might be financed. Although at least I had had childhood experience in feeding ducks and cleaning out their messy shelters.) During this time I missed out on an important part of university life. I did not join any clubs, attended very few extracurricular talks or events, failed to meet or mingle with many male university students, and scuttled back to college as soon as a lecture finished, never lingering to listen or join in discussion.

Looking back I do think there was a faint whiff of rebellion in my behaviour. Silly as it sounds, I think I decided that much of the non-academic life of the university was infantile, and that my interests were more grown-up. I suppose I felt at the time that I was a bit more sophisticated than my friends. I had lost my virginity with Peter and our weekends were planned to include opportunities for plenty of time in bed. Even among close friends, sex was rarely discussed in those days. Somehow you got to know who was having a sexual relationship and then you had furtive discussions about contraception. We shared the addresses of those few doctors prepared to prescribe rubber diaphragms for unmarried girls.

My relationship with Peter was a very physical one. In fact that was probably all we had in common – sex, dancing and the thrill of the chase. At the beginning I had done most of the chasing. Ironically, by the time I started to find the relationship a bit empty he started to be much more emotionally attached to me, and he was very hurt when I made it clear that it was over and I was moving on. I had fallen in love with one of the actors in the annual college play, someone I would formerly have described as rather 'gauche', but now saw as exciting and moody and intellectually challenging. That didn't work either!

I had a few experiences with other young men that were never serious. One of them, Tom, introduced me to many of Melbourne's jazz clubs and I remember him very fondly. We said goodbye with no regrets as I prepared to leave for Europe at the end of my studies.

I certainly had an interest in and knowledge of food that surpassed that of my friends. The energy, critical faculties and focus I brought to my food investigations was far, far greater than I gave to exploring ideas or any academic material. Not surprisingly, my academic results reflected this. I regularly spent a big chunk of my monthly allowance on dinner in a good restaurant, persuading various friends to be my guest. No-one I knew considered eating a fine dinner as a necessary experience. But then I did not want to go to a symphony concert or a lecture as some of my friends did.

The Society restaurant at the top of Bourke Street was my favourite. A friend I took there remembers being impressed by my prowess at filleting and turning a pan-fried flounder. I must have been showing off. My strong memory is my first taste of a house-prepared tartufo – an oval of silky bitter chocolate ice-cream hiding a centre of chopped liqueur morello cherries, the whole floating in a pool of cream in a shallow silver bowl. And a fruit salad served in a halved pineapple, the fruits macerated in kirsch.

From time to time over the years my parents invited which-ever children were available to join them for a special meal in the city, sometimes to be followed by a night at the ballet or seeing a musical. I remember The Topsy, a Hungarian restaurant in a small lane that ran off Little Collins Street, where I always ordered the schnitzel. I absolutely loved the chestnut Mont Blanc, a pyramid of alcohol-drizzled chestnut 'worms' topped with lightly whipped cream. In remembering and attempting to reproduce this classic preparation dish many years later I realised what effort goes into boiling chestnuts and peeling the inner skins while hot – arguably the worst job in the kitchen, but I persevered. I was amazed to receive a letter many, many years later from the daughter-in-law of the owners of The Topsy, telling me that the delicious dessert I loved had been made using tinned chestnut puree! And she con-firmed my memory that the husband, her father-in-law, always wore slippers in the restaurant.

We also went to The Latin or to Mario's, both very important establishment restaurants. It was at The Latin I tasted my first bowl of handmade ravioli and I can still remember it – I think I was about ten years old at the time and was unsure about the smell of parmesan cheese. I can also recall my first gelato at the Italian home-style restaurant Pellegrini's in Crossley Street, off Bourke Street (now Becco). Using a silver spatula the waiter pressed and pushed a wave of creamy zabaglione ice-cream up and over the edge of a silvery cup, following it with a scoop of snowy lemon gelato that chilled the teeth.

The food at University Women's College was uninspiring. My friends all told me it was much better than what had been served to them at boarding school. Well, I could not make that comparison. I had no experience of institutional life. My benchmark was the lovely, inventive, beautifully presented meals prepared by my mother.

I remember little of University Women's College breakfasts as mostly I was still in bed. Lunch, however, might have been one baked tomato, a small portion of stodgy macaroni cheese or a commercial meat pie. You were expected to fill up on a towering stack of sliced white or maybe wholemeal bread and red jam. Dinner was prepared at around four or five in the afternoon. The odour of cooking vegetables and poor-quality fat wafted through the corridors for hours until we were summoned by a bell and all traipsed in. We wore our academic gowns, which I found ludicrous and could never take seriously. Admittedly the gowns were very warm, which was great in the winter months, and they were good for mopping up spilt liquids. For an evening meal we ate stringy rolled roasts of beef, or lamb, or lacklustre stews with dried-out roasted potatoes and frozen peas, and some sort of baked pudding. There were variations, of course. To compensate, or because we were guilty about not having started on an essay, many of us ate too much chocolate or too many biscuits and became quite chubby. A reasonably regular outing with whoever I could coax to accompany me would be to Lygon Street to buy delicious and rich cakes from one of the Italian shops. So hard to choose; in most cases I think I selected two.

We also had many late-night sessions in one room or another when we toasted crumpets on electric bar radiators (strictly forbidden), washed down with a shot of my cumquat brandy (alcohol was also strictly forbidden), became briefly interested in seances, discussed love, filled in questionnaires in women's magazines – anything rather than settle down to academic work. And of course most of us smoked! There were Saturday night dances called 'hops', which I attended now and then once my relationship with Peter came to an end, and between the residential colleges there were quite formal annual balls.

It took me far too long to learn how to balance a budget, although I did become quite good at living on nothing much once I had spent my allowance in half the month. I ran up debts with my friends, mostly for cigarettes and chocolate, but I think (or hope) I always paid them back.

I augmented my allowance by setting myself up as a hairdresser. I am embarrassed to remember this, as I had absolutely no idea how to cut or dress hair, but had a good eye for creating an artistic effect with a well-placed flower! Before one of the many university balls, girls with long hair would pay me to fold their locks into elaborate French rolls or braids, and perhaps tuck in a gardenia. On one occasion I even 'set' Myra Roper's hair.

At the end of our time at University Women's College, and after the final exams, Jean, Kathy, Helen and I took a holiday cottage at Torquay to celebrate the end of an epoch. We drank Porphyry Pearl wine and I cooked I know not what. For the others it ended with congratulatory telegrams from family but I had the news that I had failed fine arts. Time to split!

I was over studying for the time being.

4

Salade Tahitienne
& Pain Poilâne

Foreign Adventures 1962

As children we had pored over the family photograph albums, fascinated by glimpses of our parents as younger beings. When my father and his brother Wilfred decided to leave Australia in 1936 for their Big Adventure, they booked third-class tickets on the *Tahitien*, a cargo ship on the Messageries Maritimes line that regularly crossed the Pacific, calling in at New Caledonia, Vanuatu (then the New Hebrides), Tahiti, Panama, Martinique, Guadaloupe, Madeira, and finishing at Marseilles.

I was already a Francophile and was determined to live in France somehow. I had read a great deal about the trials, tribulations and love affairs of the Impressionist and Post-Impressionist French painters and, during my years spent observing and talking with Malcolm's parents and his aunts, had understood that there was a rich and sensual life out there. And that artists often behaved in unexpected ways and led unconventional lives. Hadn't Gauguin run away from a respectable life as a banker and headed for the South Pacific? France seemed to be at the centre of many such stories. And of good food.

I discovered that Messageries Maritimes still followed the same route. The idea of retracing my father's footsteps was irresistible.

However, I did need to save some money before I could start the next adventure.

After university I was offered a job as a library assistant in the children's section of the Coburg Library. I discovered that a fellow student of University Women's College, Priscilla, was employed in the adult section of the same library. We planned to travel together and rented a house nearby, which we shared with yet another University Women's College student, Lyn. I enjoyed the novelty of 'keeping house' with other young adults and my memories are that we all got on well. I cooked a lot; both Priscilla and Lyn had regular boyfriends and had very busy social lives. I was still enjoying evenings with my then boyfriend Tom at various jazz clubs. I loved traditional jazz, and felt variously excited, melancholy or uplifted by the liquid notes of the clarinet and the mellow rounded tone of the saxophone. From the first notes played I felt a release of tension and a rare rush of joy.

During the time I was working in the Coburg Library I became friendly with one of the sales representatives. He was very entertaining, very well read, an enthusiastic cook and from time to time we cooked for each other. He was also gay, which we never openly discussed. This was Ian Atkins, who would become a very dear friend for the next forty years.

As the year moved along and our proposed departure date loomed closer, Priscilla changed her mind, deciding to stay and get married instead of travelling. So I set out alone for an eight-week journey on the French cargo boat, travelling 'tourist', or second, class. The *Tahitien* carried around two hundred passengers, including French expatriate families returning home and a small contingent of very posh French who travelled in the tiny first-class section. There were a few Australians travelling the long route to Europe, some of whom were taking advantage of the very cheap third-class fare that was still available, known as 'steerage'. But most of the passengers were super-fit, frisky and golden-skinned young Frenchmen returning home after doing their military service in the French colonies. I was a relatively innocent twenty-one-year-old with fluffy blonde hair and big blue eyes – I was fair game.

Within hours I had met Molly and Patsy. Molly was English, returning home after two years in Australia; Patsy was an Australian looking for an adventure before she married and settled down. Both girls were travelling steerage. My education began immediately. Before the ship had cleared Sydney Harbour Molly declared that she intended to find an officer whose cabin she could share for the journey. Patsy decided the same thing. The officers did look devastatingly handsome in their summer whites and were deeply tanned. They wasted no time casting long glances at the unattached women.

This promised to be a significant eight weeks. Not to be outdone, the seamen, waiters and bar staff also started turning on the charm. Offers of private French tuition came thick and fast. Invitations to accompany officers or sailors to a nightclub at the first port of call were also freely available. There was no shortage of dancing partners at the shipboard dances. It was enough to turn any girl's head! Molly and Patsy found their officers and moved into first-class cabins.

I was sharing a cabin with two American women of a certain age – probably in their mid-fifties – and an Australian woman in her thirties, who was travelling for adventure. Seating at dinner was allocated. The first night I met one of my dinner companions, a fascinating Frenchman, probably in his forties, who seemed to have visited every island in the Pacific. He spoke perfect idiomatic English with an American accent, declared that he worked in films, was charming and non-predatory, very well read and cultivated. I thought he was probably gay. We discussed France and French culture. My surprise was total when we landed in New Caledonia and he seemed to transform himself into a wild creature. He capered on the beach with several local girls, hair flying, shirt abandoned, reminding me of a faun in a Bacchanalian scene. And he was certainly not gay!

On my first evening in port in Noumea I went to a nightclub called Le Biarritz with Molly and Patsy. From the dance floor we looked onto a silver sea; if you stood on the balcony you could hear the waves slapping on the sand. (I revisited Le Biarritz in the early 1970s and ate a delicious terrine made from flying fox. I found it still a wonderfully raffish place, but alas, it is no more!) Most of the ship's crew, officers and sailors were to be found at Le Biarritz every night we were in port. We were rushed off our feet with offers, some of which were for more than a dance. We danced the *paso doble*, the bullfighter dance, which involved much dashing and swooping. Whenever I hear the music today I am instantly back at Le Biarritz. None of us had a very good grasp of the language, so maybe we misunderstood, but when we were encouraged into dense bushes alongside the nightclub to look at the moon on the water, it is obvious to me now that something else was intended. One crew member got very angry with me when I furiously resisted his attempts to remove my dress, and pushed me hard onto the ground. I escaped unharmed but was quite scared.

Back on the boat, Molly, Patsy and I swapped stories. There were certainly plenty of wild escapades. And some pretty rapid progress in idiomatic French expressions.

After a long stretch of being at sea, when various liaisons were entrenched, we docked at Papeete, Tahiti, where we spent an enchanted week. The island was as beautiful as I had imagined and the air was scented with frangipani. I had always believed that the purple mountains, black soil and vivid greens of the Tahiti painted by Gauguin represented artistic licence. But then I saw for myself that the mountains were indeed purple, the volcanic sand on many of the beaches was black, the vegetation was vividly green and the population did in fact dress in colourful *pareos* and wash them and fling them on bushes to dry in the sun. The hibiscus and bougainvillea were just as vivid and lush as in the paintings.

Several of us visited the volcanic black sand beach. The sand was powder soft. It was here I tasted my first *Salade tahitienne*: raw fish marinated in lime juice, then tossed with coconut milk and usually served in a coconut shell. The French crew seemed very proficient at the pelvis-thrusting local dance and danced bare-chested with the local *vahinés* (Tahitian women), gorgeous in grass skirts, flowers in their long glossy hair, hips vibrating at an aston-ishing speed.

There were many surprises on this voyage. I heard about and witnessed passionate couplings in lifeboats, respectable married women sneaking into officers' cabins, illicit after-hours meetings in the kitchens or in shadowed areas of the deck, wild dancing and lovemaking on beaches and in shrubbery during the shore stops. These French officers and sailors had the time of their lives. They turned a collective blind eye to female passengers sneaking into crew-only areas. The returning servicemen got second pick. My Australian cabin mate discovered her erotic inner life with the bosun; the older American women flirted outrageously with the captain; Molly and Patsy shared stories about their officers and compared their physical attributes in language and imagery that I found astonishing.

And what was I doing? Behaving rather badly. I remember my mother's impulsive behaviour in yielding to the urge to enjoy her shipboard romance, but at least it turned out to be the love of her life, hardly the case with my own promiscuous behaviour.

I was naïve. My first mistake was to be receptive to the charm of a crew member, Christian. I did not realise that there was a hierarchy on board. Dally with a sailor or a waiter, and the officers showed their disapproval. By about day four one officer had tried to warn me that I was effectively setting myself *hors de combat* (out of the contest). Of course I haughtily told him to mind his own business. Then Christian was involved in a nasty knife fight that ended with a serious belly wound – he revealed himself to be a little thug. Audaciously, he visited me in the middle of the night in my cabin where the others were sleeping to show me the dressing on his belly. I was horrified and shooed him away. All the problems that happen when one does not really share a language – it's so difficult to pick up the subtle signals, and so dangerous. My next mistake was to be captivated by the smile and long lashes of the barman, Serge. I cannot remember how that little dalliance ended. (Some months later, when I was living near Paris with a French family, he came to visit me. I imagine he expected to find a young woman eager to fall into bed with him. This time I found, with my improved French, that his motives were pretty transparent and frankly I had moved on.)

I then turned my attentions to the officers. Alain danced beautifully but it was blue-eyed Yves, who didn't say very much, who captivated me. By the time I had decided on Yves, he and I had had a misunderstanding, I was playing hard to get and he was ignoring me. This went on for about two weeks. We eventually made up and I was easily persuaded into a cabin away from prying eyes and enjoyed some very experienced lovemaking. I remember my surprise at viewing the skimpy cotton undies worn only briefly by my preferred officer. I must have seemed very unsophisticated in my to-the-waist Cottontails! *'Doucement, doucement,'* he murmured to me.

I spent the last few nights at sea with my lover reading me poetry in between physical activities. And then we arrived in Marseilles, in the bitter cold with the famous mistral blowing. Yves was met by his mother and that was the end of that. Molly's officer was met by his wife. Not sure about Patsy.

Eight weeks is a long time to be isolated in a small space with just a few hundred people. It had seemed like a lifetime. Now the serious travel was to begin.

Molly, Patsy and I caught a train from Marseilles to Paris. Molly had practically no money so we agreed to book the cheapest seats (wooden benches) and sit up all night. The train was full and I was sitting squashed against a strange man. As the train hurtled along I felt his fingers creeping over my thigh. I leant further into Molly on the other side, thinking that possibly it had been an accident. I suspect this was my first experience of being groped. When the contact happened again I whispered to Molly that I believed the man was touching me on purpose. Molly, far more experienced in the ways of men and the world, swapped places with me. Within ten minutes she had swiped the man very hard with her bag and he promptly went somewhere else. Another lesson learnt!

After an uncomfortable night we took the boat train on to London, which entailed taking a train from Paris to Calais, transferring to the cross-channel ferry to Dover (where I saw that the cliffs really were white) and then another train onto London. Molly and I had exchanged contact details; she gave a cheery wave and disappeared into an Underground station, leaving me, surrounded by luggage, for the first time feeling utterly alone and very scared.

The first shock was the cold. Of course I knew that it would be colder than Australia but that February morning when I met my

English cousin Rainer Burchett for the first time, he suggested a walk to the library. On my return I examined deep-red weals where the wind had lashed at my legs, which were clad in inadequate trousers. It took me a while to understand about wearing adequate layers of outerwear to protect against the elements, without them being too bulky in case the heating indoors was excessive. It was especially bad in the Underground, where the dominant smell was of sweat.

It was exciting being in London. I loved the square taxis and the Cockney drivers, the double-decker buses that seemed to hurtle along at high speed, and the street signs so familiar from the Monopoly board – Mayfair, Park Lane and Piccadilly. I was charmed by the beautiful parks with emerald-green grass edged with impeccable iron railings. In the parks the trees had the faintest fuzz of new leaves and the flower beds showed the first crocus and narcissus. My cousin and his mother, Erna, lived in Hampstead, so I was soon introduced to Hampstead Heath, where they regularly went to read the Sunday papers.

I have to go back a bit to explain my relationship to my aunt Erna. When Dad returned to Australia and met my mother on the Japanese boat, his brother Wilfred stayed on in Europe. He had taken whatever employment he could get and became more and more aghast at the political upheaval happening in Germany. In London in 1938 Wilfred had met and married Erna Hammer. Erna, who was Jewish, had emigrated to England with her two daughters from a previous marriage, correctly foreseeing what would happen in Germany. For a time Wilfred was employed by the Palestine-Orient Lloyd travel company, and part of his work was to assist Jewish families to leave Germany. He returned to Australia in 1939 with a very pregnant Erna as both of them wanted their child to be born in Australia. Wilfred left in 1941, to cover the early stages of the war in the Pacific. By this time he had started his work as a freelance war correspondent, filing stories with the *Daily Express*. Erna and Rainer returned to London in 1942–3.

On his return to Australia in 1937, and for the next few years, my father was increasingly concerned about the rise of fascism and the developing crisis for Jews in Germany. Wilfred enlisted Dad's help in trying to obtain Australian visas for certain families he met. Dad was a member of the Australia-Refugee Council, which made application to immigration officials, tried to secure employment for people and applied pressure where it could. Sometimes it succeeded. My parents befriended several refugee families, meeting them at the docks and inviting them home. Such friendships were long-lasting ones. One such family was the Sedlaks.

Erich and Magda Sedlak migrated to Australia to start a new life and subsequently had three children in Australia of whom Eva was the eldest. When my aunt Erna lived in Australia between 1939 and 1942, she and the Sedlak family became very close friends, and it is fair to say that she and Magda regarded themselves to some extent as establishing an oasis of European culture among the Australian 'barbarians'. After I got to know Erna in London, she told me of her negative feelings towards Australia many times.

I found her dismissive remarks annoying and yet understandable. I could imagine that Melbourne society at that time was very limited in its cultural offerings to one used to the sophistication of Berlin and London.

I should point out that Wilfred had left Erna, with new baby Rainer, with his parents, my grandparents, on their very modest farm in muddy Gippsland, with its outside lavatory and squares of newspaper stuck on a nail for toilet paper. Erna was appalled by country life and the general lack of refinement. She quickly moved to an apartment in East Melbourne.

By the time we met in 1962 Erna and Wilfred had been divorced for many years. Wilfred had remarried and he and his Bulgarian wife, Vessa, had three children – three more cousins I would not meet for many years.

At university I was vaguely aware of Eva Sedlak but it was not until we both found ourselves in London in 1962, both having commitments to visit Erna Burchett, that we became good friends. We were also the same age. Eva was a social worker and seemingly accomplished in all directions. She was a passionate skier, an enthusiastic patron of the arts and had relatives scattered all over Europe and in Israel. She had a respectable job in a London hospital, lived in a mews cottage and even had her own car! Eva and I enjoyed each other's company and we went to the movies together, walked in parks, laughed a lot and from time to time visited Erna together.

Erna was a tiny person with a focused interest in intellectual pursuits and the works of a select range of artists and writers. She and my cousin Rainer were both extremely hospitable, although I suspect Erna had few expectations of this child from the backwater of Australia. In her conversation it seemed she believed that life in Australia in 1962 was the same as it had been when she had been parked briefly in Gippsland in 1939. She and Rainer introduced me to many delightful London experiences, including the theatre and the ballet. I remember Erna showing me with excitement a small lemon tree in the conservatory at Kew Gardens that was covered with lemons. I was rather underwhelmed, coming from a country where it was usual to have a lemon tree in the backyard.

Erna attempted to engage me in philosophical and psychological discussions, even suggesting regular readings aloud from high-minded journals. Her attempts at cultivating and improving my mind made me very uncomfortable and I fear that I presented myself as quite frivolous. Erna wondered why I often spoke to her 'in quotation marks,' as she put it, although I was never sure what she actually meant by this phrase. Perhaps she was suggesting that I always gave evasive stock responses, not wishing (or not able) to engage in discussion at the level she hoped for. Whatever it meant, I acknowledge that I did attempt to turn the conversation to topics I found easier to engage with. Fairly soon we agreed not to force matters and I could even tease her about her intellectual hero, Jung.

My parents had once more given me a modest allowance on the assumption that I would get a job quite quickly. I am embarrassed to mention a further example of my inability to manage money. Before job hunting and while the cold was still intense, I splurged on a very smart and very expensive dress at Jaeger in Piccadilly, which turned out to be far too hot for indoors. At Liberty in Regent Street, I made the even more ridiculous purchase of a pale-blue mohair coat with completely impractical three-quarter sleeves. I had yet to discover Marks & Spencers and the suburban High Street.

Molly and I decided to share an apartment. We shared a dingy second-floor flat in what was then very unfashionable Kilburn. And we did learn how to budget very quickly as neither of us had a job. Molly tried unsuccessfully to convince me that stewed lamb's heart was edible. I countered with roasted, rolled breast of lamb with a bread stuffing. One breast of lamb cost something like ninepence. Molly also introduced me to London pubs and to 'clubbing' 1960s-style. Once again her single-minded and focused intention of finding a lover amazed me. She could sit on a single drink for a very long time until a likely candidate approached, and she usually found a companion for the night. I would return alone to the flat.

I was still very intent on finding a way to live in France. My language skills had improved on the boat, thanks to Christian, Serge, Alain and Yves. In fact I had learnt a few expressions I probably needed to forget. I decided to try for a position as an *au pair*. Molly had also decided to travel so we parted company amiably after just three months, agreeing that should we end up in London in the near future we might share again.

I travelled to Paris with an English friend of a friend who also intended to look for a job as an *au pair*. She lasted just a week before deciding that she missed her boyfriend too much and returned home. So I was alone again for another adventure. It seemed to be my lot. Without difficulty I found an agency that specialised in the placement of foreign girls with French families and I set out to meet mine.

As the door opened and I introduced myself in my best French I was greeted with surprise. The family thought their *au pair* was coming from Austria. There were few Australian *au pairs* in those days and *australienne* and *autrichienne* were not far apart. It was a good ice-breaker. Both Monsieur and Madame spoke perfect English, which was certainly very helpful in the early days when my brain pounded with the effort of finding the correct tense and the right word. I was to have charge of a six-year-old called Marie-Claire. The house was in Versailles and both parents worked in Paris. They would leave around eight a.m. each morning and Marie-Claire and I would entertain each other until it was time to take her to nursery school four mornings a week. I then did household chores, such as washing and ironing, attempted to read the French newspaper, read books, and usually waited to collect Marie-Claire before setting out for the food shopping. I needed her by my side to recall the word for 'slice' if I was buying ham, or 'mouldy' if Madame had wanted me to return the bread to the baker. I always had extremely specific instructions to give the butcher, the baker, the *charcutier*, or the attendant at the fruit and vegetable shop.

Marie-Claire was a dear little girl and absolutely no trouble to mind and entertain. Sometimes we took a picnic lunch to Le Petit Trianon palace gardens and entertained ourselves singing French songs and picking *boutons d'or* (buttercups). The family home had a lovely back garden, where we could sit under a tree or play hide-and-seek. We read lots of stories. I think it was Marie-Claire who introduced me to *Asterix the Gaul*. This comic strip had first appeared in 1959 and quickly become very popular. She also had several books of the adventures of Tintin. My French comprehension improved quickly, but the ability to converse with fluency was much harder. The everyday activities required a fairly straightforward vocabulary and I felt I was coping well, until the family had guests and the speed of conversation rapidly increased. I usually retired with a headache.

It was a very lonely time as I had no-one else to talk to. On my day off I would take the train to Paris, and even though all the delights of Paris were available, I often spent the day walking, staring into the river, admiring the mouth-watering displays of cakes or the eye-popping displays in the cheese shops, sitting in cafés and feeling utterly alone. Then I would take the train back to Versailles.

I wrote many letters home and one friend kept a few of them. On rereading them I am pleased to find that despite my solitude I was thrilled with Paris, commenting on the fashions, the flower shops, the river and the men!

For the first month all went well. I learnt a great deal about how a middle-class French family lived, especially with regard to food. These were lessons I would carry into my own life forever. In the morning there would be a short discussion about dinner. Sometimes either Madame or Monsieur would tell me they would bring some special ingredient from Paris. More often I would be asked to shop. In a notebook I recorded my surprise that Monsieur seemed to be really interested in whether we should buy carrots or beans for the evening meal. Meat or fish were luxuries and were not eaten every day. Every meal had at least two courses, usually three. There was always a bowl of fruit put on the table at the conclusion of dinner. We often ate prepared dishes from the local *charcutier*. Dishes such as stuffed tomatoes, or a salad such as *céleri-rave rémoulade* or *carottes rapées*, were always bought in. As would be a slice of a country terrine, a waxy *poutargue* – the cured roe of mullet that was a delicacy spread on hot buttered toast – or slices of ham to be eaten with small red-skinned potatoes. We ate green salads every day and the family tradition was that Monsieur would mix the dressing himself. I would have washed and patted each leaf dry before rolling them in a dry cloth and placing the bundle into the refrigerator. A warm vegetable dish of mushrooms or leeks would be cooked with butter and herbs, almost always followed by a piece of cheese.

At the weekend we would have a joint of meat or game, a chicken, or occasionally a piece of salmon. For these special meals there was always much anticipatory conversation, some discussion about how best to prepare the dish and then, when it finally appeared, modest portions of meat or chicken were served, again to be augmented by a vegetable dish, a salad, a piece of cheese and a piece of fruit. I never cooked a dessert, but on Sundays it was common to visit a patisserie and buy an apple tart or similar.

During the week Monsieur and Madame ate a substantial lunch, often with clients. They instructed me to buy myself meat if I needed it for lunch but I rarely did so. They also convinced me that I should revert to my natural hair colour, assuring me that blue eyes and brown hair were far more startling in France than fair hair and blue eyes. I think I was ready for a change and avoiding the cost of maintaining blonde hair was another compelling incentive. So I had my hair cut very, very short and returned to being a brunette.

Au pairs received a very modest allowance, bed and board, and were given one day off per week. They were expected to do light housework and care for a child or children. Sometimes in the park I would meet other *au pairs* and sometimes I heard stories of exploitation, disputes about the amount of heavy cleaning that was reasonable and so on. My family was scrupulously fair in all of these matters.

I did wonder why the family never served wine. As my language skills improved and as we all relaxed a bit, both parents started to tell me things that perhaps they should not have. Monsieur told me I should be aware that Madame had an alcohol problem and that I should alert him if I found evidence of stashed bottles or odd behaviour. Madame on the other hand told me that Monsieur had no interest in sex and that she had a German lover whom she visited several times a year and who sometimes telephoned her.

Soon after these confessions, I was alone with Madame for a day – I cannot remember why she was not at work. As the day progressed I became more and more certain that she was drinking. Her language became a bit slurred, she bumped into the doorway a couple of times, she spoke more and more about the German lover, and she started cleaning out a cupboard with manic energy. She was really talking to herself rather than to me. I opened a cupboard in the kitchen and found a half-empty bottle of Scotch, which as the day progressed became a two-thirds empty bottle of Scotch. I was unsure what to do. Late in the afternoon she went to bed and was sound asleep when Monsieur arrived home. As it happened I did not need to say anything. There were slammed doors, shouting. I just prepared pasta for Marie-Claire, who seemed oblivious to the commotion. I bathed her and put her to bed before Monsieur reappeared. He went to say goodnight to Marie-Claire and then came into the kitchen. He came over to me, put an arm around me, gave me a big hug and apologised for what had happened during the day.

I have to admit that that was the start of our affair.

I have no defence. I was lonely. He was charming. He and his wife did not like each other but were united in their love for Marie-Claire. We arranged trysts when I was supposed to be having my day off in Paris and he was supposed to be dropping me at the station and then going to spend the day at his hobby, which was flying small planes. On these days Madame would have arranged to spend the day with her family at their country property. Once or twice Madame confessed to me that she was off on a flying visit to her lover. By now I had passed on this news to her husband. He seemed uninterested in her infidelity.

He had plenty of interest in sex, just not with his wife. We would take a room in a small *hôtel de jour* for an hour or two and after our enthusiastic lovemaking we would go to a small café to muse about the impossible future. The *hôtels* were in the seedy Saint-Denis area in Paris and were more than a little sordid, but we also meandered in more salubrious areas and on one such occasion I had my first stroll through the arcades of the Place des Vosges, said to be one of the most beautiful squares in the world. It certainly seemed magical to me. He introduced me to the pleasures of *pain Poilâne* with raw ham and a glass of delicious fresh wine. These days when in Paris, I usually enjoy a sandwich of raw ham on Poilâne bread and experience a pleasant twinge of nostalgia. It was on one of these bittersweet outings that we read of the death of Marilyn Monroe. She was such an icon, and I suspect many will remember where they were on that day.

The affair was crazy, of course, and doomed to discovery. But I was in love by now and had dreams of Monsieur leaving his wife.

We took impossible risks. He would sometimes visit me in my tiny, narrow bed just metres from where Marie-Claire slept, even leaving footprints clearly outlined in the liberal scattering of talcum powder that Marie-Claire liked to use. There would be a special brush of the hand as we dried the dishes together. Occasionally we risked a kiss. Madness! And we were sprung. Madame's young brother caught us in an embrace in the kitchen and quickly passed this information to Madame. I was sent on my way.

I must have suppressed what happened next because my memory is mostly a blank. I believe that Madame left me a letter telling me to leave the house that day. My time as an *au pair* had lasted just four months. I couldn't face another family, preferring to head back to more familiar ground to nurse my broken heart. I have no recall of actually packing, or travelling to London, and no idea where I went. Perhaps I stayed in a hotel? I do know that shortly after this Molly and I met up again and found another flat, this time in an equally unfashionable part of London, near Portobello Road. Monsieur wrote, but it was over and of course I was heartbroken. I sought a job, still determined to return to France again but not immediately. I informed my family in Australia of my change of address but left out the details.

Many years later Monsieur visited Australia and sought me out. At the time I was married to Monty but feeling overworked, underappreciated and pretty unattractive. A brief fling with a still-charming Frenchman seemed like a good tonic, although I was consumed with guilt afterwards. We never had any further contact. I still wonder what happened to Marie-Claire.

5
Ackee & Saltfish

Monty 1962–4

Back in London I really needed a job. Through a friend of my father's I obtained an interview with the head librarian at the BBC's Broadcasting House in Portland Place. I had a glowing reference from my former boss at the Coburg Library and I was offered a position. The pay was appalling but the work was fascinating as the library was the research hub for the producers and I really enjoyed my fellow workers.

The BBC received review copies of many, many books. They filled a large room to overflowing and the library employees were invited to help themselves. Trying to make my nine pounds a week go a little further, I admit to taking bundles of shiny new books to a dealer in secondhand books and using this money to help make ends meet. Maybe everyone else did so too. I also took an evening job as an usherette at the Notting Hill Classic cinema for an extra four pounds a week and remember enjoying repeated screenings of early Alfred Hitchcock and Marlon Brando films.

My first Christmas away from home loomed and I started to have a serious bout of homesickness. My aunt Erna had offered to cook a Christmas lunch. I knew this was an especially magnanimous offer and not usually something she did. She was Jewish, a vegetarian, did not enjoy cooking and I am not sure whether her family usually celebrated at this time of the year. As my own family were not at all religious it was not the spiritual side of Christmas I was missing, just the gathering of family. I was rescued from what I felt would be an 'obligation occasion' by an interesting invitation from a colleague to spend Christmas in the country with her aunt. She told me that in her younger years she too had been a traveller and had fond memories of her time in North America and especially of those who had invited her to share special times with them. She now tried to extend similar hospitality to lone travellers she came across. She certainly made my Christmas memorable. Looking back on it now I wonder whether these two delightful Englishwomen stage-managed some of my Christmas surprises. It turned into the Christmas from central casting.

On Christmas Eve I travelled by British Rail to the West Country, to their tiny village outside Salisbury. I remember being most impressed by the plush seats and by the comforting foot warmer provided in the train carriage. The house was modest and comfortable, my colleague and her aunt both welcoming and interested in hearing of my (selectively edited) travel experiences. We trimmed the tree and wrapped presents and were delightfully interrupted by a choir of carol singers outside the door. They were offered iced biscuits and a silver coin each. The evening continued with more carols, this time broadcast from the famed choir at King's College Chapel, Cambridge.

The next morning we awoke to a white Christmas Day. So exciting! We walked about a mile to Salisbury Cathedral, which is awe-inspiring at any time but breathtaking with a light powdering of snow. After an invigorating walk back from church, our breath preceding us in ghostly puffs, we enjoyed a restorative sherry before tucking into a traditional lunch. The coal fire blazed, the turkey was delicious, the pudding just as it should be. After lunch we sipped port (and I don't even like port), dozed and listened to the Queen's message.

The next day we went to watch the local hunting club gather for their annual Boxing Day hunt. I couldn't quite believe that the scene was real – all those red coats, red faces, bowler hats, hounds and stamping horses. The publican's lad was busy handing around the 'stirrup cup' – the parting cup of port or sherry shared by those at a traditional foxhunt. With a tally-ho and the sounding of a horn, they were off, leaving me amazed.

I returned to London after four days of warmth and home comforts, knowing that I had experienced a very special English Christmas.

After a few months at Broadcasting House I was transferred to the Television Centre at Shepherd's Bush. There the work was even more exciting as I was often checking out books and periodicals to producers of hugely popular BBC series such as *Steptoe and Sons* and *Z-Cars*, an early police drama, probably a forerunner to *The Bill*. Most of my female colleagues were seriously starstruck and mention of then-heartthrob (later to become Sir) Cliff Richard or Brian Blessed who played 'Fancy' Smith in *Z-Cars*, would send them into a giggling frenzy.

During this winter of 1962–3 London experienced one of its worst smogs. Many people died and the weather was front-page news. Legislation was to change after 1968 but in this year the combination of industrial coal fires and fog meant that on many days visibility was reduced to a metre. I have memories that I can hardly credit, of coming out of the tube station at Westbourne Park around six o'clock in the evening to a world that was a dark-grey, smelly curtain. I would walk home with my arms outstretched in case I hit a lamppost and remember shuffling to find the kerb.

But it was also the London of the Swinging Sixties. The girl at the next desk was a clone of mod fashion icon Mary Quant, with a severe square bob haircut, white-pink lipstick, tiny skirt and black stockings. The newspapers were full of the Profumo scandal, where it emerged Conservative Secretary of State for War, John Profumo, had had an affair with Christine Keeler, the reputed mistress of an alleged Russian spy. There were accounts of outrageous parties in the country houses of the aristocracy. Carnaby Street was the hottest place for the young, and the Beatles were just about to burst onto the London scene.

It all seemed so speedy in London. My life had been pretty pedestrian in Australia, working in the library in Coburg, taking the tram home to a very suburban house I shared with two women, saving money for the big trip, and occasionally going to the movies. In the streets around Portland Place there were crowds of people and Oxford Street was always jammed. The accents fascinated me, and I was surprised at the speed with which those big red buses roared along. People dashed across streets paying scant attention to traffic signals, some men wore bowler hats. There was so much to look at, listen to and laugh about.

Molly's and my flat, just around the corner from Portobello Road markets, was on the first floor. Our downstairs neighbours were two elderly women who regarded us with deep suspicion and were alarmed when noisy friends visited. Their alarm turned to horror when I was visited by two black men some months after moving in. Monty was about to enter my life.

It was Eva Sedlak who first met Monty, always known as Monty and never by his full name, Rupert Montague. Molly and I were very curious about this black man she was seeing and even more so when we saw his photo and realised how handsome he was! Eva said very little, despite Molly's insistent questioning, so we had no idea if this relationship was important to her or not. She was always very reserved where her feelings were concerned.

Monty was a keen jazz lover and attended every concert of importance. He was a regular visitor to Ronnie Scott's and other jazz clubs. We first met at a party Molly and I held in our flat. I remember dancing with Monty briefly; I also remember drinking far too much wine and spending quite a lot of time locked in the toilet being sick! The next thing I remember about Monty was that Eva left London for a skiing holiday and one day Monty turned up at the flat (startling our downstairs fellow tenants), saying he was in the area and 'just wanted to say hello'. I was surprised but we chatted pleasantly about jazz. I recall it being a very hot London day, and very humid. I was lying on the bed in our larger bedroom, which also doubled as a sitting-room and conducted the conversation from this prone and perhaps provocative position. I don't believe I had any ulterior motives at this stage.

Monty was the eldest of eight siblings, seven boys and one girl. (All the men in Monty's family were tall. I later saw the tiny family home he grew up in and I cannot imagine how it could have accommodated so many grown strapping men.) He and his siblings had a strong desire to leave as soon as practicable in order to be independent and start earning some money. Monty enlisted with the RAF towards the end of the war and had been stationed in Scotland. He painted a graphic picture of the contrast between his sun-drenched island home of Jamaica and Scotland in the middle of winter. He also implied that he had had a marvellous time in Scotland and had enjoyed being an exotic specimen. Monty hinted at romantic entanglements. He seemed not to want to elaborate.

Once the war was over he trained in industrial glass-blowing, which was used to make television tubes and was a booming industry. But when we met he was in fact employed as a 'bagman' for an illegal gambling club organised by his Chinese friend Joe. It was Monty's job to collect the betting slips and manage the money, both in and out. He was probably on the dole as well. He seemed to have no moral scruples about this activity. He was also fascinated by business and by cricket.

The next day Monty rang me at work and suggested we go to a well-known pub in Chelsea called Six Bells. Again I was very surprised and assumed he wanted to ask me about Eva. We met at the pub, danced and had a drink or two, and it soon became obvious that Monty was, at least on this evening, interested in me and had no intention of discussing his relationship with Eva. I was excited by Monty and thought him physically irresistible but my conscience was already troubling me. Back at my flat, when it was obvious that bed was on both our minds, I made a heroic effort to challenge him and ask, 'What about Eva?' His answer was, 'What *about* Eva?' I think in retrospect he was behaving in a rather shabby way towards her. And yet in Monty's defence he said that he didn't believe he was anybody special to Eva, that he had enjoyed her company but that it was no more than that. I allowed myself to be convinced pretty easily!

We spent a very torrid two days wrapped in each other's arms, emerging briefly to eat my first Jamaican meal of pigs' tails with rice and peas, and to read newspapers. My head was whirling. I had never known such tenderness, or such 'adult' attention. Most of my serious boyfriends back home had been pretty unsophisticated, as had I been, and my ill-advised French affair and French cargo boat adventures seemed a long time ago. Monty was sixteen years older than me and he was relaxed and confident with women, but at all times an interesting as well as a romantic, passionate and considerate companion. And he was gorgeous!

The low point of this fantastic time in my life was when Eva returned from skiing. I straightaway told her I had been seeing Monty and was by now heavily involved with him. She was angry but very upset too. He had meant more to her than she had ever intimated and I don't think she ever forgave me. The next meeting between us was two years later. I was doing some temporary work at a bookshop in Melbourne that was managed by my old friend Ian Atkins, and was six months pregnant with Lisa when I saw Eva at the counter. We greeted each other warmly but warily. Eva later married and lived for a time in the United States. (After her return to Australia we met intermittently and reminisced amiably about our shared adventures in London. Monty was never mentioned.)

But that was in the future and this London year of 1962 was marvellous. Monty and I went through the stage of seeing each other every day, being together almost every night. I met his friends and cherish memories of funny Lester, serious Winston and gorgeous Gertie. He met mine. Jean Watters was now married to John Tinney, her university sweetheart, and they had arrived in Europe, about to start their posting as *assistants de langue* (language assistants) at a school in Caen in Normandy. We had a delightful weekend together in London. I have always loved having my special friends meet one other and I am sure I beamed as everyone got along famously. And Monty and I became closer and closer. There were memorable parties with fun-loving West Indians (mostly from Jamaica), lots of laughter, lots of spicy food, lots of compliments on my blue eyes and pale skin. (Oh God, how I hated my pale skin!)

Monty had taught himself to cook out of self-defence. Living alone his options had been to eat British stodge, starve, or learn to fend for himself, the last of which he did admirably. I had moved into his apartment in West Kensington where he used to carpet the kitchen with thick layers of newspaper to permit an easy clean-up after the frequent gatherings to eat juicy pigs'-tail stew, escoveitched fish (fried fish onto which is poured a vinegar and spice pickle) or fricassee of pork chops from paper plates. All three dishes were central in the Jamaican repertoire. Monty's friend Gertie brought beef patties and amazing cakes and puddings.

Monty took me to the West Indian street markets in Portobello Road and elsewhere, which were a riot of colour, sing-song voices and good humour, where we bought green bananas and plantains, sweet potatoes and Scotch bonnet chillies. I learnt to enjoy boiled bananas and fried breadfruit, and was introduced to the national dish of Jamaica, ackee and saltfish, which is always on offer at breakfast. 'Ackee, rice, saltfish are nice' was a lyric sung at the time by Harry Belafonte in his hit song 'Jamaica Farewell'. (I wonder whether anyone would sing 'The nights are gay' any more.) Ackee looks like scrambled egg and tastes a little like avocado. The capsicum-sized pinky red fruit from the enormous ackee tree bursts open when ripe to display shiny black (inedible) seeds and creamy flesh. Unless the fruits have opened naturally, it is said to be poisonous.

Erna Burchett voiced her disapproval of my lover. I think she felt that our differences were so enormous as to promise trouble further down the track. I don't think any of our subsequent problems had anything at all to do with race, background or age difference, as she prophesied. Molly thought Monty very desirable and cast an interested eye in his direction but he just laughed at her. It was no longer unusual to see black faces on the streets and I do not believe I encountered any hostility, other than with the women in the downstairs flat. Monty was very charming and had made friends with his local butcher, corner shop owner and so on, so that a wander around the shops with him met smiles and good humour all the way.

By now it was June and London was enjoying a long, hot summer. Months earlier I had accepted a contract to teach English conversation in a French teacher training college, just as Jean and John Tinney were now doing. The position was to be at Tours in the Loire Valley and to start in September. I had also agreed to a hitchhike to Greece with Molly in August, so in two months' time Monty and I were facing a long separation. In retrospect I have to marvel at my loyalty to Molly. Newly in love, facing a nine-month separation from September onwards, I did not contemplate backing out of my commitment to my friend. Perhaps I was a bit scared of the very forthright Molly, although I feel fairly certain that had the situation been reversed Molly would not have thought twice about changing her plans.

I have often wondered what it was that Monty found so appealing in me. Was it my relative lack of sophistication, or my enthusiasm for the new and my enjoyment of his lifestyle with his upbeat friends? Perhaps it was this, together with the fact that although he was of a different race and colour, it had no negative significance but was a very positive turn-on to me. And also my head was always full of projects and plans and he liked that. One of his best friends, Ossie, was also involved with an Australian girl and the two men occasionally made remarks about these 'real' Aussie girls compared with the many English girls they had known and presumably courted. I am sorry that I lost touch with Ossie's Australian girlfriend and later wife, Jenny.

Monty and I made the most of our time together over the next two months and I fell more in love every day. Molly and I then had our holiday in Greece and had a marvellous time. Hitchhiking from London to Greece seemed a bit of an adventure to us, but we did not consider it dangerous. We had a couple of unpleasant experiences with drivers who had the wrong idea, but Molly was wise to these tricks and had us out of those cars quickly. Somewhere towards the end I collected several letters from Monty and they were the sort of dream letters that a girl keeps forever (as I did for many, many years). I went on to my school in France and Molly returned to London and her job. I was now, of course, completely torn between my desire to be with Monty and the beginning of what I had dreamt of for such a long time – the opportunity to live and work in France, conquer the language and generally hone my sophistication.

Once again I was on my own and fearful of how to proceed. I found the school and on the second day discovered a note in my locker clearly intended for someone else. The someone else was female and called Ursula. The note said, 'Let's meet for a drink at L'Univers at five o'clock this evening,' and was signed 'John'. Desperate for company I decided to be bold and turn up at the bar and find John. Which was not that hard as a young Englishman was in loud conversation with a young woman whose strong accent I recognised as being from the north of England. The young woman, Ursula Chamberlain, became one of my dear friends. I introduced myself and explained my presence to John and all was well. He had got his schools confused, thinking Ursula was at the École Normale des Filles, which was in fact my school. Ursula was a wonderfully extroverted and warm-hearted girl. She made friends wherever she went, and I got to enjoy some reflected friendship.

For my first few weeks I had rented a room in the home of Madame Duval. The facilities included a gas ring, a tiny cupboard, a tap and a plastic bidet. The bath was under lock and key and could be requested once a week. Ursula remembers us having snacks of delicious cheese and baguettes as we sat on my bed and picked the fleas from the bedcover. Another lasting memory of my time *chez* Madame Duval was viewing the funeral of John F. Kennedy on her television set.

I decided I needed to move. Ursula found us a tiny flat in the old part of the town and we had a very happy time there. There was still no shower or bath and we used the public bathhouse twice a week, heading off with our soap and shampoo and hurrying home with wet hair. Our apartment was in a very old house that was in desperate need of restoration, which did happen years after we had left. Ursula was told that it had once belonged to the silvermaker for Louis XIV!

Each morning I walked across the Loire to the teacher training college. In winter the river half-froze, which fascinated me. I was completely unused to seeing frozen rivers or hearing the creaks and cracks as chunks of ice moved sluggishly through the icy river. My classes at the *école* were not very taxing. Small groups of around ten young women would sit together and we would speak in English on a given topic. My role was to correct, repeat and reinforce, and to guide the discussion. There was no assessment expected, so once the day's contact classes were over my time was my own.

I was very impressed by the quality lunch provided for the students and could not help but compare it with the college offerings I had endured. Every day there was a simple entrée, followed by a main course of meat or fish, cooked simply and accompanied by a vegetable and a green salad. Cheese was then served, and a bowl of fruit. I was astonished that despite there being afternoon classes, there was also *vin de table* on offer for these students of eighteen or nineteen. It was also noteworthy that not many of the students were interested in the wine. I usually had a small glass.

I ate at a separate table with the two *surveillantes*, women employed to look after the students' welfare in a very general way. Often these positions were taken by university students, who received bed and board in exchange for sharing meals with the students and being available to listen to their concerns and advise on personal or study issues. They were very good company for me, being about my own age.

Occasionally I was not needed in the afternoon and sometimes I accompanied Ursula to the student *resto* − a facility for all students at the university. For a small price, students were issued with vouchers that they exchanged for a meal. On Thursdays the menu was always grilled horse steaks and chips, which I found delicious. Ursula and I also visited all the local cafés. We were both quite greedy, for the food as well as for the experience. This was Tours, famous for the pork *rillettes de Tours* and the *rillettes du Mans*, which included rabbit and came from the nearby town of Le Mans. Neither of us had tasted rillettes before, or for that matter *brandade de morue*, another favourite starter, made from salt cod and potato. Cafés served coarse-cut country terrines in their original dish with a knife impaled in it so you could cut yourself a slice. And the generous selection of cheeses was similarly presented and left on the table. Of course the expectation was that a discerning French gourmet would survey the selection and cut one piece, maybe two. I fear that Ursula and I often cut more than this.

I was seduced by the sensational cake shops and ate a great number of cakes. Slices of vanilla flan; chestnut barquettes with a fluffy chestnut mousse piped onto an almond frangipane base, coated with vanilla and chocolate fondant; and in the warmer months, strawberry and raspberry tartlets. Inevitably I started to put on weight, despite my daily two-kilometre walk.

In writing this I realise that here is another bit of repetitive behaviour. Just as during my years at Melbourne University, when my romantic attachment to someone outside of university life prevented me really engaging with all that the university had to offer, here in France I was in danger of doing the same thing. In love and separated from my lover, I did a lot of mooning about and eating. I really think Ursula saved me from myself. I lived for Monty's letters. Our landlord, Docteur Assémat, came by most days, but his opening of the locked communal letterbox was very haphazard. We developed a technique whereby I would hoist Ursula up in my arms so that she could stick her hand inside the letterbox, the slot for which was too high up the wall for easy access. It was then an easy matter to pull out the letters without waiting for the docteur's visits.

I stuck it out and spent almost all of the modest allowance paid to me as a language assistant on regular fares back to London, together with eating out in country restaurants up and down the Loire Valley. I was fortunate to meet an Englishman who was engaged to a girl teaching in the North of France, and with whom I could therefore enjoy a platonic friendship. He also loved to eat. Roy was a great dining companion, and a thoroughly delightful young man. I am sorry that I lost touch with him.

Ursula greatly improved my enjoyment of the time working in Tours, as she challenged my tendencies to be self-obsessed and recluse-like, and I was swept up in her general outgoing nature and included in many outings. I might otherwise have spent the year hiding in my room writing letters to my love when not in the rather sterile classroom.

One interesting bit of trivia is that for the previous year before coming to France Ursula had danced every Saturday night at a club in her hometown, Liverpool, where a local group was getting quite a bit of attention – the club was The Cavern, and the group was, of course, the Beatles.

Before too long Ursula met and fell for a handsome American, Richard Kalt, who was studying medicine at Tours University. Ursula and Richard married and continued to live and study in

Tours long after I returned to London. And Jean and John Tinney contrived to stay in France at the end of their time as *assistants de langue* – John as a chauffeur at the Australian Embassy, Jean as a salesgirl at Le Drugstore on the Champs-Elysée.

On one trip back to London, full as ever with romance, social outings to West Indian clubs or private homes, parties of which there always seemed to be at least one every weekend, Monty and I started to talk of the future. Monty seemed just as determined as I was that our relationship should become permanent. He even became a little defensive, I think, anticipating that I might face parental opposition. Of course at this stage he had not yet met my liberal, tolerant, trusting parents. Judging anyone on the basis of their race or colour would have been unthinkable for either of them. But I suspect that despite his outwardly positive attitude Monty had experienced negative reactions somewhere in the past.

To this point Monty's career had been going nowhere. I have always been able to fantasise quite convincingly, and it seemed to me that if Monty and I were living in Australia he could develop a business somehow. He was interested in trying his hand at importing West Indian products, principally rum, ackees and tinned breadfruit. I convinced Monty that in order to introduce these delicacies to the Australian public, we would have to have an outlet where they could be sampled, such as a coffee lounge.

It is hard to remember what preceded 'coffee lounges'. And I don't remember coffee lounges in London, which was all about clubs and pubs. In my mind coffee lounges are inextricably linked to the growing Italian character of Lygon Street in Melbourne in the early sixties. Perhaps there were no places for young people to congregate and chat other than pubs before this? Coffee lounges in the sixties did not inevitably involve an espresso machine, even though the first such machine was operating in Carlton's Caffe Sport in 1953 and the popularity of coffee drinking escalated from the early sixties and has not declined since. They differed from restaurants in that they were open and offered food all day. Until Melbourne sorted out its licensing laws the beverages drunk were mainly coffee or soft drinks.

Monty's knowledge of Australia was restricted to what he had read in the enthusiastic newspaper reports of the cricket Test series held in Australia in 1960–1. The exuberant West Indies team, captained by Frank Worrell (later Sir Frank), had charmed the crowds. Ironically at the time West Indian cricketers could be invited to play in Australia but they would not have had a chance to migrate to the country due to the restrictive and shameful White Australia policy. Monty adored cricket and felt that a demand for West Indian produce would be inevitable given the love affair that seemed to have developed between Australians and West Indians during the cricketing Test. The loophole in the immigration laws would permit Monty to enter permanently as my husband. He also held a British passport due to his long residency in the United Kingdom.

Planning was necessary and I still had six months of my French contract to run. Monty was eager to start investigating how he could become an importer. My next trip to London would be at Christmas, when I would have a longer break than usual. The first decision we made was to marry then, so that there would be no delay in seeking visas for Monty when the time came to travel. We planned to travel to Australia via Canada, where Monty had three brothers he had not seen for about twenty years, and then on to Jamaica to set up contacts for the planned import business. Luckily Jean and John Tinney could be in London for the ceremony, which was set for 4 January 1964. Somehow their being present made it seem connected with my Australian life.

My parents were no doubt startled when they heard the news of our intent to marry. Christopher tells me that I telephoned from

London with the news when both brothers were home from school for the long Christmas holidays. That must have caused panic as telephoning from overseas was very rare and only to be done in times of great urgency. Clearly I thought this was one of those times. Christopher answered the phone and I said to him, 'Get Mum. I am about to marry a Jamaican.' He decided to get Mum but not give her a heads-up. He says that there was no general alarm, but he has the impression that despite my parents' belief in the brotherhood of man, they wanted to be reassured that I was going to be cared for and that Monty would be a suitable partner. They behaved marvellously, writing letters of encouragement in which they introduced themselves to Monty. They decided to come to London for the wedding and were really very gracious when I countered by saying maybe it would be better to pay our fares back to Australia! They no doubt swallowed any disappointment and agreed. That was the first of many such injections of funds over the next few years. Diana remembers being excited at the thought of a wedding in the family and looked forward to meeting her new brother-in-law.

With my very limited funds I bought a plain blue woollen suit and a furry hat as it was likely to be freezing on the appointed day. Monty bought a new suit and looked very suave. We were both pretty excited. I had a beautiful heavy gold ring that had belonged to my maternal grandmother – I do wonder why I had a wedding band in my travelling possessions! There was a slight hiccup when Monty's friend Ossie, who had offered to drive us to the registry office at Hammersmith, had forgotten to fill the car with petrol and it stopped. We almost had to break into a run to take up our allotted appointment. The ceremony was pretty impersonal and very short. I signed the register as Stephanie Montague. We emerged with big smiles and had a very few photographs taken.

Erna, who had chosen not to attend the ceremony, had insisted that we visit her afterwards, so Jean, John, Monty and I had a rather stilted afternoon tea before retreating to our apartment, where there was a rather more joyous celebration with several of our Jamaican friends.

I returned alone to Tours as Mrs Montague to continue my contract before our planned departure for Australia. Monty flew to Paris for Easter towards the end of my time in France for four days of loving. The weather was mild and sunny and when I look at the pictures we took, of Monty and me laughing as we straddled the balustrade on the Seine, or the next day when we had a marvellous picnic with the Tinneys in the Bois de Boulogne, of John Tinney upending a bottle of Beaujolais straight into his mouth as we all sprawled in the park, I can still feel the sunshine on my back.

Travelling to Australia via Canada and Jamaica was really our honeymoon. Although by now we had been together for more than a year we had spent a good deal of that time living in different cities, so travelling together was enchanting. And yet I can recall only fragments of this journey.

Monty had not kept in contact with his family during his twenty years in Britain and had never returned to Jamaica in that time. I found both things surprising as contact with my family had always been so important to me. So meeting brothers not seen for twenty years was rather stressful for Monty to anticipate. It was almost like meeting strangers as they had so few shared experiences. We flew to Toronto and were met by Monty's brother Spurgeon. I was interested to note the family resemblance. Spurgeon's charming wife, Lyn, also originally from Jamaica, introduced us to her three very young children. Next we met brother Volney and his wife,

Ruth, resident in nearby Windsor. Ruth was white and they had no children. A third brother, Anthony, was presumed to be living in the United States but the Canadian brothers had lost contact with him.

I remember visiting Niagara Falls, where I ate fudge for the first time and found it overwhelmingly sweet and its slightly grainy texture weird. There is just a glimmer or splash of memory regarding the falls themselves. I can hear a mighty roar. And I have a memory of eating fried chicken in a diner and being underwhelmed by the taste but overwhelmed by the size of the portion. I also remember driving in supersized cars.

On to Jamaica and my memories are all in technicolour. We travelled to Monty's family home, where he was born, in the deeply green and lush countryside of the Parish of St Elizabeth. I sat on the porch and dandled a baby on my knee. (Recently, forty-five years after that first visit, I again sat on that porch and chatted to that 'baby', now a sophisticated and charming woman and mother of a twenty-year-old daughter.)

The house was small, set high on its block and reached by a long driveway. Each day there seemed to be more family to meet, including brothers Mervyn and Lindy and their wives and children. And there was a similarly strong family resemblance in each of the brothers I met here. Mervyn's wife, Lee, and Lindy's wife, Una, were very welcoming.

Religion was very important there. I don't think I went to church but I remember grace being said before each meal. I was intrigued to read the bumper stickers on many of the cars on the road: 'I am blessed', 'Jesus is coming soon', 'The Lord is my life and my salvation'.

Our base was in Kingston and we stayed with Barrington Watson, a painter friend of Monty's whom I had met briefly in London, as well as his gorgeous, sassy wife, Gloria, and their two young children. Monty set about visiting business contacts. I wanted to explore Kingston with the two children – they babysat me rather than the other way around. In 1964, unlike today, Kingston appeared to be quite safe. We travelled on the local buses and had outings downtown and to the beach. I had a few strange looks cast my way and I was told later that no white person would ever use the buses. And probably no white person would ever line up as we did to buy spicy beef patties from a street stall. With my young companions I was oblivious to all of this. The beef patties were delicious.

Barry and Gloria had a maid who showed me how to make rice and peas. The peas in this dish are actually red kidney beans, cooked with rice and coconut milk. She also showed me how to roast a breadfruit. In days gone by families would have buried the breadfruit, which is about the size of a coconut, in the coals of a fire until the skin was well blackened before peeling it away to get at the dense flesh. The modern approach was to stand it on an open gas flame and keep turning it until it was thoroughly blackened all over. I also learnt more about the curious ackee, which originated in Africa but by now was very common throughout the island. The national dish of ackee and saltfish was eaten most days at breakfast, usually with slices of fried plantain and 'bammys' – small cakes made from grated cassava and cooked in buttered rings much as we might cook a fried egg or a home-made crumpet on a hotplate. Avocados were eaten as an accompaniment to many meals, and slices called 'pegs' were cut to sit alongside a dish of curried goat. Cakes and puddings were made from bananas, breadfruit, coconut or sweet potato and were very sweet. And there were stunning mangoes. I also saw my first West Indian limes – the tiny, bright-green fruit needed to make lime cream pies. One recipe I have for a Jamaican pudding includes a curious ingredient – '1 cup breadfruit blossoms'. I have yet to see a breadfruit flower.

Monty's friends drove us around the island. In the countryside we stopped at a food stall. A fire burned, fed by long boughs from the pimiento tree, and various iron pots were balanced on the coals. We could have had tripe or calalloo, rice and peas, or curried goat, but the real treat was the 'jerked pork' or 'jerked chicken'. The meats are marinated in spices including the diabolically hot Scotch bonnet pepper and lots of pimiento (allspice to me). Then they are barbecued over a smoky fire that is built in an iron drum cut in half vertically to make a curved base and a lid. It was delicious sticky finger food at its best, horribly dry at its worst. We experienced both at different times.

We went to many parties, always outdoors in the tropical warmth. We danced to calypso rhythms or to the newly fashionable 'ska' music – I particularly remember Little Millie and 'My Boy Lollipop', which preceded reggae. We tried to do the limbo, we also drank a lot of Appleton Estate rum diluted with ice and water or ginger ale. Our days were filled with lots of laughing and our nights with lots of loving. We planned the future.

Monty reported on his positive meetings with suppliers of canned breadfruit; and tamarind, ortanique (a citrus that is a cross between an orange and a tangerine) and guava juices; as well as the more difficult issues surrounding the importation of Jamaican rum to Australia. This part of the plan never eventuated. We were both impossibly naïve about what we were contemplating. The import and export of alcohol – especially overproof rum, with an alcohol content much higher than the standard forty per cent – was complicated, tightly controlled and would require a level of financial backing we could never hope for.

Everywhere I was welcomed warmly and my memory is that I floated through the days in a state of sublime happiness, cuddling up to Monty every night, sure that life would be perfect forever.

6
Solomon Gundy

Lisa and Jamaica House 1965–8

Two and a half years after I had left, I was back in Melbourne with my new husband. I was very excited and eager to be reunited with my parents and siblings and to introduce them to Monty. I have much-treasured home-movie footage of our arrival, with me looking so young and *thin* (and so like my second daughter, Holly) and Monty looking tall, imposing and just a tad apprehensive.

It took a few weeks before Monty met the rest of the family. My brother John, who was fifteen at the time, recalls Monty coming to his school with my parents and encountering many curious stares. And he met my younger brother, Christopher, when we visited Geelong Grammar's extension school, Timbertop, where Christopher was spending the school year. Both brothers remember a subsequent family picnic in the You Yangs National Park. Family footage shows all four siblings, Mum, Dad and Grandpa, tucking into one of Mum's famous rabbit pies.

Within a short time we had settled into an apartment in Flemington, in north Melbourne. An urgent imperative was that Monty learn how to drive a car – a skill he had somehow never acquired to that point in his life. I had soon got a job at Preston Technical

College in the library and once Monty had his driving licence he was able to look for work, even if it meant travelling some distance. We bought a second-hand Volkswagen car and soon after that Monty found a job as an industrial glass-blower at Highett, a half-hour's drive away. Our aim was to start saving money and to find suitable premises to open our coffee lounge. I had also decided to complete my degree, so I enrolled in evening classes for my remaining subject. I decided to take ethics and, with the benefit of four years' maturity, thoroughly enjoyed the lectures and tutorials.

I was prejudiced in favour of Carlton as a likely location for our coffee lounge, having spent my formative student years roaming Lygon Street. It did seem to offer access to the perfect clientele for what were to be reasonably exotic tastes. I introduced Monty to my favourite haunts in Carlton and he wholeheartedly agreed that this cosmopolitan mix of easygoing and extroverted Italians, with young, rather alternative families, and a sprinkling of radical students and academics, did seem the ideal location for a business that promised to be new and different.

Both of us wanted to have a family and, with little thought as to optimum timing or the implications, enthusiastically put in a lot of enjoyable effort to that end. I became pregnant almost immediately and was overjoyed at the prospect of a baby, although it did add a bit of urgency to our planning. We needed to have found our location before the baby was born, and ideally would open the coffee lounge a couple of months after the birth. I had decided the name of the coffee lounge would be Jamaica House, with its suggestion of an embassy or a custodial location for all things Jamaican. Monty was very easygoing and had plenty to do with establishing the business contacts he needed. He was all too pleased to give me free rein to organise and manage the 'creative' bits. I finally graduated Bachelor of Arts when I was seven months' pregnant.

Some parts of the plan worked. We found our premises, a simple shopfront in Lygon Street with even more simple accommodation above. We started sanding back forty bentwood chairs for our customers. My mother's unpublished memoirs remind me that I enlisted the help of family and friends for this task. I seem to have always needed my nearest and dearest to be involved in my schemes in some way, and how amazing it is that this so often happened. And how grateful I am for their loyalty and support, not to mention elbow grease! My enthusiasms have always been very persuasive and once I am engaged with a project my energy seems boundless. I worked very hard too and was fortunate in having a pregnancy without complications.

My old boyfriend, now friend, Malcolm Good, designed our striking logo. We bought a few pieces of second-hand furniture to convert the dingy back room into a space suitable for the preparation of sandwiches and salads. Monty scrubbed the beautiful old terrazzo floor and we moved our meagre possessions upstairs.

In planning the very first menu in the very first Jamaica House I had to design dishes that could be prepared in the tiny, ill-equipped kitchen, which was never intended to be a restaurant kitchen. I also had to summon up a flavour of the West Indies that offered a tenuous link with my memories. And another imperative was to use the products that Monty was importing. Already cases and cases of exotic products had arrived and were stacked along the upstairs passageway. The original intention had been to create a coffee lounge where customers would come for a juice (tamarind, ortanique or guava), a coffee (Blue Mountain, of course), a sandwich (roasted lamb with guava jelly, ackee and crisp bacon), a snack (a salted herring spread called Solomon Gundy on hot toast, or another of flaked salted codfish with onion served with crackers, and chilli on crackers) and something sweet. I was sure I could manage this as well as a new baby. The 'something sweet' was a challenge, as in those days tropical fruits from the north did not make it as far as Melbourne, forbidden because of the fear of fruit fly infestation. I decided on a chocolate cake drenched with Appleton Estate rum. At least I had the sense to realise that I could not possibly keep up with baking sponge cakes as well as all the other things, so I rang Ferguson's bakery and spoke to a Mr Ferguson, who was absolutely charming. He seduced me at once by saying that theirs was an old-fashioned business. 'Our sponges are made with twelve eggs to a pound of flour – none of those aerators,' he said. 'They're not as high as some but they're real.'

And they were. Right to the last incarnation of Jamaica House, a chocolate rum cake was always on the menu. Each layer was split, drenched with rum mixed with a little sugar syrup, then sandwiched with fresh cream, and a rich chocolate ganache icing spread on top. The cakes needed twelve hours to develop the proper squidginess, and were absolutely marvellous.

We had an advertised opening date but the baby refused to be born. I had arranged for a friend, Kristen, to help me in the kitchen. She was due to have a baby a couple of weeks before me. Her baby son arrived and still I was at home, this time with three weeks to go before we were due to open. She did gently tell me that it had taken her a good few weeks to recover physically from the birth. I would have pooh-poohed that. I knew that I would manage! After all, women had babies all the time and my doctor had suggested that I was carrying a neat little bundle that should not prove to be a problem.

We had had elaborate opening-day notices and invitations printed. Perhaps that is why neither Monty nor I considered delaying opening day. It does seem absolutely crazy. I think my mother might have said that once Stephanie had set her mind on something you might as well save your breath.

My planning for the birth had been rudimentary and consisted of gathering together some pretty baby clothes and creating a nursery. I had lovingly painted the walls of the nursery and spent quite a bit of time staring at the bassinet and imagining what it would hold in just a few weeks. I don't think I attended any antenatal classes. By the time I was two and a half weeks overdue my doctor became concerned. He suggested that I wait for the weekend and then on Monday he would induce the baby.

On Saturday I started to feel mild contractions. I was very excited. They grew a bit stronger and we decided to head for the hospital. It was late afternoon before I was settled. The contractions continued but not very strongly. I was moved back to the ward. The labour sister was not very encouraging and told me crossly, 'You have come in too early and now you are getting too tired.' She sent Monty home, leaving me feeling very miserable and, as she said, exhausted. The doctor came very late in the day, gave me a quick inspection and prescribed some drugs. This certainly speeded things up, and about two hours later, the baby was born. I was very befuddled from the drugs and was told that I had plenty of stitches.

It wasn't until Monty came rushing back to the hospital and we both had a good cry over this exquisite little bundle that I realised we now had a precious daughter. She was very beautiful. She weighed just six pounds, had silky black hair and creamy skin and resembled no-one but herself. We named her Lisa.

We opened the original Jamaica House in June 1966 when Lisa was three weeks old. She was loved. She was adored. It simply was not fair on any of us what happened. We were caught on a rollercoaster of our own making and could not stop it.

The pattern of our days in those first few months was appalling. We still needed cashflow, so Monty continued his work at Highett. He had established an excellent rapport with his boss, who agreed that Monty could continue to work an eight-hour shift on his own in the factory commencing at around four-thirty in the morning. At about one p.m. Monty would return from Highett, and straightaway become the jovial host to those having their lunch. For some reason I can't fathom now, we were open until the early evening. Monty mopped the floor after the last customer left, put out the rubbish and went to bed somewhere between ten-thirty and midnight. He then arose at four a.m. and it started again.

Meanwhile, I wrapped my darling baby in a bunny rug and wedged her in her basket between a chair and the wall in the tiny room between the dining room and the kitchen. This heart-squeezing memory reminds me that my little six-pound baby needed feeding every three hours. I started in the kitchen at around eight o'clock. My friend Kristen arrived around ten and parked her own two-month old baby in the same small space. We alternated feeding our babies, making toasted sandwiches and tossing salads until mid-afternoon. She went home, I fed the baby, attempted to make some food for Monty and myself, continued in the kitchen and then rapidly put the baby to bed. At the end of the shift, having cleaned down, I would crawl upstairs and debate with myself whether to wake the sleeping baby for a feed in the vain hope that she would then sleep through, or fall into bed only to be woken about two hours later by her cries. Sometimes Monty would be woken too and he would come into the freezing-cold room where I was trying to feed Lisa without disturbing him. We would have a big hug, all three of us, and there were plenty of tears.

It could not continue like this.

An extra pressure was that we were not making any money, although more and more people were clamouring to come to Jamaica

House, and they wanted more diverse offerings. That elusive bot-tom line haunts all those who work in hospitality. It is so easy to allow the costs to get out of control, and our spend-per-head was very low. There was a limit to what we could charge for a salad and a sandwich, and the waitress and dishwasher still needed to be paid. We had so much to learn! Monty's original plan that he would develop a business as an importer never eventuated: the demand for Jamaican flavours was never going to be more than a trickle. Early attempts to interest the few retailers that specialised in exotic goods were not encouraging. It became obvious that the imported tins of food would be used almost exclusively by Jamaica House. As the quantities needed were not huge, the paperwork and time taken to organise these shipments was out of proportion to their value. Nevertheless, Monty discovered the appeal of hospitality and realised that it offered the possibility of an alternative career.

Monty was a celebrity in Carlton. We had to decide: do we become a café and maybe employ someone to help or not? I was thinner than I had ever been. I could count every rib. Food choked me. I couldn't swallow. Three months into our new business I developed dermatitis all over my hands. I wore cotton gloves all day and smeared my hands with black tar ointment at night. My milk disappeared and we then had to deal with boiling bottles and making formula.

Kristen has a special place in my heart for her part in this story. In an earlier life she had had experience running a very hip coffee lounge in a seaside town. Of course, I had no experience at all. She was also an actress with an eye for the exotic or for a charismatic personality, and our venture promised both. Newly pregnant, she was a bit bored and keen to get involved in something she believed would be easy to manage with a new baby, at least for a few months. Neither of us was very realistic about the demands of motherhood.

Kristen remembers her sister chastising her about the long hours she was working and telling her she didn't deserve to have a baby. But we loved our babies! I was so caught up in the web I had created that I was quite unable to stand back and think of a rational solution. How could I be a loving and effective mother as well as learn how to manage a small business, not to mention be the main worker in it? And with Monty getting so few hours' sleep each night he had no energy for creative solutions to our domestic trauma.

Into this mess came a young woman, Rose, who was pretty needy herself. She had great reserves of energy, no experience at all with either catering or babies, but was willing to do whatever was asked of her. Pretty soon that included taking both babies to the health centre for their vaccinations, doing incidental shopping, washing dishes in the kitchen, leading to helping with the cooking. Soon she became indispensable.

We decided to try a bigger menu, hoping to 'up the spend'. I tentatively planned a limited lunch and dinner menu to include an ackee and saltfish cocktail, a rich pumpkin and allspice soup, a coconut pepperpot soup, a beef curry (we could not find goat meat in our first year) with a raw cashew and bean side dish, a basket of fried chicken with fried breadfruit, and an extra dessert. It was a very simple menu but very popular. This menu, which I designed to be possible with only two burners and one tiny fryer, remained the backbone of the Jamaica House menu for many, many years.

Now I found that when I had a day off, usually a Sunday, all I wanted to do was sleep. Monty needed to do paperwork, and Rose was always asking if she could take Lisa to the park or on some outing for an hour or so. Sometimes I returned home to Rosebud West for a day at the weekend and my sister Diana would scoop Lisa up and take her to meet a friend. Or Monty would take her to the market with him. A combination of events and people started to mean that when there was spare time, when once I had rested I would have liked to play with my daughter, I was left alone to sleep and my family amused themselves without me.

Lisa was being passed around like a parcel. She was a beautiful and a happy child with soft brown curls, sturdy limbs and creamy skin. I loved her so much. Somehow I needed to get my energy back to assert myself as her loving mother. I wanted to play with my baby too. I wanted to roll on a rug in the park with her or play in the sandpit. But for those first few months both Monty and I confused our priorities and found ourselves sucked into whatever crisis seemed most urgent at the time.

Looking back I do not think I had post-natal depression. In no way was I rejecting my daughter or resenting her birth. I certainly felt depressed. But my depression was, I believe, a result of physical exhaustion, rapid weight loss, and a growing awareness that I was not coping with anything very well.

And there was always a crisis. There always *is* a crisis in hospitality. It seems that whenever a couple with young children works together in a business that has such un-family-friendly hours, there will be stresses and choices. Without sufficient income to provide quality assistance the relationship will almost always suffer.

Relief came when Monty stopped working at the glass-blowers, giving us a bit of time to smile, to hold each other and to play with Lisa. We spent happy times with my family at Rosebud West and I have wonderful photos to help me remember. Mum loved being a grandmother, Diana enjoyed being an aunt, and I think my brothers enjoyed playing with Lisa on the rare occasions that we all coincided at Rosebud. Lisa beamed with happiness during our weekends with the extended family. She was now walking and was an absolute delight. And Monty and I also rediscovered earlier interests. We went out to dinner and to a few jazz concerts. This must have been the year when Duke Ellington played in Melbourne.

Financially things seemed to be creeping ahead. We decided (or probably I decided) to rent a proper house and try to have a domestic haven away from what was becoming such a demanding business. Our upstairs-downstairs life was also unsuitable for a curious toddler. We employed a trained chef to help in the kitchen and I found 'Homeville', a large and lovely old house in North Carlton with a big garden. The idea was that I would have most evenings free to spend with Lisa and recover my health and good humour. I will always remember the garden for its glorious magnolia tree that burst forth every spring and a magnificent Moorpark apricot tree that was covered in fruit each December and into early January.

My friend Jean Tinney was in Melbourne between postings. Her husband, John, had been most recently working in the trade office of the Australian Embassy in Paris, and they were waiting to be posted again. Jean was pregnant with her second child and needed to earn some money, so we discussed the idea of her doing a bit of childminding at our house. Jean looked after four little children, four days a week, for about six months, until just before the birth of her son Michael. There was two-year-old Lisa; Jean's own daughter, Catherine; Kristen's son, Jonathan; and another friend's little boy. Jean reminds me that my friend Lyn, with whom I had shared a flat so many years before in Coburg, did the fifth day of the week.

This arrangement worked wonderfully well and Jean remembers how much all the children enjoyed playing in the garden and eating lots of apricots in the summer. This time was much easier on Lisa. She was in her own house with her own toys even if her mum and dad were still in and out.

Later in life it was suggested to Lisa that she and I had never bonded properly. When I look back over her first three years of life

I feel I should apologise to her and repeat that despite how it might have seemed she was deeply loved by both parents.

Years later I was reading *Changing*, the extraordinarily honest and revealing autobiography of Liv Ullmann, actress and partner to director Ingmar Bergman, with whom she had a daughter. She writes of her own feelings of need, at the same time acknowledging the needs of her daughter. It seemed painfully familiar to me. 'I was to give a child security and tenderness, but didn't feel I received enough of this myself,' she wrote. And a little later on:

> I know I can never make amends for the wrongs I have done her. All the choices I made that were not to her advantage. Every time I left her in someone else's care . . .
>
> What memories and experiences lie buried deep within her and will place their stamp on her in later life? Will bring to her fears and insecurity that she will never understand? Longings that can never be fulfilled? Because they belonged to an early childhood and could only have been satisfied at that time.

Money was still tight and I took in a couple of boarders. I thought it was a constructive way forward but it proved to be a bad choice. I cannot remember any discussion between Monty and me regarding this decision, which is probably indicative of how things were heading. Monty, who valued his privacy, did not like it one bit. He sometimes drove home from Jamaica House so tired that he would pull up outside the house, turn off the ignition and fall asleep in the car. And Helen remembers that he sometimes made cheesecakes for Jamaica House in the kitchen at 'Homeville' late at night if they had run out.

Monty shopped at the Queen Victoria Market each week and became very friendly with one of the market vendors, Jim Vlassopoulos. One thing led to another and the two men discussed going into business together in a bigger and better Jamaica House. Jim had money he wanted to invest in something more challenging than selling vegetables. Monty had the charisma and the 'brand' and he needed a hardworking business partner to help with the workload and more importantly to inject some cash. Jim, his wife, Melita, Monty and I had several dinners together and looked forward to a creative partnership. It was a total shock to me when shortly afterwards Monty confessed that he had hidden our true financial situation from me and that things were really bad, that there was considerable unpaid debt. This was the only time in our relationship that I can remember Monty being absolutely crushed by events. I was very hurt that I had had no warning of what was happening. To this point my father had been the person we turned to on several occasions to help us out of a financial hole. And true to form, my wonderful father borrowed money to help us pay bills and establish what was to become the second Jamaica House.

I felt that as I was the creative side of the partnership, Monty should be responsible for the boring business of money. I have to acknowledge how foolish I was. This was the first but not the last time I ignored the financial implications of a business I was helping create, and with dire consequences. It took some horrible shocks years later before I truly realised that if you are running a business, the bottom line is critical.

So in late 1968 the first Jamaica House closed and Jamaica House number two opened further down Lygon Street, south of Grattan Street, above a pizza parlour. Now there were three active partners: Monty, Jim and Melita. And they employed a young chef destined to go places, Tony Bilson. I blush with embarrassment when I recall interviewing an unknown-to-me Bilson for the job as chef. Tony had been working as a labourer for a landscape gardener so it is perhaps understandable that I needed him to convince me that he knew how to tell if a steak was well done, medium or rare. My recall is that he answered pleasantly and did not reveal by word or gesture how absurd he probably thought my question was. Needless to say Tony cooked the pepper steaks brilliantly and they stayed on the menu for years. He also turned his hand to more unfamiliar dishes such as stews of pigs' tails with beans, and a goat curry. He and I often talked food. Tony was fascinated by the classic dishes of the French repertoire and pretty soon moved on to open his own French restaurant in Hawthorn called La Pomme d'Or.

I was considering returning to work as a librarian to ease the cashflow situation and to provide that essential bit of normality for Lisa every evening. I was told that the position of school librarian was vacant at the local high school, which was within walking distance of 'Homeville'. I applied, was immediately accepted and within a week or so was installed at Princes Hill Secondary College, where I spent the next six years.

Looking back I am not sure really what happened to our marriage. Since the decision to close the first Jamaica House and the reality of Jamaica House number two opening, the relationship was in difficulties. I think that Monty felt somewhat ashamed of the mismanagement of the first business. Maybe he resented the fact that he had to go to my father again, cap in hand. Certainly with our Box and Cox existence – with my working in the restaurant mostly in the daytime, and he being out and about most of the day and then back in the restaurant in the evenings – and then me moving to a day job that actually supported the family, our lives were diverging.

Monty and I were both stretched to near breaking point after eighteen torrid months establishing the first Jamaica House. I still needed to be reassured and to feel loved. It must have been at this time that my French lover from my *au pair* days turned up in Australia and I allowed myself to be distracted for a few days. Monty knew this had happened and was not at all pleased. I pleaded for things to change between us. He said he could not promise to offer all that I needed. We separated for a couple of weeks and I cried myself to sleep every night. At the end of the fortnight Monty came back and we had a loving reunion and agreed to try again. But things were not the same. Within another few months we had agreed to separate. I cannot say how Monty felt about it but I was absolutely devastated. And our new business partners were very nervous.

In hindsight who knows what would have happened if we had not put ourselves through such a dreadful eighteen months after two and a half years of bliss. Neither of us had spare emotional resources to support the other. We just fell over.

7

Clanking Milk Bottles & a Jam Doughnut

Getting on with Life 1968–71

Living with a broken heart is horrible. And nobody can make it better. Probably having a two-and-a-half-year-old helps a little as one still has to get the breakfast, do the washing, read the bedtime stories and so on. Lisa suffered a great deal through Monty and my separation and it took many years for her to deal with it, or even acknowledge all the hurt and feelings of rejection.

When Monty and I separated she became quite disturbed. She would not sleep alone for a long time. Once when she had a cold a doctor prescribed a cough mixture that gave her hallucinations. They terrified her and they terrified me. She screamed, pointing at 'someone' or 'something' behind the door, her body arching stiffly in my arms, trying to get away. Soon neither of us was sleeping at night. She became scared of the sound of the milkman delivering bottles of milk that clanked together early in the morning. Another doctor prescribed sedatives for us both, claiming that this pattern of sleep deprivation had to be broken.

I did read her stories and hug her very tightly but as I had a broken heart myself I think I was a sobbing mess some of the time and she was well aware that things were not right. I don't think I was a very good playmate for her. She hung onto her piece of blanket. And then when Monty came to collect her or to bring her back from a visit, she clung to him crying. It was horrible for all of us.

Jean had returned to Europe by this time. One saving grace was that the University of Melbourne had an outstanding day care centre in Drummond Street, North Carlton, and I was able to enrol Lisa there. Lisa loved the staff and they loved her. Her daytimes were spent with plenty of friends and plenty of activities. I could get on with the job of earning our living at Princes Hill Secondary College assisted by the money I was being paid by my two lodgers.

One of my closest friends from university days, Helen, was going through her own separation and had come to live with me. She was a marvellous support, both as a shoulder for me to cry on, but also as an extra mother for young Lisa.

Lisa would be put to bed and would appear to be absolutely sound asleep but within minutes of my going to bed, she would run down the passage in a speedy dash, take a dive into my bed and would be asleep again before her head had touched the pillow. Popular wisdom at the time cautioned parents not to allow their child to sleep in their bed. But I snuggled gratefully up to my warm bundle, ignoring the smell of a wet nappy. We were both very miserable.

My parents were also saddened as they were very fond of Monty and of course they hated to see my pain. They also had concerns about recovering the money they had invested in the business. The repayment difficulties were complicated after Monty and my personal relationship broke down.

Once I realised that there was no future for the relationship I had dramatically insisted that I sever all connection with Jamaica House. My father was aghast at my decision that was so foolish in the light of his ongoing investment in the business. Monty also suggested that I should remain as a partner for Lisa's sake. I expect he hoped that if I remained as a partner, there might be a financial benefit for her eventually. Maybe I should have done, but I have never been good at looking backwards, and once I have stepped onto a different path I cannot bring myself to retreat.

As would happen more than once in my life I made an important decision without giving due consideration to the bigger picture. My father was only too aware of the financial consequences of my high-handed action whereas I was not. The loans Dad had offered required my parents to borrow the money and pay interest on it. He had difficulty recovering that money and I am ashamed of the financial burdens I placed upon him.

For my first two years at Princes Hill the school library was in a standard double classroom and the work was pretty routine. Students had a regular 'library class' where they got on with assignments and used the books to research. I supervised these sessions, processed new purchases and checked loans in and out. It was not very challenging but at that stage I was still miserable every evening and was not looking for a challenge. And then in 1971 the school was half-destroyed by a fire, including the library. The students endured an unsettled two or three years traipsing from what was left of the school building to temporary portable classrooms erected on unused railway land, pushing supermarket trolleys filled with their books. A brand-new school with a ground-breaking library design was completed in 1973. This was very exciting and it was a very beautiful building. School libraries were one of the first beneficiaries of the investment in education of the recently elected Whitlam Government and they were now known as Resource Centres.

I was now really enjoying the work. It was an exciting time in education. Contemporary educational thinking was embracing new ideas such as team teaching; general studies were replacing geography and history; interdisciplinary approaches to topics became popular; and the curriculum broadened to include performance studies, photography and mixed-media art departments. In this pre-digital age the first multimedia teaching materials and equipment became common in classrooms – such as film loops, slides, projectors, tape recorders and video cameras. The hardware had to be stored somewhere and the supporting material needed to be catalogued. Within months the Resource Centre became a very busy place indeed, and my work as the teacher-librarian, along with my assistants, included helping teaching staff and students locate supplementary materials and even suggesting linked items.

Looking back on these changes in education of the early seventies I note that the pendulum has swung again. While there is currently considerable emphasis on literacy and numeracy, in recent years we heard a lot about 'enquiry-based learning': students investigate themes and multidisciplinary projects, then display their work using new technology. It all looks and sounds very familiar to me.

Rather than just being a processor of book loans, the new, expanded role of a teacher-librarian included being aware of educational thinking. This meant I needed to gain an additional qualification. The assistant appointed to care for the Resource Centre while I studied for a Diploma of Education was Angela Clemens, who was destined to become a lifelong friend.

Angela was warm, friendly and energetic, and we liked each other immediately. Angela was in her element talking to and helping the students. I loved working with the teaching staff, selecting and combining materials to broaden the scope of whatever theme they were working on. Together we made a great team and soon the Resource Centre really did seem to be the hub of the school. It was very stimulating and collaborative and got me through Monday to Friday pretty well. But the weekends were still bleak. Angela and

I continued to work together for more than twenty years through Angela's four pregnancies and in many varied capacities.

The late sixties and early seventies were turbulent times. The war in Vietnam was dividing opinion everywhere. There were riots and demonstrations, and staffroom conversations were full of discussion about the Vietnam War. Most of the young staff were vehemently opposed to the killing of conscripts and Vietnamese civilians, and horrified at the reported defoliation of the country using Agent Orange, as was I. More than twenty thousand people marched in the streets expressing their opposition to the war. I marched too and joined the masses sitting in the streets.

The war was a constant point of discussion within my family. My uncle Wilfred Burchett wrote several books condemning American foreign policy during this period. His commitment to reporting the conflict from 'the other side', indeed from within the tunnels of the Viet Cong, made him very unpopular with many. He believed that the Vietnamese people would fight to determine their own destiny. His best-known work from this period was the book *Vietnam Will Win*.

Lisa had begun at the local primary school. Monty would collect her after school on a Thursday for his trip to the Queen Victoria Market, where she had her weekly treat of a jam doughnut, and they also ate together every Sunday, often in a Chinese restaurant. Lisa did not comment until years later that she was teased about her non-European appearance by a few of her schoolmates. Children are so often cruel to each other. She also told me many years later that she did not want her friends to see her Dad, flamboyant as he was in flowing brightly coloured shirt or scarlet jumper. With his dark skin and long beard he certainly stood out from the other parents. There was no question that she loved her father very much, but like most primary-school-aged children, she desperately wanted to be like everyone else. (Nowadays at the same school there would be parents from many, many countries all happily mingling but it was a very different society in the early seventies.) For a long time Monty was seen as an exotic specimen and Lisa, aged seven, was not sure how to react to this.

Despite my personal unhappiness I was still very interested in cooking and in foods of the world. I talked a lot about cooking in the staffroom and my enthusiasm led to frequent dinner parties. In many cases I assisted colleagues plan a meal they intended to pre-pare. One thing led to another and I was asked if I would teach a few of these young women to cook. I was thrilled to do so and have happy memories of those Saturday-afternoon sessions. Occasionally I meet one of these women and they tell me they have kept the typed notes I prepared. I have not and I cannot quite remember what was in them. I think I included advice on handling ingredients as well as recipes, along with personal comments reflecting my own experiences in making this or that. All perhaps a forerunner for the style of *The Cook's Companion*.

During this time a brief romance with a dashing artist helped restore my confidence, but it ended quickly. I had heard from 'well-meaning' acquaintances that Monty was seeing other women and I suppose it really mattered to me that someone find me desirable. It didn't seem to matter that we had little in common other than enjoying a sexual fling. But it did mean that the affair just petered out without much heartbreak.

I still needed to have boarders at 'Homeville' to help meet all our living expenses. I had firm friends and Lisa had good friends from school. There were plenty of people around us both, but they all seemed to have someone special in their lives. I believed I faced the future alone and felt desolate.

8

Grilled Trout & Wilfred's Pot-au-feu

Maurice and a New Home 1971–5

I was invited to dinner with a college acquaintance early in 1972 and among the guests was Maurice Alexander. I had vaguely known of his existence during my university days, as his father had been the vice-master of nearby Ormond College, but I do not think we had ever met. Maurice was a lawyer who had just completed several years as a crown prosecutor in Hong Kong and was newly returned to Melbourne, contemplating going to the Bar. He was interesting on the topic of his Hong Kong experiences, and he was attractive, with sparkling hazel eyes and thick, wavy dark hair. Maurice had travelled extensively through Europe once his posting in Hong Kong had finished and I was intrigued that he had seen so much of the world and had done this on his own. Clearly this man was very self-sufficient, with plenty of initiative and a taste for adventure. He seemed to enjoy talking to me and I was not too surprised when he called me the next day to suggest an outing.

He recalls that he was startled to hear me go on about all the arrangements that I would need to make for Lisa before I got to a yes. He probably wondered if he had made a wise choice contacting this single mother with so many domestic concerns to be sorted out before she could agree to a drive in the country.

On this first outing I met some of Maurice's family at a lunch in a small weatherboard cottage in the Dandenongs. The cottage had been in the Alexander family for two generations and was used as a retreat for whichever of the siblings was in Victoria at any time. There were five in all, including Maurice's sister Jenny, who was married to Graham Little, an academic and writer. Our talk over lunch was fascinating, friendly and funny. I must have been relaxed, as later on Graham told me that they were intrigued Maurice had met such an 'interesting' woman.

I loved spending time with Jenny and Graham. Graham Little was a beguiling talker and a deep thinker. He was a lecturer in the Department of Political Science at Melbourne University with a special interest in leadership and the how and why of political thinking. An evening at their table meant having one's brain stretched with new and fascinating thoughts, as well as being hugely entertained. Both Jenny and Graham were excellent hosts and they did care about offering a good table along with their marvellous conversation. Graham was Irish and had the charm and the eloquence associated with his countrymen.

So started a new romance. Maurice was open to new experiences, friendly towards Lisa and quickly became very fond of her. Although Maurice and I were of a similar age and had shared certain important experiences, such as university, travel and living in a foreign country, and had friends in common, in many other ways our backgrounds could not have been more different. My family had never been interested in games or physical exercise, other than digging in the garden or building something. Maurice, on the other hand, loved being out and about and enjoyed going for a run, playing beach cricket, swimming in even the coldest water or climbing the nearest mountain. I found this physicality very appealing, especially as it was such a contrast to my own preference to curl up with a book or gaze at the faraway hills rather than wish to climb them. Lisa was seven at this time and very much enjoyed sharing the fun times with Maurice. I have a favourite holiday snap of the two of them, bronzed and beaming after a snorkelling outing on holiday in Queensland.

In those days, whenever we visited friends for dinner, or they came to us, the tradition was that the children would come too; they would all bed down together and chat and giggle before falling asleep. When it was time to go home, the sleeping children would be scooped up, sleeping bags and all, and transferred to the car for the drive home. Few people had cars with seatbelts and there were certainly no restraints for children!

As the son of a Presbyterian minister Maurice learnt at a very young age that every penny spent should be carefully considered. A clergyman's stipend was not generous and Maurice's mother, Margaret, had had to manage a large family on very limited means. Economy and frugality were stamped very deep in this family. I suppose many families would have shared this concern when bringing up hungry children so soon after the war years. My own mother's preparedness to spend a little extra on, say, a specially matured cheddar or a little-known vegetable was unusual. I had battles with Maurice even early on about what I perceived to be his stinginess. I was not a wild spendthrift but I did not want to recycle yesterday's green salad or serve liquid from a rinsed-out cream bottle, as he had been taught to do.

We enjoyed taking country trips on the weekends, visiting places of interest. I remember a magical weekend camping alongside the Howqua River with two friends. It was very, very cold but we built a huge fire, grilled trout, drank wine and looked at the stars. And

on another occasion we explored the Coorong, admiring the sweeping sand dunes, the saltwater lakes and the plentiful birdlife. We
had many delightful weekend escapes to the family cottage in the
Dandenongs, where typically I would settle in with a book while
Maurice took a long walk, or cleaned out the gutters or chopped
wood so that we could have a crackling fire in the evening. Other
adventures took us much further afield: to the Snowy Mountains,
the wine country in South Australia, Wilson's Promontory and many,
many beautiful places. Maurice was a true adventurer and was
always excited to see what was over the next ridge or round the
next corner. He always chose the scenic route.

Sometimes Lisa came on these trips but more often I left her
with friends. I was mystified that although Monty included Lisa in
many social outings at the weekend, he seemed reluctant to have
her stay at his home overnight. As a contrast, when the marriage
of two of my close friends collapsed and each established a new
household, they encouraged their children to regard each home as
equally 'their' home, with toys, clothing and books in both places,
and where they were always welcome. Such an approach might
have helped Lisa cope better with the absence of her adored father.

In planning a weekend away I usually constructed a picnic lunch
with the expectation of finding a wonderful country restaurant
where we could enjoy a romantic dinner. Maurice believed that a
counter tea in the local pub would do. We would argue about this
decision, although I would almost always win. I think Maurice
would admit he could not sustain the battle as long as I could.
Whichever way it went, the atmosphere was usually spoilt by one
or the other of us sulking or behaving in a resentful manner. This
pattern was repeated over and over again.

Ridiculous, really. How sad that commonsense and rational
discussion were entirely absent from these damaging arguments

from entrenched positions. These days I would often go along with the choice of a pub meal, having learnt that the fancy country restaurant does not always exist or does not always live up to my fantasy. And that a simple grilled steak and chips without other embellishment can be pretty good. Realistically, thirty-five years later, the traveller is as likely to happen upon a great pub as a good restaurant. But things were very different in the early seventies.

One day in 1972 I went looking for a new dress for a party. I happened to drive down Fenwick Street in North Carlton and saw a tiny and pretty house for sale. Typically I made an instant decision to try to buy it. Astonishing, really, as I had eight hundred dollars in the bank and the asking price for the house was thirteen thousand. I went to see my friend Kathy's husband, Bruce, who was a bank manager. He sighed and we went through my assets, which were nil. I did, however, have my full-time job and felt I could manage a mortgage. He asked if my father would be prepared to guarantee a loan. Dear old Dad came to the rescue again, agreeing to go guarantor, and in a remarkably short time I was the owner of the house. (Typically I had no idea that it was not usual bank practice to lend to a woman. I remember telling Bruce that I had an unsettled but agreed insurance claim for a few hundred dollars due and some other small debt about to be repaid. In all I felt I had, or would have soon, just about the full ten per cent deposit and did not anticipate a problem! Bruce must have been relieved that my father agreed to go guarantor.)

Soon after I took possession of my new house, and when Maurice was still a regular visitor rather than a full-time resident, we had a carefree holiday in Bali while we were still getting to know one another. This was Bali without sealed roads, with one or two roadside stalls on the sandy track leading to the beach at Kuta, where one could buy banana pancakes and drinking coconuts and the highlight of each evening was to sit and watch the sunset with just a dozen fellow travellers and the locals. No-one sold souvenirs, or touted for business of any sort other than to offer a bed for fifty cents a night – a clean bed in a room with a fan and access to a scrubbed Indonesian-style bathhouse and squat lavatory. Roadside stalls sold the delectable *babi guling* (roast suckling pig) to locals – and I was quick to taste it too, carrying my portions away inside folded banana leaves – or goat curry aromatic with coconut milk. Brown ducks wandered along the roadside. A young boy proudly displayed his catch of bright-green dragonflies that would be fried. Dance performances were for the villagers themselves, not for tourists. Local buses were the only way of visiting temples and other than one international hotel near Denpasar there was not a single elaborate resort to be found.

I returned to Australia and to my job at the end of the holiday, which was also the end of the school holidays. Maurice travelled on in other parts of Asia for at least another month. It was not until he returned that we started to discuss the future. Maurice moved in to Fenwick Street and we surprised our families with a decision to marry. We still squabbled childishly about all manner of things but we also recognised our shared experiences and similar values, and I wanted a partner. Maurice had fitted easily into my family and he and my father frequently discussed world politics, both, fortunately, having similar viewpoints.

Maurice had been admitted to the Bar and spent quite a bit of time waiting for work. I was still at Princes Hill as the teacher-librarian and enjoying it. We had a simple registry-office wedding in May 1973. I recall arriving at the Old Mint building in Graham Little's vintage Bentley, feeling very grand and smart in a delicious Prue Acton blue and fuschia-pink suit with Chanel-style jacket and an A-line skirt. Lisa was an enchanting bridesmaid in a long black velvet tunic with a frilly white blouse. It seemed logical to become Stephanie Alexander as my previous surname was no longer relevant. It did not occur to many women in 1973 to keep their maiden names.

After the ceremony we had an elegant lunch in my parents' home in East Melbourne, catered for by my mother. I remember a beautifully boned, stuffed and reassembled chicken galantine among other delights. My parents had sold the family home at Rosebud West and had moved to East Melbourne, wanting to be closer to the life of the city now that all their children had grown and were scattered.

All of the siblings of both families were present at the wedding. Seven siblings, many with partners, meant that we had quite a large official party. Later that night we had a big party in Helen Pyke and her new husband, Jim Murray's, North Carlton garden, again with wonderful food.

The little two-bedroom house I had bought just two years before, which was ideal for my daughter and me, was a squeeze once there was another adult. Once again I made an instant decision – this time a very bad one. I had seen a huge and admittedly neglected-looking Victorian-style villa in an excellent position on the hill at Northcote with stunning views towards the Dandenongs. It did need extensive renovation and repair. Maurice would have been very happy to stay squashed in Carlton but once again I argued strongly for a fresh start and more room. To help the argument I was pregnant and the prospect of a new baby and nowhere to put it was the clincher. We were both thrilled to know that soon we would have a child together. I was determined to try for a natural birth and we both started to attend childbirth classes. Helen had successfully followed the current guru Sheila Kitzinger's advice during her pregnancy and she and I were both very taken with her analogy of the labouring mother as a ripe camembert, oozing with the flow as the contractions hit!

Fenwick Street was sold in 1974 at an astonishing profit. Carlton house prices were soaring each week. I had been there less than three years and the resale price was nearly three times what I had paid. We moved to Northcote and started slowly to renovate it. I was reminded of these tortuous renovations recently. We employed the boyfriend of the mother of one of Lisa's friend's to chip away at the badly cracked plaster on a wall. He rang me at the library one morning to inform me that he didn't want to proceed with the plaster removal as the entire wall was moving! My father came to the rescue and reinforced the wall with a steel strap. The handyman was Howard Jacobson, winner of the 2010 Booker Prize for his novel *The Finkler Question*. (There was a lot of multi-skilling going on in and around the inner suburbs, and plenty of home renovation. In his other life Howard was a tutor in the English Department at La Trobe University.)

Lisa was ecstatic with the news that she would soon have a brother or a sister. She was just over eight years old. I was determined that this time around the first few months of my baby's life would be very different. I resigned from my job and enjoyed a relaxed month or so before the birth in December. Once again the baby was overdue and once again my doctor gave me a deadline and once it passed I was ordered into hospital to have the birth induced. The membranes were ruptured by the doctor and away I went at lightning speed. I was much more alert this time and refused any painkilling drugs. I was triumphant at achieving the drug-free labour I had hoped for and in about two hours produced a perfect little girl we named Holly. Most thought we had chosen the name to evoke Christmas. In fact we had taken the name from *The Forsyte Saga*. Holly was adorable from the first day of her life. And Maurice was an adoring father, patient and helpful. Lisa was equally adoring as the older sister and loved to cuddle Holly and push the pram when we went for a walk. This was a very happy family time.

When Holly was three months old we decided to take a three-month trip to Europe, believing that it would be easier to travel with a very young baby than with a toddler a year later. Maurice at this time was exhibiting a very lacklustre interest in his legal career. We hoped to link up with Jenny and Graham Little, who were then living in Chicago, and to convince them to share an apartment somewhere in the south of France with us. Jenny has kept a batch of letters I sent to her in Chicago, where Graham was deeply involved in a psychology think-tank and was initially reluctant to leave to join our month in France. I wrote seductively of what it would be like to be on the road in France, anticipating tucking into trout in country *auberges* alongside rushing streams, and enjoying bottles of local wine in the small hotel-restaurants we would carefully select from our trusty red Michelin guide. It was great fun rereading all of this, of which I had absolutely zero recall.

I have never been good about keeping letters but really I wish I had been. They record so much detail, much of it trivial. For example, I mentioned that I needed to save some extra money for the trip so had agreed to return to Princes Hill Secondary College to help with the backlog of cataloguing due to the avalanche of spending that was a corollary of the Whitlam Government's invest-ment in school libraries. The magnanimous offer was three dollars per hour, and I could breastfeed my baby in the sick room. At the time it was an offer too good to refuse!

As my parents' financial state had improved they too increas-ingly planned holidays abroad. The caravan park was now leased and managed by Dad's brother Clive. My father had progressively subdivided and developed the rest of the property as building blocks. Each time a block was sold there was a sigh of relief and the gradual sale of all of this land secured my parents' income for the rest of their lives. Dad also enjoyed several years working as the assistant librarian at the local library he had helped found all those years ago. From time to time throughout the land development phase Dad needed to arrange a loan and he usually went to his family lawyers. Peter Boothby and his son Brook over and over again acted generously and wisely and supported my father during at least one credit squeeze. This extraordinary firm has continued to offer friendly and sensible advice to many members of the family.

When travelling, Mum would write a short article relating her food discoveries, which after 1966 would appear in the pages of *Australian Gourmet* magazine. Dad would record the trips on his super 8 camera and we were all required to watch endless replays of Mum admiring this or that famous sight. We were not very respectful of these showings, but they remain an amazing record of travel during the sixties and seventies. I think my parents' travel influenced me more than I realised at the time. I wanted to gather my own souvenirs and build my own store of happy memories. And besides, Maurice and I got on so well when we travelled.

Lisa, at the age of eight, had travel plans too. She and Monty were to travel to London, Canada and Jamaica, so some of our time away would coincide with her travel. I was so happy for her and was curious to know how she would interact with her hitherto unknown Jamaican aunts, uncles and cousins.

Lisa remembers her holiday as a wonderful experience, having her father all to herself. He showed Lisa his old flat in West Kensington, where we had been so happy. In Toronto she met two of Monty's brothers and several cousins. There was more family to meet in Jamaica: aunts, uncles and cousins. She and Monty spent time in Kingston and Montego Bay but also in the country at the family home. It was here, while they were sitting on the porch, that a telegram was delivered, advising the family that Monty and daughter would be arriving very soon. The telegram, sent from London, had taken two weeks to be delivered.

Via Jenny's letters I had my memory jogged regarding my fruit-less efforts to buy a special baby carry-cocoon that was being made by Mothercare in England at the time but not available in Australia. I tried via one of Maurice's sisters, Robyn, who was living in London, but the London Mothercare shops had sold out. I was pretty desperate: I had to have something for Holly to sleep in over the next three months. My letters record a trail of enquiries and false starts until I was finally directed to a seamstress in the outer sub-urbs of Melbourne, who said she was making exact copies of the cocoon. I was thrilled and bought one. Fortunately we tried it out at home a few days before leaving and were dismayed to find that the baby next morning was sleeping unravelled on the wooden floor about two metres from the cocoon. It was simply not as strong as the original. We had no time to think of another clever idea (I do remember wondering whether she could simply be wrapped tightly inside a pulled-out bottom drawer of the chest of drawers I felt sure would be in every bedroom. This was quite rightly pooh-poohed by her father.) We had to take a very cumbersome and heavy wicker basket, and we borrowed an American-made cloth pouch, a Snugli, for daytime use. Nowadays every baby equipment shop would have many sensible options. Not so in 1975.

We did meet up with the Littles in Paris. Maurice and I had been met by my uncle Wilfred, who was living at the time in Meu-don, just outside Paris. Wilfred insisted that we stay in his lovely but compact house. It was not for several days that I realised

Wilfred and his second wife Vessa had vacated their own bed for us! I discovered interesting cousins I had never met before. I do remember the delicious meals Wilfred cooked and the lively conversations we had around the dinner table. We ate rabbit with prunes, and another favourite, a pot-au-feu made with oxtails. For many years afterwards Graham Little recalled the evening he had with Wilfred and family at Meudon. Wilfred helped us pack our small hire car – four adults, a baby in a basket, and we still needed to fix luggage to the roof. The phone rang as we were thus engaged and it was Henry Kissinger. 'Tell him to call back,' Wilfred instructed. 'I'm helping my niece prepare for a long drive.'

And so we drove off and spent a memorable fortnight in Beaulieu-sur-mer, about ten kilometres from Nice. By chance we drove past a classic shuttered mansion right on the Corniche with a sign *Apartement à louer* (Apartment for rent). I dashed in and fell in love with it at once. With the shutters flung wide we overlooked the glittering Mediterranean. But it was more than our planned budget and both Graham and Maurice were reluctant to take it. Jenny and I went for a walk and discussed tactics. I had a bit of a tantrum and pointed out that this was exactly what we had hoped to experience, not some miserable, dark apartment tucked away in a town. Jenny supported me and the decision was made. And what a wonderful decision it was! We visited markets and I cooked. We sat on the beach and paid for sun lounges and I breastfed Holly discreetly. Graham sat in cafés in small towns and corrected the proofs of one of his books, a glass of red wine at his elbow and a beret on his head. He perfected a Gallic shrug and as long as he was not expected to speak was the perfect Frenchman. For our outings we squeezed into our tiny hired car with baby Holly tucked behind the back seat in her basket, our luggage tied to the roof. In remembering this I do wonder at myself. No restraints – no-one wore seat belts in France in 1975. My memory is that she travelled without much trouble, with a doting aunt to give her a cuddle or a rusk if she complained, and was parked under many a restaurant table, the draped cloth covering the basket as one might drape fabric over the cage of a canary! Our budget is recorded as forty dollars per day per couple.

Jenny and Graham continued with their travels and Maurice and I went on to Italy by train. We went to Assisi and struggled up the hill in the stinging cold of late autumn, with Holly in her wicker basket, to find a small hotel, before strapping her into the pouch and setting out for the basilica. The Italian love of babies is well known and they are particularly attentive to blonde and blue-eyed babies. Everywhere we went someone chucked her under the chin, cooed at her and, a few days later, on a Venetian ferry, when she was wailing with hunger and being carried by Maurice, she was whisked from the pouch by some solicitous nuns who seemed to disapprove of such a way of carrying and caring for a baby. Or maybe they thought she should have been with her mother.

Away from the workaday world Maurice and I were so much nicer to each other and recognised that our different strengths were both needed. Maurice had an unerring sense of direction whereas I could hardly tell my right from my left so I depended on him in foreign places. He was unfazed by driving on the opposite side of the road – I quailed at the very thought. I had the French language so could interpret. I had the food knowledge and by this time we had fewer battles about where to eat. Both of us wanted to have a good experience and Maurice had developed an interest in really good wine. We had forged a shared interest in restaurants, which was the background for our next great adventure together.

My maternal grandparents, Emily and John Bell, with my mother, Mary Elizabeth Bell, 1932.

My father, Winston Burchett, and Uncle Wilfred in Poowong.

My father with a friend in Tahiti in 1936.

Mum and Dad getting to know one another onboard the *Kamo Maru*.

Mum on her wedding day.

Mum and me, in about 1942.

Exploring the garden, 1943.

Mum with Diana and me, aged four, 1944.

Mum in her kitchen at Essendon.

Diana and me, in about 1946.   John, me and Diana, 1948.

The extended family, in 1950. Back row: Uncle Clive, Dad and Uncle Wilfred. Middle row: Aunt Molly with baby Valerie, me, Mum with John, Grandpa George with Christopher. Front row: Helen, Wilma and Diana.

Grandpa in relaxed mode.

Christopher (aged two and a half) and John (four).

Receiving a good citizenship award at Rosebud High School, in 1956.

Diana, Christopher and John with the family cat.

The family home, 'Greenslopes', which my father and grandfather designed and built at Rosebud West.

Wilfred temporarily set up in Dad's study.

Mum and Dad travelled overseas regularly throughout their lives. Here they are at the Acropolis in the 1970s.

Setting out for a day in town,
aged about fifteen.

Me with a student friend in about 1959.

Me with my newly blonde
hair in 1959.

Aged twenty-one, about to leave for Europe.

Me with a fellow student at University Women's College, in 1959.

Clockwise from back left: John Tinney, me, Kathy Chester and Jean Watters, in about 1960.

Onboard the *Tahitien* in 1962. Some charming Frenchmen with Molly and Patsy.

Ursula Chamberlain and me enjoying a *citron pressé* in Tours in 1963.

Me with the '*surveillantes*' and friend Roy in the garden at the École Normale des Filles, in Tours, France, in 1963.

Jan Patrick and me in London in 1963.

Monty and me on our wedding day, 4 January 1964.

John and Jean Tinney and friend Mike Ferris were our witnesses at the wedding.

Monty and me in Paris, Easter 1964.

A picnic in the Bois de Boulogne. John and Jean Tinney, Mike Ferris and Monty are all enjoying the sunshine.

Me and Monty with Monty's nephew Christopher in Toronto, in 1964.

I graduate with a Bachelor of Arts while seven months' pregnant, in 1966.

Publicity shot taken of Monty and me at the opening of Jamaica House in 1966.

The menu cover of Jamaica House; the logo was designed by my friend and former boyfriend Malcolm Good.

Portrait taken at the opening of Jamaica House in 1966.

Bringing home baby Lisa, in May 1966.

Monty and Lisa at Rosebud West.

Monty comforting Lisa after she fell over and tore holes in her tights.

Lisa, aged two or three.

Lisa helping in the kitchen, in about 1971.

Helen Murray and I were bridesmaids at Diana's wedding to Marcus Clarke in 1970. Lisa was an adorable flower girl.

The Alexander and Burchett families at our wedding in 1973.

Maurice and my wedding day,
with Lisa, in 1973.

Maurice and me enjoying the French countryside in 1975.

Baby Holly in London, 1975.

Me in a London park during our 1975 trip.

Holly in the baby pouch during our
European trip in 1975.

Our new house at Northcote in 1975.

Me with Maurice and Holly in 1976.

With good friends Janni Kyritsis, Damien Pignolet and Josephine Pignolet.

Janni Kyritsis and his partner, David Bradshaw, tucking into a seafood platter in Paris in the early eighties.

Holly and Lisa on the beach at Port Douglas in 1979.

A publicity shot of me in the first Stephanie's Restaurant, taken for *Home Beautiful* magazine.

Tansy Good and me in the kitchen of the first Stephanie's.

Me, Tansy Good and Helen Murray in the kitchen of the first Stephanie's.

The family table at opening night of the first Stephanie's Restaurant in 1976.
Clockwise from front left: Diana; Dad; a friend; Diana's husband, Marcus; and Mum.

9

Radishes with Butter

The First Stephanie's 1976–8

In Melbourne in the early seventies there was a stirring in the restaurant scene. At that time a few families owned and operated the best-known establishments such as Mario's, The Latin and Florentino's. Most of these families were Italian. Other than that there was just a handful of serious restaurants, my favourites being Two Faces, owned and operated by Hermann Schneider and his wife Faye; Fanny's and Glo Glo's, owned by Gloria and Blyth Staley; and Tolarno French Bistro, owned by Leon Massoni. The leading hotels had dining rooms of varying quality. For a time, Whiting Caprice at the Hotel Australia had seemed the height of sophistication. There were many small ethnic restaurants with loyal clientele; technically they were not permitted to serve alcohol but quite a bit of wine was served in coffee cups at such places until in the late sixties a loophole in the law saw the beginning of BYO licences. Anyone who could satisfy council and health requirements could open their own establishment and take their chances.

The infamous six o'clock swill ended in 1966 when pub trading hours were extended until ten p.m. A few publicans started improving their premises and many enthusiastic amateur cooks opened

BYO establishments. They still could not sell liquor, however. It took another twenty years until the 1986 Nieuwenhuysen report to the Cain Government recommended liberalising the requirements to obtain a liquor licence, and from that time the bar, restaurant and café scene boomed.

By 1977 there were enough restaurants in Melbourne offering varying styles of cuisine and ambience for newspapers to run weekly restaurant reviews and to warrant the publication of the first food guide, entitled *Eating Out in Melbourne* and edited by Peter Smark, which reported on more than one hundred and thirty restaurants. In the list of the top rated twenty-two restaurants in the 1977 *Eating Out in Melbourne*, more than two-thirds were French, and the other five were Italian or Cantonese. One year later the guide reviewed one hundred and sixty establishments, but no longer included a list of the top-rated restaurants. From the index the offerings were more varied. The largest category was 'International'!

There was also change brewing in Europe and the new thinking influenced some restaurateurs in Australia. In 1973 French food journalists Henri Gault and Christian Millau used the term '*nouvelle cuisine*' in their monthly magazine *Guide Gault et Millau* to describe what they saw as a new style of cooking being practised by some of the great French restaurateurs – specifically Paul Bocuse, Alain Chapel, Jean and Pierre Troisgros, Michel Guérard and Roger Vergé. They identified the characteristics of this new style of cooking, which can be summarised as: simpler cooking, implying less complex dishes than in classical '*haute cuisine*'; reduced cooking times, especially for fish and green vegetables; shorter menus, implying fresher ingredients; abandoning the 'mother sauces', such as *espagnole* and *béchamel*, in favour of light jus and sauces based on cooking juices or herbs, often bound with butter; new and inventive combinations; and the introduction of new techniques and new equipment, among them non-stick cookware and the microwave oven. This 'revolution' received a huge amount of global attention. And whether they wanted to jump on the bandwagon or not, a chef could hardly fail to be influenced to some extent.

I had become friends with Tony Knox and his partner, Mietta O'Donnell. Mietta belonged to one of the original Melbourne restaurant families, the Viganos, who owned Mario's restaurant. Her childhood had been spent around good food and her family had always celebrated and gathered around a fine table. My experience at Jamaica House had left me shuddering at the idea of owning another restaurant and yet in 1973 I found myself dropping in more and more frequently to the newly opened Mietta's, which was located in a double-fronted old butcher's shop with wide windows onto Brunswick Street. I was fascinated by the business. Tony was a genius at creating interesting spaces at minimal cost and adept at locating and recycling discarded wood panelling or Victorian painted glass panels or light fittings. The first Mietta's had a moody, glamorous atmosphere with its dark-panelled walls, wine-coloured undercloths on the table and glorious and extravagant jugs of flowers. I could feel an itch developing as Tony and Mietta chatted on. Tony had many theories, many of them extreme, but he was a fascinating character. Mietta was more studied in her remarks but there was no doubting their commitment to quality and innovation. They saw a need to shake things up and intended to be the catalyst for change in Melbourne's restaurant scene. Initially they felt that their restaurant should reflect Melbourne's growing diversity.

In its early days the menu at Mietta's changed weekly and its parade of dishes, referencing the widest possible range of culinary influences, was extraordinary. Here one could eat a freshly boiled artichoke, spread open like a flower with excellent olive oil; an Indian-style curry; slow-cooked lamb shanks; or a classic

Piedmontese *vitello tonnato* (veal in tuna sauce). Pasta was served frequently and parmesan was shaved from a block. There were luscious desserts too, and delicious cakes: at Mietta's I tasted my first-ever dessert made with lightly sweetened mascarpone. *Amaretti* biscuits were offered with coffee. I remember with pleasure Mietta serving a red berry salad, which was nothing more than an opulent bowl of blackberries, raspberries and probably strawberries but it was memorable for its generosity and simplicity.

Mietta and Tony asked me to help out in the restaurant on a Sunday evening so that the chef could have a night off. I didn't have to do much original cooking as mostly I was reheating food. This experience introduced me to the routines of a busy kitchen, with the need to get the food out fast and correctly. I was given no training whatsoever, so was really learning on the job. Despite the stress, despite Tony's cutting remarks when all did not go as well as he hoped, I loved the work and the camaraderie, thrived on the bustle and soon started to consider seriously how I could do something similar myself.

Neither Mietta nor I had had any formal training in cookery. And yet in some ways we had both had the best of all possible training. We had been raised in families where good fresh food was highly valued, where seasonal specialties were home-grown or sought out and where family gatherings around a table were a high priority.

In a pattern that ought to have become familiar by now, I speedily found an empty shop further down Brunswick Street, convinced my father to guarantee yet another loan (twenty thousand dollars in 1976 was sufficient to get us started) and talked my dear friend Helen Murray into becoming a partner in this new business. She was a trained teacher and social worker with no experience whatsoever in running a business. But it promised to be different, and Helen loved new and different. Besides, she felt under-utilised at home with her two young children being wonderfully cared for at the Salvation Army day care centre in North Fitzroy, as was Holly. The curiosity, compassion and openness that had served her well in the years she worked as a social worker stood her in good stead in the first turbulent year of Stephanie's Restaurant. I also asked Malcolm Good's young sister, Tansy, to be my assistant in the kitchen. I had known her since she was a baby, and had watched as she grew from a rebellious teenager into a strong-willed young woman with a growing interest in all things culinary. She was as passionate as I was and it seemed like a good idea that we should work together to create beautiful, memorable food that would delight every customer at this new business.

It is hard to believe that Brunswick Street, which today is so crammed with cafés and restaurants, was virtually a desert in 1976. Other than Mietta's at the far northern end, a pizza place across the road, a small café called Mother Tuckers near the Johnston Street corner, and a lively and sometimes scary brothel next door, there were few shops. But I shouldn't forget the delightful Italian general store/delicatessen owned by Mr and Mrs Pizzaiola, both of whom were charming and of very generous proportions. They made us equally generous sandwiches stuffed with provolone and mortadella, which kept us going in the early days of the renovations and clean-up. The previous tenant had kept a huge doberman, apparently without bothering to take it outside for exercise or evacuation. We shovelled many loads of dog excrement. The rest of the street I remember as having a few small factories, some general shops, the post office, and at night it was quite dark.

The first Stephanie's lasted four years. Four momentous years, both for me and for Melbourne. I had been cooking non-stop all through my six years at Princes Hill Secondary College, including the classes I held at home. My friends were accustomed to endless invitations to eat at my place. Maurice and I had also visited almost every restaurant of repute in Melbourne, often with Tony and Mietta. We would discuss other people's menus, their décor, their service staff and their prices. The restaurant that stood head and shoulders above all others as far as we were concerned was Hermann and Faye Schneider's Two Faces in South Yarra. Here were restaurateurs who knew how to construct a menu with style, could always surprise, always used the freshest, best-quality and most appropriate item for the season. The cloths were crisp, the wine list extraordinary and the food was almost always sublime.

True food lovers always looked at the specials list first of all. You might find a civet of hare, a duck with black cherries, a goose, something garnished with braised celeriac or unusual mushrooms, or a dessert that featured fresh green almonds or white currants. And I cannot forget the poached figs in Armagnac syrup.

I rather hoped I could eventually come somewhere near what was being achieved at Two Faces, a daring thought from someone who had never had a formal cooking lesson in her life.

What was in my mind? I loved to cook, I loved planning menus. After my time in France and especially in its family-style country restaurants, I felt impatient to express myself in a similar way. I had supreme confidence in my ability to cook for a crowd and do it well. I found it surprising that others doubted I would succeed – failure did not even cross my mind.

Not for the first time I am puzzled that I could have boundless confidence in my abilities on the one hand and, within minutes, or when faced with a serious hurdle, could plunge into a feeling of despair, which rapidly morphed into believing that the project was doomed and pointless. Fortunately once I had plunged to the depths I usually resolved to fight back and develop a new strategy.

In the early months the plan was that Maurice would continue as a barrister as well as manage the finances of the business and act as host in the evenings. I do not recall that we ever sat down and discussed how to manage family life in any detail, other than that we needed to make arrangements for someone to live in the tiny flat at the rear of our Northcote house, so they could care for the children in the evening. My determination to just plunge in was typical, possibly also reckless. I wanted to do it, so I would do it, and would cope more or less well with the consequences.

For Maurice as a young barrister the road ahead was always going to be highly competitive. What work there was was handled by the clerks assigned to the various legal chambers. It seemed to me that young barristers were required to sit around early in the morning to find out if they had a brief, and by ten or so, if nothing was offered, it was unlikely to happen that day. In the early days, before the restaurant opened, Maurice often went to the movies at this point. Sometimes he then missed obtaining a brief for the next day. Having been absent from Melbourne for those three years in Hong Kong he had also distanced himself from his legal contemporaries and was probably at a disadvantage when he returned. These observations are mine; maybe he would see it differently. I felt that Maurice was pleased to move into a new field that offered prestige, contact with interesting people, and the opportunity to manage relatively large amounts of money.

In France I had been particularly delighted by the multiple-course meals I had enjoyed in private homes and small country restaurants. One started with a little something, went on to another, more substantial dish and finished with a sweet but not too sweet flourish, perhaps with a single piece of cheese tucked between main course and dessert and, of course, a carefully turned green salad. So my restaurant would be a *restaurant prix fixe*. We would make everything ourselves: bread, stocks, petits fours, puff pastry. We would churn our own ice-creams and sorbets. Dishes would have brief descriptions and not be given fanciful names. I would search out little-known edible ingredients and surprise guests with violet petals in a sorbet or in a salad, with lemon verbena scenting a fish or a sorbet, or I would infuse a custard or line a sponge cake tin with rose-scented geranium. My fish soups might come with lightly dried marigold petals, faintly reminiscent of the muskiness of saffron.

The original tablecloths were made from an unserviceable but pretty sprigged floral cotton, which we changed to a Liberty lawn with a pattern of rioting pansies two years later after our first exposure to European style in the starred restaurants! My mother came once a week and made tiny posies for each table, picking most of the flowers and herbs in her own garden. We offered a small dish of olives as guests sat down and one or two petits fours at the end of the meal.

The influence of *nouvelle cuisine* was faintly noticeable in those first years, although some elements had long been present in my cooking. I never overcooked vegetables. I loved presenting vegetable combinations sauced with the last spoonful of cooking juice shaken to bind with a knob of unsalted butter. And I had often created first-course *salades composées*, where green leaves were combined with something crunchy or crisp, or the leaves were nestled around something small and succulent such as a quail stuffed with duck liver parfait, or a fat piece of smoked eel. I also liked to preserve the shape of small green beans, removing the tops but leaving the dainty curved tip in place. This detail was criticised by an early reviewer of the restaurant and I was predictably enraged.

The first Stephanie's was BYO. We opened with two menus, the cheese and a second entrée being extras on the more expensive option. The original menus were nine dollars and twelve dollars per person. Within the first month the prices escalated to ten dollars and fifteen dollars. Twenty-one years later the closing price was an all-inclusive eighty-five dollars per person and the cheese course was listed as an alternative to a sweet dish.

The opening twelve-dollar menu at Stephanie's Restaurant in 1976 was as follows:

Mushrooms à la grecque

or

Fish soup as in Marseille with croutons and rouille

or

Galantine de volaille

(boned chicken with pork and veal forcemeat,

pistachio and green peppercorns)

Boudin blanc

(delicate sausage of pork and chicken)

or

Feuilletés au Roquefort

(layered puff pastry with a melting Roquefort cheese filling)

Aioli garni

(hot and cold vegetables and poached seafood with garlic mayonnaise)

or

Beef and walnut ragoût with pasta shells

or

Noisettes of lamb with stuffing of mushroom, sorrel and lamb kidneys

Salad

Cheeseboard

Crème brûlée

or

Florentine oranges

or

Strawberry shortcake

Reading it now I note that the influence was one hundred per cent French.

At the end of the very first service came one of my worst-ever mistakes. Wanting to establish exemplary habits, I intended to drain the oil from the small deep-fryer so it could be filtered before being reused. That I was very tired is my only excuse. I put a plastic bucket under the drain tap and watched in horror as the hot oil splashed in and the bucket immediately sagged and collapsed, allowing all four litres to flow over the beautiful new vinyl floor. Towels and strewn salt and hours of work later, I eventually went home. The floor was never the same.

Many of my friends were caught up in the excitement of the first months and wanted to help. Helen Murray as an initial partner was a solid rock of friendship and commonsense. Other friends washed dishes, carried plates, cooked alongside Tansy and me, peeled shallots, and in the early days we all sat down to a lavish supper at the end of the night. Angela Clemens, my friend since library days, was a regular, as was her doctor husband. He recalls washing dishes, no doubt after a gruelling day with patients! And my sister Diana, who was now living in Melbourne, also came to lend a hand.

Soon after opening, compliments began to flow from the dining room back to the kitchen. An early supporter of my cooking was a young man named Damien Pignolet. I was actually a bit unnerved by his enthusiasm for my little restaurant. He raved about our radishes served with unsalted butter and salt. And the calves' liver crisply sautéed but still pink in the middle. Few other customers had 'got it' as he had. Damien ate in the restaurant at least once a week until he moved to Sydney in 1978 to develop his career as a restaurateur. Shortly afterwards he married fellow chef Josephine Carroll in 1980, and Josephine and Damien became special foodie friends. Our friendship strengthened over the years. In 1981 they opened the incomparable Claude's restaurant in Oxford Street, Sydney, designing and executing exquisite food and achieving great acclaim.

We had a high percentage of return custom. Word of mouth was delivering more and more business. Other restaurateurs came to see and taste.

One of our first private dinners was organised by a friend of Maurice's from the Victorian Bar, Jim Kennan, who was at the time an office-bearer in the organisation Lawyers for Labor. Jim will always be remembered by all of his friends and colleagues for his astonishing laugh, his dimpled smile, his irreverent humour and his deep compassion. It meant a lot to Maurice to have so many of his peers assembled in the restaurant and I was impressed and delighted to see so many distinguished and recognisable politicians and lawyers enjoying my food. The after-dinner speaker on this evening was then barrister now the Honourable Mr Justice Michael Kirby.

Any account of Stephanie's Restaurant has to make mention of significant members of staff. Some stayed for years, others came, went and came again, some were more transient.

Tansy Good worked alongside me for the first eighteen months or so before travelling to Europe. Later she returned to the second

Stephanie's for a short time before leaving to open her own restaurant, Tansy's. Then there was Jenny Cousins, who had a wonderfully light hand with pastry. She also returned to the second Stephanie's after marrying and having a child. Her sense of the ridiculous kept us all amused.

Julian Desailly was an important kitchenhand and he introduced a friend, Janni Kyritsis. Janni stayed for five years, making the transition to the second Stephanie's. He was always ready to try something different and had an ingenious mind. No matter how odd my idea was, Janni would help me realise it. I missed him dreadfully when he moved to Sydney, where he worked for many years with Gay Bilson at Berowra Waters Inn and at Bennelong at the Opera House before operating his own Sydney restaurant MG Garage. Janni was an outstanding colleague and remains a good friend.

Steven Pallett came and worked with precision and focus and offered me great loyalty and friendship. He came and went more than once, and was head chef at the second Stephanie's for several years before leaving to take up a teaching position at William Angliss, Melbourne's major hospitality training college.

One of the most challenging aspects of running any small business is dealing with the staff. A restaurant is a bit like a theatre. It has a nightly performance with a great deal of work leading up to the moment the guests arrive. In both back of house (the kitchen) and front of house (the floor staff), there is palpable tension as the time approaches for the curtain to rise, or as one waits for 'service' to begin. There are many routine preparations to complete but staff must always be able to deal smoothly with the unexpected. There is little room for mistakes. There is even more tension in the kitchen once the orders start to flow; commands must be clear and the team must work well together.

There were always issues to do with personalities. Fortunately Dur-é Dara had joined the staff as a casual waitress. She had done some social work training and was very good at smoothing the waters and sorting out the issues. Feuds between this person and that (resolve it after service), a staff member in tears because of a personal crisis (go home, deal with it and then come back), bossiness or rudeness (discuss it after service), a challenge to a superior (needs one-to-one discussion the next day), cliques developing that threaten the team effort (discussion the next day), love affairs between staff members (if they cannot work effectively together they must leave). I was ill-prepared for all of this and was often resentful and angry at what I saw as petty distractions that could upset the whole team and impact on the service of my beautiful food.

I had spent many a happy hour dreaming about preparing and cooking delicious food but had not spent much time planning how to deal with some other aspects of restaurant management. Much of our original equipment had been purchased secondhand to stretch our dollars. Maintenance issues loomed right from the beginning, ranging from leaking pipes, greasetrap hygiene, blown-up power points and dishwashing machine breakdowns to name a few. Janni was very handy with a spanner or even a coathanger to fix this or that. A roll of gaffer tape was always at the ready.

I remember two special incidents from our time at the first Stephanie's in Brunswick Street. One night, after all the customers had left, Dur-é, Maurice and I were seated in the restaurant deeply engaged in debate about something or other, when two men appeared from the direction of the now-deserted kitchen, wearing balaclavas and holding iron bars. They directed us to lie down on the floor while they searched for money. It all happened so quickly that my primary emotion was surprise rather than fear. Once they had found the cash they disappeared quickly. The police arrived very speedily and we spent the next few hours giving statements to a young constable. Other than the humiliation of being forced to the floor, my strongest emotion was outrage that, while we had been talking, the robbers had systematically gone through our bags, removing anything of value.

On another occasion I had decided to sleep upstairs rather then drive home. (In the upstairs area, alongside the storeroom and staff toilet, we had installed a comfortable bed in case of illness and also as a crash pad if anyone needed it for any reason.) In the early years of Stephanie's I often sat around with the staff at the end of the night and reviewed the service. Wine flowed and, coupled with the exhaustion that follows a busy night in the kitchen, there were many occasions when I should not have driven home. This was probably one of those occasions and this time I decided to sleep upstairs. Dur-é and her partner, who lived on the topmost floor of the building, were intending to travel very early the next morning to Sydney to play in a concert. (At this stage in her life Dur-é was also a percussionist and played with her musician partner.) In the middle of the night I was woken by the stamping of heavy boots on the stairs, thought to myself that they were making a colossal racket and hoped they would go quickly. Fortunately Dur-é's partner remembered (or was alerted to the fact) that I was in the building, because I found myself being pulled out of bed and hustled down the stairs. Once out of the door I walked into a waterfall and realised all at once that not only was I in the middle of Brunswick Street in my flannelette nightgown, but that the next-door brothel was on fire. The fire brigade was pumping water into the restaurant as well as into the brothel, though there was never any danger of the restaurant catching fire. When Maurice was summoned his concern seemed to be for the water damage in the restaurant rather than that I might have been overcome with smoke. I was not pleased with his reaction.

Predictably, being an owner-chef brought with it very long hours and worries. I had to adjust to the relentless repetition of tasks and learn how to direct others. I wonder if I had imagined I could do everything myself. The restaurant was booked to capacity right from the start, for every service. I was working ridiculous hours and the memory of Jamaica House was becoming stronger by the week.

By this stage Lisa organised herself in the morning and caught the tram to school without any help from me. I don't think I made her lunches. My day began with a call to the fishmonger to check on the morning's arrivals. Then I would drop Holly at day care, zoom past the fish shop to pick up the order and then a supermarket to buy the inevitable items that had run out the night before, such as extra milk, cream or butter. I tried to be at my bench checking work lists and reducing stocks by ten in the morning. And the restaurant did not open for lunch. Meanwhile Maurice was either up and out if he had a legal case, or if not, sleeping in. 'Sleeping in' was a concept totally foreign to me and still is. I condemned it as a waste of time and it frequently provoked a row between us. Maurice would often collect Holly from day care and spend an hour or two with her before turning up at the restaurant to be the host in the evening.

Before Damien Pignolet left Melbourne for Sydney in 1978 he bequeathed me his cleaning lady, an extraordinary woman named Maria. Maria was Latvian and for the next twenty-five years she cleaned my various houses and became part of the family, and I could not have done without her.

Various friends and acquaintances at different times lived in the tiny flat attached to our house at Northcote and babysat the two children in the evenings. Some of these arrangements were excellent and some were not. Life became more pressured for Holly once the restaurant opened. She did love day care at the Salvation Army centre, though. The matron and her husband were absolutely delightful and seemed to truly love each one of these little children. Holly was always pleased to arrive and although delighted to see me in the afternoon, was sometimes reluctant to leave the games or the sandpit. She does enjoy reminding me of the day I delivered her still in her pyjama bottoms. Probably true to say that I was thinking of two things at once. Happily we both find the story funny.

One of the excellent although short-lived arrangements was when a young woman named Alannah and her dear little girl Claire stayed in the flat. There is a sweet picture of Claire and Holly in the back garden, wearing matching red cardigans. The girls and I remember Alannah fondly for her friendly nature and her excellent cooking.

Sometimes Holly came to the restaurant before going home to bed. She enjoyed making cubby houses under the tablecloths as the dining room was being prepared for the evening service. We had family holidays, and she played with the Murray children as often as possible. On weekends Maurice would take the girls to the swimming pool or on some other excursion. Sometimes I went. Other times I grasped at solitude and read books or planned menus.

Lisa was ten years old when the first Stephanie's opened and Holly was just two. It was probably during these years that Lisa and Holly became so keen on watching television. Without much else to do in the evenings, without any parental assistance or guidance, both girls became entranced with the world of popular culture, especially anything to do with America.

Most evenings I made it home to cook for the family but not always. I have a memory of whipping my little green Volkswagen around the roundabouts between Northcote and Fitzroy, hurrying to get back to my restaurant kitchen. Maurice had his own car and probably followed at a more leisurely pace. Sundays were for family and friends. Mondays the restaurant was closed but as it was a school day and the only day to catch up on paperwork, planning and menu writing, not a lot of time was spent on family relationships. In my heart I knew this was not satisfactory and I think I just thought that Lisa was a sensible girl with plenty of friends and that she would be all right – whatever that was supposed to mean. Holly being so much younger had a more structured routine. Neither daughter was given much encouragement to take up regular sporting activities other than swimming.

For a time my friend Betsy Bradshaw and her then husband lived in the flat and babysat Holly and Lisa. The children loved her. Lisa remembers that Betsy took her to see Abba at the Myer Music Bowl in 1977. Lisa was a passionate Abba fan. The Abba phenomenon of the time passed me by, as I was deep in activity in my kitchens. I did, however, attend the end-of-year concert at Princes Hill Primary School and was startled and somewhat appalled to see a troupe of nine- or ten-year-olds, all dressed in purple shimmery flapper dresses, dancing and gesturing to the Abba hit tune 'Money, Money, Money'. (I wonder who made Lisa's costume. Probably my mother.) It didn't seem right, the provocative hip thrusts and stabbing fingers of these little girls. Many, many years later I enjoyed the film *Mamma Mia* with adult Lisa and loved seeing her eyes shine with excitement, knowing that she was inwardly singing along!

Maurice was still at the Bar, with the added responsibility of managing and looking after the finances of the restaurant. My friend Helen was realising that her skills were not suited to the kitchen of a professional establishment even though her wise guidance was crucial in other areas such as the accounts. She recognised that emotions were running high between Maurice and me and after the first six months very wisely opted to withdraw from the partnership, suggesting that Maurice and I should work to operate the business as partners. At this point Maurice gave up being a barrister.

Mostly I had stacks of energy and stamina. Standing at a bench chopping while directing others, thinking, discussing, tasting and reflecting for fourteen hours at a stretch was not a problem. I loved it. I loved the camaraderie of the kitchen. I loved the sense of being at the centre of a creative enterprise. What exhausted me was emotional conflict. And there was plenty of that.

I was driven by my ambition and the excitement of my work, and probably a need for recognition. My children trailed along, happy enough, with plenty of friends, but not really getting enough from their mother. Maurice took Holly to swimming lessons, drove her here and there, took her to the park, read her *Alice in Wonderland* and other stories. My special time with her was taking her to day care in the morning. She chatted away and snuggled up to me as she went inside. She was always happy to be with the other pre-schoolers and grew to be very confident and sunny-natured.

Lisa struggled to achieve the same self-confidence, given that she had a distracted but loving mother and intermittent contact with her father. By this stage Monty was living with a new partner and they had a son, Simon, born in 1975. Monty still spent time with Lisa on Thursdays after school, and their Sunday restaurant outings were highly anticipated. Lisa was also included in outings with the extended family of Monty's partner. Monty was a well-known and well-loved personality around Melbourne and Lisa glowed in his company. She remembers a particular Sunday outing to the popular Eltham Barrel Restaurant with her father and cricketers Clive Lloyd and Viv Richards. She was proud to be in the company of these extrovert and huge personalities, and recalls that a hush fell over the entire restaurant as they walked in. The West Indies cricket team made a huge impact in Australia during the seventies.

I do have treasured photographs of a happy family holiday we took in New Caledonia when Holly was about three or four, and Lisa eleven or twelve. The framed photo of the two girls on the beach, both looking straight to the camera, still sits beside my bed. Lisa's arm is around her little sister, and both are laughing with expressions of pure happiness.

Thank God for my own wonderful friends. So often they filled in for me and Maurice, and for Monty. Jean and John Tinney, Helen and Jim Murray, Kathy and Bruce Wright were the stalwarts. Our friendships had grown stronger over the twenty years since we met at university. The men had come a bit later in some cases. Betsy Bradshaw, who was now married to my former boyfriend, Malcolm Good, and Angela Clemens and her husband, Duffy, had joined this group a bit later on. I must have contributed something to these friendships because they were mutually valued (and still are after fifty-plus years). I think we all laughed a lot and I know that they were there for me when I cried.

But in among all this emotional turmoil, heat and grease there was the food!

I started out reproducing dishes I had eaten or remembered from my visits to France, becoming more ambitious as I proceeded. Many of the classic dishes of *cuisine bourgeoise* appeared, cooked with love and care. I made savoury navarins of lamb with spring vegetables, which were sent to the table in individual lidded casseroles. I made pork with prunes, as I had enjoyed from my days in Tours, and a simple pot-au-feu that included poached lambs' tongues. There was a version of *boeuf bourguignon* where the sauce and garnish were classically correct but the *boeuf* consisted of fillet steak sauteed rare. And one of my favourites was (and still is) a poached boned chicken stuffed with a well-flavoured stuffing of ham and chicken livers and with a creamy enriched velouté sauce.

Such were the limited offerings in most Melbourne restaurants at the time, and the limited overseas experience of Melbourne diners, that I found that I was being hailed as 'innovative' by preparing beautifully made rabbit and pork rillettes and serving them with *cornichons* and grilled house-made toast, as I had enjoyed them during my year as a language *assistante* in Tours; or grilling a trimmed slice of calf's liver and serving it with potatoes fried in duck fat and home-grown green beans; or making a smooth sorbet from tree-ripened peaches. I found this then, as I still do now, embarrassing, revealing the lack of understanding of some of the customers and food critics. I moved on to more ambitious preparations.

Of course the specialist produce available in 1976 was very different from what is available today. Parsley, mint and chives were the principal herbs available. French tarragon, unobtainable. Coriander, not on the horizon. Most ginger came already peeled and sliced in small tins. Iceberg lettuce was the sole salad green offered. Fortunately I had a few friends who had a few friends and here and there a European family was growing greens of a more interesting sort. I remember the first time I was offered a waxy potato. Small zucchini were unheard of and forget any notion of stuffing zucchini flowers. Slender beans were obtainable only if you grew them.

At the Queen Victoria Market some of the Chinese market families saved the day. They sold Asian greens and other interesting vegetables that never made it to the suburban shops. Hermann Schneider could always be seen on market days carefully inspecting and selecting for Two Faces. If there was ginger travelling down from Queensland, the Chinese had it. One Chinese couple cultivated oyster mushrooms.

For a brief moment in the mid-seventies French cheeses were imported, but this stopped when the system became too complicated. Goat's cheese was unheard of. Janni and I determined to try to make our own and we did, a simple cheese made with pasteurised goat's milk that was delivered to the back door. We served our hand-moulded goat's curd with fresh herbs, some of which were grown by friends.

On the other hand scallops were very inexpensive – no-one appreciated them. Calamari was almost given away – few non-Asian customers were interested in trying it. But octopus – forget it! We had plenty of beef and lamb, very young veal (sold as 'bobby' veal), wild rabbits, chickens and ducks. For the production of squab pigeon we had to wait until the late eighties and early nineties for Ian Milburn from Glenloth Game to develop his business, but I do remember being offered my first quail in the mid-eighties. Jack and Josie Canals ran an amazing fish shop in North Carlton (Canals Seafood is still owned by family members), so our fish was always very fresh. The salmon industry did not start until 1985.

Other ingredients chefs take for granted today were also unavailable. A short list would include abalone, blood oranges, chorizo, eel, exotic mushrooms, guinea fowl, hare, marrons, Australian extra virgin olive oil, cultured butter, sea salt, sea urchins, truffles, venison, white asparagus, yabbies, specialist breads. And many more.

With the end of the Vietnam War in 1975 Melbourne's Victoria Street was about to be transformed. Within two or three years shining roast ducks, soy-dipped chickens and bubbly-skinned roast pork hung from hooks in the windows of small restaurants, mountains of unknown green vegetables were stacked outside the rapidly proliferating fresh food stores, and hitherto unavailable items such as fresh lemongrass, kaffir lime leaves, bundles of the freshest coriander, and dried noodles of bewildering variety filled the colourful shelves. For many cooks this opened a new and fascinating world. Dur-é was more familiar with how to use many of these new resources. I loved going with her to small tucked-away ethnic eateries and always left the ordering to her.

I read a great deal about food. The ever-expanding local food media reported from time to time on the great European restaurants. Every newspaper now ran a column or a supplement with a heavy emphasis on food and restaurants. There were several locally published food magazines – not nearly as glossy as today and with less emphasis on lifestyle and expensive hotels. I subscribed to *Cuisine et Vins de France*, an important food periodical, as well as certain British and American food magazines, and gazed entranced at the beautiful plates of food. I eagerly purchased a copy of Michel Guérard's seminal book *Cuisine Gourmande*, first published in English in 1978, and found it totally inspiring and revolutionary. Here was one of the best practitioners of the *nouvelle cuisine* movement identified by Gault and Millau. His salads included surprising combinations of ingredients, many then unknown or unavailable to Australian chefs. All featured a selection of salad leaves such as endive, lamb's lettuce, batavia, watercress and radicchio, the salads garnished maybe with quails' eggs, streaky bacon lardons, smoked fish, foie gras or truffles, and with asparagus tips or fresh garden peas and plenty of picked herbs.

The book described combinations of meats or poultry with vegetables that were novel for the time but are now unremarkable, such as hare with beetroot, or rabbit with spinach and baby turnips, partridge on a bed of crisp tossed cabbage, ham with a mushroom puree, ox-cheek with orange; on and on went these exciting dishes. It all just made me want to rush to the stove.

Other cooks such as Tony and Gay Bilson were also impressed by the movement. Tony had cooked at several restaurants since the days of Jamaica House and we were still friendly. He had met Gay in Melbourne and they formed a strong partnership for many years, starting at Tony's Bon Goût in Sydney and moving onto Berowra Waters Inn on the Hawkesbury River.

Other books by French starred chefs followed. Ideas came thick and fast. I filled notebooks with concepts to be explored further – many with sketches beside the descriptions as I imagined how the dish might be presented. Many are so abbreviated that I am not sure what I meant. 'Mussel mousse', 'stuffed turnips braised in cider', 'geraniums in ice' – what could I have meant? Others I recognise as being the start of what later became a successful dish: 'gratin of aubergine', 'yabbies with salad burnet', 'green tomato gazpacho', 'flounder stuffed with crabmeat and fish mousseline', 'stuffed duck neck en brioche', and on they go. There are hundreds of entries. Only a small percentage ever made it to the table. At this time I taught myself to bone birds and rabbits, to fillet fish, to separate a leg of lamb into separate muscles, to mount sauces with butter (*beurre montée*) and a hundred other *trucs* of the trade.

Food, chefs and restaurants were claiming more and more media attention. In 1979 wine promoter and writer the late Len Evans planned an annual dinner to be held in the Hunter Valley at Rothbury Estate, the vineyard he co-owned. I do not recall many other grand dinners before this, other than the regular calendar of Wine and Food Society gatherings for which many of us cooked. Len Evans had hand-picked a few chefs and asked them each to come up with a course that together would present a harmonious and outstanding dinner for guests who would be asked to pay quite a lot to attend.

I was thrilled to be included and was asked to produce the dessert. I thought and thought. Of course I wanted my dish to taste wonderful, but it should also represent the style I was trying to establish. After considerable thought I decided to offer a plate of *trompe-l'œil* (literally, 'deceive the eye') frozen 'fruits'. Fresh fruits were hollowed and their shells frozen to provide rigid containers. I had bowls of pureed pear, tamarillo, passionfruit and kiwifruit. Individual sorbet mixtures were made, sugar levels adjusted and the shells then filled with freshly churned sorbets. We practised the dish in the restaurant. The *coup de grâce* was placing a red rose on each plate and adding a 'rosebud' made by infusing red rose petals in syrup and churning it to create a deep-red and aromatic sorbet.

This all took place before any small restaurant was using an electric ice-cream churn. We churned every sorbet and ice-cream by hand in a barrel churn that had a steel canister in the middle. The space between canister and barrel was packed with ice and salt. A great deal of elbow grease was needed to turn chilled mix into a smooth sorbet. For the dinner we had arranged to borrow two additional churns.

Janni Kyritsis was my chief assistant and we set off for the Hunter Valley confident that our dish was going to be a hit. Our syrups were packed into the bladders from wine casks. Our hollowed shells were frozen solid, providing their own chilled protection.

We arrived at the venue and immediately packed the available churns with ice and salt and started churning. As each sorbet was finished we spooned the mix into tray after tray of shells, and settled them all carefully in a chest freezer. Our preparation was finished so we went back to our accommodation, relaxed, swam and wondered how the other cooks were faring. Within an hour there was an incredible storm. Thunder, lightning, rain, and the venue lost all power. We hurried back. One cook was in despair as her choux puffs had been in an oven and were now ruined. We opened the freezer to discover that our trays were awash with brightly coloured syrups. With just an hour to go before more than one hundred guests would arrive, panic ensued. Candles were found for the tables. Electricians were summoned and worked frantically. Power was restored but not in time for our products to refreeze. Janni and I sent out for lots more ice and had to churn each sorbet *à la minute*, scooping it into the shells as waiters stood by to rush the plate to each guest. It was one of the most stressful evenings of my cooking career, but miraculously the dish was well received by the diners. It provided a salutary lesson that a successful event does depend on many details and that even the best-laid plans can be undone by events beyond our control.

One machine that was in every restaurant kitchen was the food processor. Up till this point few chefs would undertake the time-consuming task of forcing fish or chicken through the finest sieves to create ethereal dumplings and mousse (although Hermann Schneider did). All at once everyone could create a mousse, and seafood terrines or *boudins* and quenelles of fish or fowl were every-where. These preparations might be plain, herb-flavoured, striped, or layered with other ingredients. It was a significant breakthrough. Pureed sauces and vegetables became ubiquitous, as did *coulis* of berries and herb pastes, now all possible at the flick of a switch. At the time of writing this, once again new technology has delivered the ability to do all sorts of things not possible before. Even though my professional cooking days are well and truly over I find myself intrigued by the Pacojet, which minces, purees and makes a creamy mousse out of frozen products at astonishing speed. I may have to buy one! And I am fascinated by the Anti-Griddle, which instantly freezes a product, making it possible to offer a semi-frozen crea-tion with a crunchy surface and a creamy middle. I also meet more and more home cooks who have invested in the semi-commercial wonder machine, the Thermomix.

But back in the late seventies, I decided it was time to return to France, to visit some of the restaurants I had only read about, and see and taste for myself. At this time Maurice and I were having lots of tense arguments. He regularly accused me of extravagance, whenever a large bill came in from a providore. He was always emotional when dealing with large sums of money and found it impossible to stand back from a bill and consider it as part of the bigger picture. On the other hand I was unable to discuss the topic constructively. Whenever someone raises their voice at me I am always struck dumb. These regular confrontations were doing damage to our relationship. But Maurice loved adventuring and we had always travelled well together, so it seemed a good opportunity to do something we both loved. And importantly the cashflow was healthy, we were answerable only to ourselves, and we were able to close the restaurant for a month in May 1978 and travel to France.

Three-year-old Holly stayed with my parents. I remember the disbelief on her face as we said our goodbyes at the airport. Her face crumpled into horror and she wept, as did I. And yet I knew she adored her grandparents and would be very well looked after. Ten-year-old Lisa was more stoic as we kissed goodbye. She travelled once more to Jamaica at this time with Monty, his partner and their toddler son. I was home again in time to greet them on their return.

10

Saumon à L'oseille

Inspiration from France's Grand Restaurants 1978–9

In 1978 Maurice and I had the first of several extensive holidays in France. They were research trips but they also recharged all our batteries. Our pleasure in each other's company returned as we sat on sidewalk cafés in Paris far from the stresses of the book-keeping or staff issues at our restaurant. We breathed in the scent of honeysuckle as we strolled down walled lanes in the south of France or travelled through the deep-green forests of the south-west; we picnicked in flowery fields, sometimes sitting on cushions of wild thyme; and we ate in beautiful dining rooms that might look over the sea or onto a mountain or towards a distant town with lights twinkling. We also caught up on romance and sleep. We talked about matters not always connected with the restaurant. Maurice climbed a few mountains, always preferring the distant view. I preferred the close-up perspective, noting the drift of flowers from a linden tree, or the creamy flowers of the false acacia (*Robinia*). I was always captivated by the first sight of a field dotted with scarlet poppies and I joyfully picked small posies of wildflowers. In villages I peered into the *potagers* attached to almost every house. Maurice visited every church and every place of interest. We both

enjoyed markets and impromptu surprises. Sadly we still squabbled about money.

My regular notebook habit seems to have started from the time
of this European trip. I have trawled through them for details of
dishes tasted or comments made but I must say that I think my
notes are pretty poor. Of course we did not have a computer in
those days and I probably scribbled my thoughts after too much
wine and before falling into bed.

We started the trip at Beaulieu and the first entry is on
Maurice's birthday, 16 May, with a description of our wander
through a French food market. The first visit to a food market on a
trip to France is always uplifting, especially in late spring. I noted
the slender green beans, called *aiguilles*, meaning needles. And the
purple artichokes, bundles of asparagus, tiny turnips (unknown in
Australia at this time), tiny pearl onions (ditto), and pink-skinned
and waxy *ratte* potatoes. And I was enthralled by the strawberries
tumbled opulently in loose mounds, a glorious still-life arrangement
wherever one looked. Fish gasped their last on marble slabs, wet
seaweed lined the tubs of oysters, tightly closed as they should be,
next to all manner of shellfish, from tiny *tellines* (a type of clam like
a very small pipi) to crabs and lobsters. I have seen many a French
market since this time but they never fail to thrill me. Quite apart
from the sensational produce, it is the banter between seller and
buyer that delights. The pleasure of being among all this good food
seems to communicate happiness to all.

I wrote myself a reminder that day after our meal in a tiny café
in the square where I ordered my first fish soup. Ordering a fish
soup early on in a trip to France remains a ritual for me to this day.

A good fish soup must be thick but not too thick, rust-red
in colour, the smell must be of the freshest fish with no

suggestion of that awful aroma of overcooked fish stock with its chalky bone taste, and it should have crunchy garlic croutons and a powerful *rouille* to swirl into the soup. The only downside is that the French often serve gruyère cheese grated a long time beforehand so it can be sweaty and hard.

At Roger Vergé's Moulin de Mougins in the south of France, we were delighted with both the food and the restaurant. It was a warm day, the tables set under umbrellas in the garden, with pink cloths and massed flowers. The dish that I attempted to reproduce at home was a section of lamb loin, trimmed of every vestige of silverskin, sauteed and then cut into long strips as one might carve the loin from a saddle of lamb. It was served with a small quantity of a delicious lamb jus whisked with a puree of garlic and accompanied by a small and exquisite female zucchini (*courgette*) with flower attached. Very refined. The meat was butter-tender and evenly rosy-pink.

The complimentary appetiser was a slice of a vegetable layer cake (that food processor at work!) that alternated tomato, spinach, tomato and onion served with tiny Niçoise olives. This sort of mousse/custard/mousseline filling became a bit of a cliché by the end of the holiday but this first one tasted fresh and delicious.

On this trip we ate at La Pyramide at Vienne, in the Rhône Valley, the home of the late Fernand Point, considered by many of the revered chefs of the day as 'the father of modern French cuisine'. It was scary approaching the actual restaurant; so often intense anticipation leads to disappointment. I need not have worried. Every diner was greeted at the door by the tiny and tottery Madame Point, who had apparently observed this practice since the death of her legendary husband in 1955. (Madame Point died in 1986 but the great restaurant has survived under various changes of ownership, although I have never had the opportunity to revisit it.) Like many other Francophile chefs I had read and reread Fernand Point's memoir *Ma gastronomie* and been inspired by his love of life, the number of chefs he had trained and influenced, and by reports of his delicious food. My copy of the book has little pencil marks beside certain recipes I thought to try. Needless to say, without truffles, *foie gras*, plentiful scampi or European lobster, many of the recipes were impossible to attempt, but some were possible. His generosity of spirit is shown in the number of dishes included that are named for his apprentices who went on to become great chefs in their own right. Thus we have *Paté de grives des Frères Troisgros* (The brothers Troisgros thrush paté), *Paté froid de saumon Alain Chapel* (Alain Chapel's cold salmon paté), *Dorade Louis Outhier* (Louis Outhier sea bream), *Truite à la façon de Paul Bocuse* (Trout the style of Paul Bocuse), and many more. Point's *Gratin de queues d'écrevisses* (Gratin of freshwater crayfish tails) was said to be his greatest creation, but then there was his *Foie gras en brioche*, the *Gâteau marjolaine* (thin layers of almond and hazelnut meringue sandwiched with chocolate cream, butter cream and praline butter cream, the entire log finally spread with more of the chocolate butter cream), which we had already attempted at Stephanie's. Every dish we tasted was delicious. The service was attentive. The restaurant was elegant and, once again, had exquisite flowers.

Next stop was Les Frères Troisgros at Roanne near Lyons. Pierre and his brother Jean ran the restaurant that their father Jean-Baptiste had established back in 1930. Here I was impressed by their famous truffled vegetable *mosaïque* with its nuggets of truffle and colourful vegetable against a background of pale pink ham mousse. It did indeed resemble a mosaic.

And I simply had to try the *saumon à l'oseille* (salmon with sorrel), a dish so simple in concept that it was sweeping the world!

Jean Troisgros proudly showed me the menu sent by a Brazilian *stagiare* in whose restaurant the dish now featured prominently. It relied on the recently available non-stick pans and cutting the salmon into thin escalopes that cooked in less than a minute. The sauce was a classic *sauce vin blanc* built on a reduction of shallots, vermouth and white wine, with plenty of excellent French crème fraîche. This master sauce was then enriched with a knob of butter and a large handful of sorrel. The dish was ready to be served in maybe three minutes from being called away by the chef. Brilliant.

We had stunning beef with chunks of marrow and an intense red wine sauce and, to finish, a pineapple sorbet to accompany chunks of fresh pineapple dipped in hot toffee as the Chinese do with apples. The final parade of petits fours that seemed obligatory in these three-star restaurants was always delicious but in my opinion excessive. Of course I tried them but came away feeling that this big hit of sugar was not the best way to finish a meal.

Alain Chapel was my hero. I loved his restaurant at Mionnay most of all. It was different. His food was different. Like all the three-starred restaurants his menu offered plenty of *foie gras*, truffles and luxurious seafood, but he moved beyond what the others did with these ingredients. He surprised. There was a freshness, an originality, even in the way he described his dishes. Almost all the restaurants we visited to this point exuded extreme formality, even though the staff were very friendly. Chapel's restaurant was in a low stucco building, partly covered with a climbing vine. It looked like a lovely country house. Through the arched entrance you looked into a cool courtyard with glimpses of a green garden beyond that. I think the floor in the main restaurant was flagstones. There were bowls of simple garden roses and a carpeted anteroom where you sat to read the menu and enjoy an aperitif. As we did just that a basket lined with a cream napkin was put down in front of us. It held crisply fried sardines and inner leaves of celery, also deep-fried. Both morsels were greaseless, piping-hot and delectable. As we looked appreciatively at this treat the chef himself hurried from one room to the next and gently scolded us, urging us to eat them at once while they were still hot.

It was at Chapel that I first tasted hot *foie gras*, which in the words of a friend who had already tasted this product, was like 'moving molecules'. The specially fattened livers are chilled, sliced thickly, sautéed very briefly on both sides in a hot pan, which makes the outside of the slice crisp and almost caramelised, and then a little alcohol or reduced stock is dribbled into the pan together with any simple accompaniment, which might be figs, sultanas, peaches, or pre-cooked and glazed onions, and then it is served. Too long in the pan and the liver will melt to nothing.

It was also at Alain Chapel's that I tasted the best main course I can remember from the trip. It was described as '*salade de roquette, reine des glaces, feuilles de chêne et éclergeons, de pintadons de bresse aux chapons et huile de noix*'. There were no translations at Chapel, so I tried hard to work out what the dish might be. I knew that the bird was a guinea fowl. I loved rocket leaves, which were available in Melbourne at the time only if you grew them. I loved walnut oil, so I decided to order the dish. I wondered about oak leaves and confess that when I returned home I gazed at many an oak tree, wondering at what point the leaves of the tree should be picked to add to a salad. They always looked tough and unpromising to me. It was not until a few years afterwards, probably in the very early eighties that I heard of oakleaf lettuce. How silly I felt. Thank goodness I had not tried to include oak leaves in a salad for my customers!

So many years later, while writing this, I am trying to piece together an exact description of this very favourite dish. I remember butter-soft slices. I remember a tangle of soft lovely leaves.

I remember a slice of country-style bread cut on the bias, grilled and flavoured with walnut oil and a suspicion of garlic, and with a splash of deep crimson red wine reduction roughly mixed with a game sauce so that the two marbled on the plate, looking dramatic and tasting deeply intense. But what are *reine des glaces* and *éclergeons*? Neither appear in my dictionary. The former I guessed might be iceberg lettuce, but the latter is a total mystery. I asked my friend John Tinney, an excellent French scholar. Not only did he discover that *reine des glaces* is Batavia (a broad-leafed slightly frisée-style salad leaf) and *éclergeons* refers to 'thinnings', but he found online the actual recipe for the very dish I enjoyed at Chapel's in 1978. I can now definitively say that the portion included four thin slices of breast meat without skin, and two pieces of the thigh meat cut following the shape of the muscle, and that the handful of baby salad leaves were drizzled with a vinaigrette that included some of the roasting juices. Three cheers for the Internet!

From that time on I became very interested in creating main course salads based on poultry and leaves. Sometimes it was grilled duck with tiny corn pancakes studded with duck confit; sometimes it was rosy slices of squab breast, with a little 'haggis' of its minced liver, legs, and soaked cracked wheat all encased in caul, which crisped to a golden-brown; sometimes it was free-range chicken with slices of pickled peach or grapes; but always there were leaves, and something crisp or crunchy.

Maurice's main course was another dish to make one gasp. Sweetbreads, brains and spinal marrow of lamb with baby spinach, double-peeled broad beans and a delicious lamb jus. At another table were some fellow Australians who were having the *poulet en vessie* – a truffled free-range chicken cooked inside a pig's bladder in chicken broth. Most dramatic. I was surprised to see it being served with what I considered to be very overcooked snow peas.

After visiting some of the grand restaurants of France, it was time to think about returning to Melbourne, to wonder how much, if anything, of what we had seen or tasted would have direct relevance to our restaurant. I felt buoyed to have discovered that much of what we were cooking reflected European standards, and looked forward to getting behind a stove again.

Once I returned from our holiday, with my head full of elegant interiors, massed flowers, lovely plates and fine glassware, I became convinced that we had to move Stephanie's, to find somewhere bigger and better that would allow my lovely food to shine in more appropriate surroundings. Maurice was not convinced of the need to move. He disliked change at any time and would dig in over something until I forced it to happen and frequently would then enjoy whatever it was. Rarely did he ever acknowledge that the decision had been a good one, which rankled. However, it is fair to say that once I was determined to make the change he would reluctantly decide to involve himself in the selection of whatever it was.

We had two false starts in 1978 and 1979. We inspected one restaurant where the previous owners had simply turned off the power and walked out, leaving a coolroom full of prawns. They were alive with maggots and the stench was powerful. The second was a historic property with holes in the roof and a bird's nest in one room. Then one day I noticed an advertisement in *The Age* for another historic property known as 'Kawarau', to be auctioned in Hawthorn. It looked huge and imposing. I arranged an inspection and it seemed as if it was meant to be. I was beside myself with excitement. The rooms were all in the right places, we could live upstairs and the children would have a more normal family life. The art nouveau billiard room, with its warm timber panelling, striped parquet floor and swirling iris-shaped plasterwork, was breathtaking. Typically my mind swept past the difficulties and likely cost

of completely rewiring every room, that every room had ugly fluorescent lighting and cumbersome heat banks, and that the entire
building breathed neglect. It was a stunning building and I was
convinced it would be a wonderful restaurant. Even my financially
conservative husband agreed with me. We did sums on the backs
of envelopes, calculated what we could hope to get from our house
in Northcote and went to the family solicitor, Brooke Boothby. He
advised an immediate letter to my parents, who had been enjoying a carefree holiday in Europe. In it we described the 'perfect
building' we had located and asked if they would act as guarantor
again, or, even better, invest in our dream. My euphoric letter was
tempered by a more realistic page written by Maurice giving the
likely financial deal.

I felt the omens were good as the building was to be auctioned on 12 September, my mother's birthday, and settlement was
requested on my birthday, in November. As usual, I immediately
plunged into planning mode. Memory tells me that, after agreeing,
my parents hurried home to view their investment.

By the end of 1979 the building was ours. Now we had to start
the work to turn it into our dream restaurant.

11

Beef on a String

The Second Stephanie's 1980

The relocation of the restaurant to Hawthorn could never have happened as smoothly as it did without, as usual, the help of my parents. For the first few years after moving to East Melbourne my father worked as a librarian at the Brunswick Library, eventually encouraging this small library to amalgamate with the larger Moonee Valley Regional Library. At this point, with computer technology already transforming library work, he sensibly decided to leave it to the new generation of trained staff and switched his energy to researching the history of East Melbourne. He published two books: *East Melbourne Walkabout*, which is still used by walking groups interested in Melbourne's early days, published in 1975; and the more scholarly *East Melbourne, 1837–1977*, published in 1978. While Dad spent days in the basement of the Melbourne Town Hall studying old rates notices, Mum was giving cooking classes and had at last joined a painting group as well as the Embroiderers Guild. My parents also joined the East Melbourne Group, Melbourne's oldest residents' group, which has met regularly since 1953, and soon made good friends who shared their interests in good talk, books, theatre and food. Their life was full and interesting. I am sure childminding was not on their agenda.

Maurice and I, with the help of my parents, purchased the building in September 1979 and planned to open the new Stephanie's in the middle of the next year. By the beginning of 1980 Lisa had spent her first two years of secondary school at Princes Hill Secondary College and would now have to transfer to John Gardiner High School. Holly was due to begin school in February of that year at Auburn South Primary School. For both daughters the move meant big changes and for each of them it was pretty traumatic. Both the primary school and the high school were within walking distance of the new restaurant (and our home), which would be a bonus once the girls were used to the changes.

For financial reasons we had to keep trading in Brunswick Street until the very last day. Every morning either Maurice or I would dash to Hawthorn to keep track of the extensive works being undertaken there, taking the girls with us in order to drop them off at their respective schools. 'Preps' – the children in the first year of school – were required to attend only in the morning for first term. Parents would pick up their little ones before lunch so that gradually they became used to the full day at school, managing their playlunch and being the schoolgirls or schoolboys they needed to be for the rest of their school careers. Ever the absent mother, I could not be there at lunchtime for Holly as the kitchen preparation continued regardless at Brunswick Street. Her teacher agreed that she could stay later and sit with the older children until I could come for her. After a week or so the teacher contacted me to say that something would have to be done as little Holly was spending the afternoons sobbing uncontrollably.

Mum and Dad stepped in and for the remainder of the term Holly spent her afternoons with Nanny and Grandpa. It was the

perfect solution for me, and my mother and father told funny stories that suggested they really enjoyed her company. I know she
loved her time with them in the afternoons and I am certain that
Mum would have made a big fuss of her. I do wonder what Holly
ate for lunch. Despite my belief in the persuasive value of good,
fresh food, or maybe because I was too often absent at mealtimes,
Holly had become a very picky eater. Lisa, who also spent many
afternoons at Gipps Street with my parents, was more appreciative of my mother's cooking. They were happy days for both girls.

I did accompany Lisa on her first day at the new school. I was
sick with nerves. She was pale and very tense. She hissed at me to
go and leave her and, taking this to mean she intended to wade in
and find her feet without me, I went. Her closest Carlton friend
had left Australia to live in the United Kingdom, so Lisa had a new
house, new school and new friends to make. It was a miserable
time for her. Lisa had the prettiest soft curly hair but at the time
she hated it. She took to wandering around the house wearing a
long-sleeved skivvy over her curls, pretending that the swish of the
fabric was long straight hair. I failed to register the significance of
this, believing that she was just being a moody teenager. I thought
she knew how much I loved her and enjoyed being with her, but I
think I was giving out mixed signals and probably seemed impatient
with her moods or at least abrupt a lot of the time. She needed
more from me but I was too busy boning ducks to empathise with
my child's needs.

Happily Lisa made wonderful friends at school fairly soon. Her
three special female friends continue to have a central place in her
affections, just as my University Women's College friends do for
me. During her final year at school she had her first big romance,
which was a serious distraction. Writing this I am suddenly aware
that she was repeating my behaviour!

There was a very confused time while the house at Northcote had been sold but we had not yet moved, and none of us is quite sure who slept where during those weeks, although we are all certain that we moved into the upstairs at Hawthorn several weeks before the restaurant opened. The works did continue for some weeks after the family moved in. I have vivid memories of quite a long period when every morning I would be woken by one workman or another halfway up the stairs yelling for Maurice to come and make a decision or interpret a drawing.

We have photographs that show the unloved state of this wonderful building we now owned. The grand house originally stood in twenty-two acres of gardens and was constructed by Robert Robinson, a grain and produce merchant, in 1893. It was known as 'Warrington'. At the turn of the century it was added to by the second owners, the Cato family, of grocery fame, and was renamed 'Kawarau'. But we purchased the neglected building from the Commonwealth of Australia as for years since its occupation by the Catos it had served as offices for the Postmaster-General's Department. The building was classified by the National Trust as having historic importance, mainly due to the art nouveau billiard room and to the significant painted glass panels throughout the building.

For four or five months it was a construction site. Every floorboard except the parquet in the billiard room came up; every external conduit was yanked out, leaving holes in the beautiful plasterwork; ugly heat bank units were hauled out; fluorescent lighting was removed; plumbers and electricians fed pipes and wires under and through rooms; and carpenters hammered and installed a gigantic exhaust fan in what would be the kitchen. At one point a truck fell through the back garden and revealed a small cellar inconveniently located exactly where the eventual car park needed to be. We were introduced to a craftsman plasterer who resculpted the ornate plasterwork repairs.

The walls were painted a dark Cabernet colour. Metres and metres of inexpensive copper-red lining material became under-skirts for the tables and curtains. We ordered embroidered heavy cotton cloths from China. I scoured op shops for old silverplate and had it all replated. I bought antique gaslight fittings that had to be converted to electric. I insisted on very expensive Villeroy & Boch plates with a rim of pastel poppies. We commissioned high-backed fully upholstered chairs and selected a tapestry to cover each one. I worked with an architect to design a state-of-the-art kitchen. I had a great shopping spree buying new pots and pans. And in the kitchen I now had a beautiful Carpigiani electric ice-cream churn, an expansive marble slab in a separate pastry kitchen, a free-standing electric stockpot and many other refinements. It was all very exhausting but very, very exciting. We applied for a liquor licence. I wanted this restaurant to be beautiful, comfortable and better than anything else Melbourne had to offer.

Needless to say the bills were exorbitant and Maurice had frequent meltdowns about items he considered unnecessary. As seemed to be our way we could not manage proper discussions, we just had angry disputes. I mostly won the battles, but none of them without emotional damage. And Stephanie's Restaurant still operated every night in Brunswick Street. By this time I had employed a chef to better control the workflow, which gave me more headspace to plot and plan. All staff were now partly occupied with planning the pack-up and move.

Maurice decided to designate himself as the building supervi-sor or foreman responsible for much of the subcontracting. This decision was intended to save money and it probably did. The arrangement worked reasonably well, but once again there was a fair amount of shouting from Maurice with icy replies from me as we disputed decisions.

In July 1980 we served our first meal to Melbourne's Chaine des Rôtisseurs, a society that describes itself as having 'centuries-old roots dedicated to fine dining and the preservation of French cuisine'. It was forty dollars a head and BYO while we waited for our liquor licence to arrive. The menu included a sweetbread, celeriac and pistachio salad dressed with walnut oil; a brioche-wrapped coulibiac (thick fillets of trout – in lieu of the traditional salmon, which was not yet available – layered with savoury rice and dill wrapped in crepes and then brioche dough); a clear tomato jelly with nasturtium leaves as a palate cleanser (it was the eighties!); a braised veal chop with *artichauts barigoules* (globe artichokes braised with a ham and mushroom stuffing); a house-made goat's cheese; and a peach soufflé accompanied by a peach sorbet.

I think it is fair to say that the opening of this new Stephanie's upped the ante for many other restaurants in town. We had decided on beautiful glassware, generously large cloth napkins, a pepper grinder on every table, hand-blown glass dishes for the sea salt, and to spend considerable sums on stunning flower arrangements in every room. None of this was the norm in Melbourne in 1980 but the public loved it and other restaurants quickly followed suit.

There were initially four dining rooms in the restaurant, so that while we would serve eighty-five diners every night it didn't ever feel crowded and the noise level was that of pleasant animated conversation. Thanks to the carpet on the floor, no-one had to yell to converse. How different that is from restaurants today!

In the first few weeks we all had to adjust to more space, more staff and more preparation. I retained my preferred structure of a fixed price for three courses. In each section of the menu I offered first eight, then six options. The design of the seasonal menu was my favourite task. I would sit at a cleared table with various books and a notepad and allow my mind to range over all the possibilities. The dishes had to be appropriate to the season and highlight some significant produce; they had to cater for diners who wanted a substantial meal or preferred delicate flavours or wanted to experiment or were happier with the known. But each dish also had to carry my own stamp and every dish had to be something I would enjoy eating.

Early on I discovered the delight of poached meats, especially rare beef fillet. This 'beef on a string' or *'filet à la ficelle'* was well known in France but not in Melbourne in 1980. The idea was that you tied a chunk of fillet to the saucepan lid and allowed it to barely simmer, suspended in a pot of clear meat broth. Vegetables were either poached separately in broth or steamed. The beef would look an unappetising grey but after resting for a few minutes would be sliced to reveal a rosy-red interior. We served it sliced in a deep dish, an *assiette creuse*, or 'hollowed dish', so that some of the wonderful broth could be ladled around the meat. It was always served with a small side dish of condiments – sea salt, tiny pickled cornichons, horseradish, mustard and capers. This is still one of my favourite dishes: I find it clean, restorative and full of flavour.

Dishes often had an interesting garnish, such as quickly fried sea lettuce on steamed oysters; or a touch of whimsy, such as a few violets tucked among dark-green leaves as a bed for a stuffed quail together with a cracked-open empty speckled quail eggshell showing its blue interior; or a component that reinforced the cultural tradition that had inspired the dish, such as purple pickled turnip with a puree of eggplant to reinforce its Middle Eastern heritage, or a spoonful of black rice alongside a baby chicken rubbed with lemongrass and turmeric, in reference to a delightful Balinese dish.

After the menu was designed to my satisfaction, and the major ingredients costed, new dishes had to be cooked with senior members of the team in order to decide if they would be possible to execute perfectly in the middle of a busy service. This breaking-down of a dish into what can be prepared or completed ahead of time without loss of quality is at the heart of the 'magic' that many think operates in busy kitchens.

Domestic life did improve dramatically once we were all under the same roof. No more babysitters or live-in helpers. Once the transition to their new schools had taken place successfully, with Holly now moving into Grade 1, both girls trooped into the restaurant after school and chatted to me, raided the bin of chocolate, made friends with the staff who were setting up the dining rooms and then went upstairs to 'their' part of the house. We had some sort of family dinner each evening at six o'clock, although it is fair to say that I was never very relaxed at this time.

Lisa was a restaurant veteran from the age of three as a result of her weekly outings with Monty and enjoyed good food from whatever culture. She was a delight to feed and always appreciative. Holly was different. She seemed to exist on lots of milk and rye-bread toast with peanut butter. Her repertoire extended to small portions of lamb chops, the occasional egg and she loved chocolate cake. This was not always what was on offer. Our evening meal was often the same thing that was served as the restaurant staff meal. Speed being one of the main considerations, the wok was frequently employed to stir-fry peppers, onions, eggplant, chilli, garlic and ginger or some such combination. Holly would poke a piece of this and that about the plate and then ask to be excused from the table. A little later we would smell the aroma of fresh toast. To some extent I could sympathise with Holly – the staff meals weren't exciting and toast was a favourite of mine too. I didn't need any more battles in my life.

It was lovely to be able to say goodnight and just go downstairs to work. As soon as she could read Holly would curl up and lose herself in a story. Maurice still read to her at night before he joined the service team around eight o'clock, and they both loved *The Wizard of Oz* and *Alice in Wonderland*. Holly also loved reading my own childhood favourites, among them *Anne of Green Gables*. Lisa did her homework with one eye on the television. Weekends were more relaxed and Mondays were family nights as the restaurant was closed.

On the infrequent occasions that I read to Holly, my favourites were the stories by Laura Ingalls Wilder, such as *Little House on the Prairie*. Wilder wrote so beautifully about her pioneer family's lives as they moved from place to place in the American West. Each book in the series dealt with resourcefulness and good management, and detailed the ingenious ways that Ma made bread or pancakes, stored food for the winter, or gathered wild food. The books included hundreds of evocative, beautifully described incidents that set out a panorama of family life lived in close harmony with the weather and the seasons. I think Holly enjoyed these books. I absolutely loved them and remember them as deeply satisfying. I felt a little envious of the happiness and contentment that was so evident in this family. It never read as cloying; the stories were of good people who helped one another through all manner of difficult times, whether the family was living in a log cabin or crossing the country in a covered wagon.

Dur-é was by now front-of-house manager and knew exactly how to charm the customers and add to their experience. She had the ability to communicate the essence of a dish in a sensual and engaging way in order to assist diners with their choice. Over and over again I heard and have continued to hear how Dur-é's explanation of menu detail was appreciated and remembered by our customers. She managed to become the confidante of me, Lisa and almost every member of staff. Only Maurice and Holly seemed unresponsive to her need to know all.

As with Stephanie's in Brunswick Street, it is the staff that I remember so very fondly. There were so many over seventeen years. First Craig Fothergill, then Christoph Kleinhenz and then Brian Wane ran the bar and glided smoothly around the floor. Angela Clemens worked as my personal assistant, and John Smith and Mark Bowdern both managed the office at different times.

There were so many wait staff, too many to remember accurately. Some of those who stayed for a long time were artists Julie Patey, Brian Stroschien and Viva Gibb, and I have works by each of them on my walls. Surprising William Evans tried to teach me to tap dance and introduced me to many wonderful books; beautiful Sonia Cooper ran the floor staff for some years; Andrew McNeilly waited and is now a dedicated primary school teacher; Peter Lortz broke many hearts before he came to join the cookery school run by Maggie Beer and me in Tuscany then stayed to learn to make wine and eventually married an Italian woman. And there were so many more.

My kitchen years preceded the fashion of extensive body piercing, sleeve tattoos and stubble. There were not many shaved heads either (other than Janni's), and although we had several issues with staff and drugs, including alcohol, I suspect that there was less drug-use than in today's kitchens. I can admire a well-shaped shaven head, I can tolerate discreet tattoos, but I hate the full sleeve look, and I shudder at nose rings, imagining all those nasal fluids mingling with the ring. We all got very hot and sweaty and red in the face. Although the language was sometimes colourful, it was rarely abusive.

In the kitchen there was a succession of marvellous talented and loyal friends. I cannot forget Janni's first day. I asked him to bone and stuff some quail. He made a mathematical division of the stuffing into neat little cubes, dissected the quail with the precision of a surgeon and, after stuffing each one, sewed them up perfectly with neat stitches, all in record time. We missed him when he left for Sydney and Berowra Waters Inn.

Many of the Stephanie's kitchen chefs later followed their own careers in hospitality, including Michael Potts, Geoff Lindsay, Steven Pallett, Robert Castellani, Annie Smithers, Cath Claringbold, Sally Roxon, Gabrielle Shing, Nicole Riemer, Justin Dowd, Jeff Wilson the big Texan, Tom Milligan, and again many, many more.

Day-to-day life in the kitchen was never dull. Our yabbies were delivered live, each in its own beer can to prevent cannibalism. Often they escaped and took over the entire coolroom. I think we recaptured them all without too many nipped fingers. A year or so later the fabulous marron from Western Australia took over from the yabbies on the menu. They were so popular that frequently we had to run to the coolroom for more in the middle of service. There was no time to be fainthearted or to be a Buddhist. They were split in seconds with the thump of a heavy knife and the intestinal tract flicked out, quickly painted with seasoned butter and slipped into the raging-hot oven for five minutes. The cook's board had to be scrupulously cleaned between each kill. Work space was always at a premium. One learnt to tuck in one's elbows, work clean and fast and be very organised.

For a long time Sally Roxon was in charge of the upstairs kitchen, which became a furnace in the summer months. The small air-conditioning unit in the window made very little difference. All cooks in this kitchen worked with their trousers rolled up to their knees, with tea towels soaked in cold water around their necks, taking care that the sweat did not drip into the food.

I cannot forget David Backwell, who interrupted his life in Perth to come and save me during a crisis. David undertook to behead and skin the eels, and clean the wild duck that 'came' our way once or twice. Both tasks were very grisly. Elena Bonnici came and went constantly and never did make the pretty hats she said she was going to.

Simone Quinn came first of all as a work experience student and over the years came and went and at one stage was in charge of the kitchen. For one entire season Simone was in charge of sewing up pieces of honeycomb tripe with sheep gut and a craft needle to make pockets we could stuff for tripe boudin. She later confessed that the smell lingered even when she went home.

Nothing was ever too hot to handle. All staff were expected to be able to rip out bones from a pigeon or a quail or slice a duck breast perfectly despite the piece of food having come straight from the grill or the oven. Reduced fingertip sensitivity was more or less expected.

I now have an arthritic thumb joint that I date from years of snapping back duck legs to prepare them for salting. These days I have to ask for help to twist off a jar lid, and any repetitive action that involves that thumb joint results in pain and puffiness in a very short time.

The work day was divided between the hours of preparation and the much shorter hours of 'service'. Cooks were used to doing large quantities of often very mundane tasks, and they needed to do them well. Whether the job was peeling twenty sets of brains, cleaning and skinning ten kilos of calamari, shelling a kilo of boiling hot chestnuts, podding a box of spring peas, or double-peeling a box of broad beans, the task was done cheerfully. The peeling and shelling jobs were often shared and taken outside in the fresh air for a rare social moment around our staff table.

I remember Rosa, our extraordinary and diminutive Spanish dishwasher who was training to be an aerobics instructor. She was beautiful and always wore a headband that matched her tiny shorts. She had long painted nails underneath the rubber gloves and did the work of two. While Rosa was in charge the kitchen was always spotless and in her spare time (usually a ludicrous concept in the pot wash section) she told me tales from her home in Spain, of how she collected snails from the wet grass, and braised them on a barbecue plate without any purging and winkled them out to serve with a garlicky tomato sauce.

And I still laugh when I think of Sue-Ellen prancing into the kitchen with a brace of well-hung feathered pheasants draped around her neck as her grandmother may have worn a fox fur. Or of the apprentice who resigned telling me: 'I'm sick of doing things perfectly!' (Not surprisingly he has sunk without trace.)

Then there were days when things went spectacularly wrong. A bolt from our large mixer somehow ended up in someone's salad. We discovered that we had preserved a bee in our apricot chutney. Once when a very competitive fellow restaurateur was dining with us the waiter delivering her main course touched her main course plate against her wine glass. The plate broke in half, depositing pigeon, sauce and garnish neatly on the tablecloth, leaving the astonished waiter holding two pieces of plate. And once an apprentice added sodium nitrite to a pot of veal pie filling instead of salt. Fortunately I noticed the strange pink hue of the meat and it was despatched to the bin.

There were personal accidents, including a spectacular burn when chef Tom tipped a bain marie of boiling water over his shod feet. Despite his leather shoes Tom was off work for weeks. Cuts and burns did happen quite regularly but rarely required stitching or hospital attention.

Now and then I have a very brief moment of nostalgia for that amazing adrenalin rush that happened between eight and ten-thirty every evening: sweat trickling down your legs into your clogs so your feet were clammy, body on fire, face bright red, everyone into the rhythm. A certain amount of swagger and crashing was part of the drama and the pride in a job well done.

One of the strangest aspects of owning and operating a restaurant is that, in my experience, it never became easier. The number of variables that needed to be cared for constantly was astonishing – from maintenance to daily ordering, keeping an eye on the bookings book, and all this before you even think about the menu and how the food will be cooked.

Rightly or wrongly I have been the sort of owner who wanted to be involved or at least informed about all of these things, and to have a benevolent dictatorship in place in the kitchen.

This story should be not about Stephanie's Restaurant but about my life. But for the next seventeen years Stephanie's Restaurant *was* my life. The pressure and the challenges of trying to create something so special meant that everything else became subordinate. It was not that I did not value my family and friends – I absolutely needed them. But I could not find a way of managing and operating the restaurant without it sucking every gram of energy from me. My connection with the real world of political issues of the day and of contemporary culture became superficial. All these things I recognised as important but I had set myself an all-consuming task.

Looking back it is a wonder I had any friends at all. I did invite each of them, and my parents, as often as possible to come and eat in the restaurant with Maurice and me. Too often these evenings would start well and then, after a few glasses of wine, my exhaustion would lead to an outpouring of disappointment about the night's performance, or a rehashing of some rankling issue or invective, usually directed at Maurice. It is pretty horrible to recall, and perhaps fortunately I do not recall the content of too many of these evenings. Some friends found them hard to handle but I believe that my closest friends were sad rather than angry or embarrassed, realising the misery that lay beneath my unkind remarks.

Every waking moment was filled with activity. There was never time to stop and reflect on priorities, or attempt to slow down. I couldn't stop. There was always a pressing need in the kitchen to attend to.

12
Duck Gizzards & Some Heroes

Eye-opening Experiences of the Eighties

The eighties was the very best decade for the restaurant. My creative juices were flowing. We were fully booked every night. The kitchen was an exciting place to be. The team of cooks experimented; we read and talked excitedly about all things culinary. Alongside new thinking I never forgot to read and discuss the classics. I introduced my staff to the work of Elizabeth David and established a tradition of giving a copy of *French Provincial Cooking* to each apprentice when they completed their apprenticeship. Nothing was too hard in our kitchen; everything had to be handmade. I had absolute focus when in the kitchen. In fact my mind switched to restaurant mode as soon as the girls had kissed me goodbye in the morning on their way to school. I would spring out of bed, shower, climb back into last night's jacket and checked pants, and be on the phone to the fishmonger within an hour.

As first in the kitchen every morning I had to lie on the floor with my head right inside the oven to light the pilot with a flaring spill of paper, hoping it would not go boom in my face. The automatic self-light on our ovens lasted just a few weeks. We worked those ovens really hard; they were always cranked to the maximum.

We would kick them shut with one foot while moving pans on top with both hands. It was our own service ballet and I became quite addicted to it.

Once the fish was ordered came the ritual of straining stockpots, setting out stock to reduce, starting to prepare ducks or chickens or whatever it was – the rhythm of the day was soothing and reassuring, and I felt confident that what I was doing was good. I enjoyed the status and attention that came with being known as an influential and creative restaurateur.

In 1980 I cooked at the banquet for the Great Chefs' dinner at Rothbury Estate in the Hunter Valley, New South Wales. This time I presented one of the two entrées. I stuffed honeycomb tripe with a chicken mousse studded with fresh morel mushrooms, sweet-breads and ham. The tripe 'boudins' were crumbed, fried, sliced and served with a fresh tomato sauce – a daring offering for one hundred guests. The guest of honour was Jean Troisgros from the three-Michelin-starred restaurant Les Frères Troisgros, which he owned with his brother Pierre at Roanne, and where Maurice and I had eaten three years before. I plucked up the courage to ask if I could come and be a *stagiare* for a week in his restaurant a few months hence. He agreed!

That week was one of the seminal experiences of my life as a restaurateur. Most of the prestigious restaurants of France during the eighties would have had many, many requests from young cooks from all over to come and work for no money to learn. To be a *stagiare* was to receive very valuable work experience. A *stage* might last for a week, as mine did, where I basically observed and helped with any task needed, or it could last a year, where the young cook was treated as one of the team but was not paid a cent. In my time at Troisgros there was a Japanese, a Cambodian (who had seen his entire family killed by the army of Pol Pot) and a Dutch *stagiare* all working very hard. The Japanese and Dutch *stagiares* would also have had to learn basic kitchen French.

As I set out for my *stage* at Les Frères Troisgros I was very nervous as well as excited. I wanted to find out how a large and famous kitchen was organised. Did they have 'magic' equipment? What did they know that I did not? And how much of what I observed would be helpful in my own restaurant? Maurice was to meet me at the end of the week and we would have another of our meandering French holidays.

After arriving in Roanne, I was in the kitchen of Les Frères Troisgros, bleary and jetlagged, at six-thirty the next day. The pastry cook had already begun. His *feuilletage*, or puff pastry, had been started the night before and the ball of dough left on the marble. He began by incorporating butter into the flour – already a method that was new to me. It was a Swiss method, I was told, which results in pastry less crisp than the classic puff pastry, but gives more protection to the butter, making it less likely to break through the dough.

The *fonds de veau*, the veal stock, was started by the chef at eight a.m. Another surprise – he didn't brown the bones. They had experimented, I was told, and browning the bones made no difference to the finished dish. (From the date of my return no bones were ever browned for making veal stock during the life of Stephanie's Restaurant.) No vegetables were added until all the rising scum had been generously skimmed, its volume replaced with cold water. The stockpot that had simmered all night was drained and set to reduce to a deep-coloured *demi-glace*. A spoonful of this added to almost any sauce added maturity of flavour and an unctuous quality.

The fish cook arrived and unpacked the morning's deliveries at eight o'clock. Live lobsters emerged, sleepy and unscathed: one box from Brittany, one from Canada. They were tucked, still wreathed in seaweed, into rolling refrigerated drawers. (I did envy them those refrigerated drawers.) The fresh salmon for the *saumon à l'oseille* arrived from Scotland, along with other fish with unfamiliar names, and the filleting began. A crate of prickly sea urchins had to be snipped open with scissors. Their roe was destined for scrambled eggs.

The larder cooks were all chop, chop, chopping, and all by hand. Meat was being trimmed. The beef was Aberdeen Angus. Jean Troisgros cheerfully confided, 'We don't tell the French. They're convinced it's their Charolais but the Scottish beef is better.'

Ice-cream and fruit sorbets were churned again from the day before after being allowed to melt completely on the bench overnight. I was startled. What about bugs? Did they just not worry about it? In Australia the health inspector would become apoplectic if he or she saw a cook tasting without using a spoon. What would they think here, where Jean's large dog followed him into the kitchen, where a bowl of pastry cream and a bowl of *gratin dauphinois* sat uncovered all through service?

Jean and Pierre were in and out of the kitchen and among the tables in the dining room. Pierre brought in *Robinia* (false acacia) blossoms to turn into fritters for a special friend, pastry supremo Gaston Lenôtre. In two reference books, including the *Oxford Companion to Food*, I had read that acacia fritters are made with wattle but I knew that this was not correct. It is a simple botanical mistake – confusing Australian and South African wattle species (*Acacia*) with *Robinia*, which is known as 'false acacia' and is a common street planting tree in Australia. Once you have seen the clusters of pea-shaped cream flowers being dipped in batter you could never imagine it being done with fluffy yellow or cream wattle flowers.

Jean and Pierre both loved to eat and seemed to enjoy simple food. Jean shared with me one of his favourite dishes: a salad of duck gizzards on *frisée* leaves with a grilled slice of sourdough bread. The cleaned gizzards, cooked very slowly in duck fat, were soft and quite delicious.

Several dishes at Les Frères Troisgros were garnished with *pommes maxim*, paper-thin wisps of potato brushed with butter or duck fat and oven-baked until golden and crunchy. This is a slow and meticulous process. I noted with horror how Pierre would pick up a handful from the bowl and crush them if he deemed them not crisp enough. The unfortunate cook would have to start again.

My eyes were everywhere. I saw thrush that had arrived from Spain, with feathers still intact, being plucked and the meat ground up for the pâté. I watched as different fish and shellfish dishes were finished with *sauce vin blanc*, variety achieved with a handful of something different – a julienne of root vegetables in one dish, a shower of herbs in another, a spoonful of browned cucumber in yet another.

All staff worked quickly and precisely. They took no shortcuts: their techniques were exemplary. They worked exactly the hours necessary, and not one extra. Their break in the afternoon was sacred. Here at Troisgros it was for football and then a meal before the evening service. I found this very impressive. These cooks were in the industry for the long haul and had worked out how to manage this job. There were no martyrs here, no-one working late or complaining about never-ending tasks.

I concluded my week having discovered that the success of the wonderful Frères Troisgros restaurant did not come down to some magic formula, just marvellous produce, brilliant equipment, tight organisation and very well-trained staff.

The nearest thing to magic was when Jean took me to meet a supplier, Monsieur Pralus, who was experimenting with cooking under pressure with food sealed in vacuum pouches. The Trois-gros brothers had been convinced to trial this machine for cooking whole lobes of *foie gras*. They discovered that by using this method the very expensive *foie gras* lost less weight, which was financially very attractive. Nowadays every small restaurant would have a compact vacuum machine and would cook food sealed in these pouches. In 1980 my memory is of this prototype machine nearly filling an entire room.

I went to the market with Pierre. Everyone seemed to be his friend. No doubt the Troisgros brothers were excellent customers. Pierre's wife, Olympe, said to me sometime during that very special week that as restaurateurs, '*Nous sommes vraiment les marchands de bonheur*' ('We are really the sellers of happiness'). This remark has always seemed to sum up what we mean by hospitality. We are in the business of making people happy.

On our travels after the Troisgros week Maurice and I spent a few days on the wild Atlantic coast. It was so beautiful, with long white sandy beaches that were totally deserted in early June. At a café right on the seafront at Biscarrosse-Plage, a rather raffish small town, I ordered my first ever seafood platter. First the equipment arrived: a large tripod stand to support the platter; a finger bowl; a cork stuck with pins to extract shellfish from their curly shells; a pair of crackers; a seafood pick; and a very large cloth napkin. Then came the accompaniments: a bowl of real mayonnaise; a quartered lemon; a bowl of finely chopped shallots mixed with red wine vinegar and a few drops of oil; a slab of creamy unsalted butter; and a basket of thinly sliced rye bread. And finally came the seafood, piled on shining black seaweed and smelling like the freshest, briniest seashore: half a rock lobster; an entire crab, quartered; six oysters, with top shells just levered open, still swimming in their own juices; a dozen raw mussels; a dozen sea snails; about a dozen each of clams (pipis) and winkles; a handful of tiny pink crevettes (shrimp); and six scampi. In 1981 this feast for two cost the equivalent of ten Australian dollars.

What was happening in Europe was discussed by many of the local restaurateurs. It seemed that everything to do with restaurants – the food, service, décor – was becoming a hot topic. A small group of Melbourne restaurateurs decided to meet on a more or less monthly basis to discuss development in the industry during the early eighties. I think this was a Tony Knox initiative. I know it was a very volatile group with now and then a verbal stoush between two or more participants. Tony Knox had verbal battles with everyone at one time or another, and Iain Hewitson enjoyed being provocative. Gloria and Blyth Staley came along, as did Faye and Hermann Schneider, Tony and Adriana Rogalsky from Rogalskys and several others. And of course the wives, husbands and partners came too. There was a lot of hot air talked and a great deal of wine drunk. But on balance I look back fondly on those memories and on some excellent shared moments. I think Tony Knox hoped the group might become some sort of ginger group for the Melbourne restaurant scene but we were all too different for shared action.

Consistently ours was regarded as one of the best restaurants in the city and was an excellent training ground for many fine young people. The famous came. The eighties was the decade when people started to talk about 'lifestyle'. My children had a special vantage point at the top of the stairs from where they could see the front door but could not be seen. If a well-known actor or other celebrity was expected they would get a tip-off from whomever was managing the bookings, and they would be watching. Mick Jagger and Jerry Hall had them very excited.

We all enjoyed knowing there were celebrities in the restaurant. The waiters would relay a running commentary to the kitchen on how this person or that person looked, whether they ate all their food, were friendly or smiled and, most important of all, whether they made some positive remark as they left. I remember Jerry Hall's lipsticked cigarette butt was souvenired by an infatuated waiter. And I remember Richard Olney came and raved about his stuffed artichokes. It is true that sometimes I had no idea who the celebrity was.

Holly, in particular, tells me she loved being a nightly *voyeur*, cosy in her pyjamas, unseen, listening and looking down on another world. Part of this ritual was that she would ring the bar and order an iced water for the fun of having it delivered to her spot at the top of the stairs. It would be duly delivered to her either by Maurice or a dinner-suited waiter. Both girls remember that the hum of conversation and clink of glasses floated upstairs as they lay tucked up in their beds.

There were approximately eight full-time staff in the kitchen at this stage. Inevitably there were dramas, confrontations, affairs and even feuds, as well as plenty of good humour. I tried to maintain a calm kitchen. I abhor violence and especially hate shouting. Our kitchen worked as a team, and although some members of staff were more senior than others, with corresponding responsibilities, I did not encourage any strictly observed hierarchy such as operated in many other kitchens. I felt courtesy to all was essential. The only staff member who seemed lacking in respect towards me was European. I suspect that he did not believe a woman could run a professional kitchen. On another occasion a French chef tried to bully one of the dishwashers. In egalitarian Australia this was not going to work. The six-foot-two dishwasher loomed over the much shorter Frenchman and suggested he control his language.

I had not learnt how to assert myself and any sort of anticipated confrontation caused me stomach-churning and sleepless nights.

My inner thoughts went something like this: 'Being a leader is scary. Confronting others is very scary. There are always two sides to be considered. This can lead to sitting on the fence. But not confronting and letting bad things happen is not an option. It's them or me. Remember Dad's mantra: "Nothing or no-one is as good or as bad as it/they first appear."' In later years I became tougher and knew that unacceptable behaviour had to be challenged.

I think my staff fully appreciated my drive to present the most perfect food possible. They also shared some of my excitement as I winkled out of my suppliers even smaller beans, younger lettuces, or milk-fed lambs, larger squab or calves' feet. And if we managed to capture the bubbles in a champagne jelly, achieve perfect clarification of a crab stock, or make the silkiest puree of celeriac, we all rejoiced at our success. I guess I oversaw the kitchen with a velvet glove, but over the twenty-one years of operation there were fewer than five occasions when I had serious problems with a member of the kitchen team.

There were plenty of eye-popping events that happened on the other side of the doors. Word spread instantly if there was something dramatic happening. I remember one night a woman took off her clothes from the waist up and continued to sit with her companion in a chilly silence. The waiters were flustered, not knowing what to do. Maurice calmly asked her to put her clothes back on and she did. We all wondered what could possibly have been said that caused her to strip.

The restaurant was the setting for plenty of marriage proposals, sometimes on bended knee. One night roses were delivered, champagne was pre-ordered, the special table had been booked but no-one turned up. That was sad. And I was often told that there were quite a few Stephanies or Alexanders conceived or even born after an evening at the restaurant.

One week when I was serving an Australian-themed dinner that started with kangaroo-tail consommé, the restaurant was picketed every night by a group opposing the eating of kangaroo. 'Stephanie is a murderer' the placards claimed, or something like that. Worse was to follow with the placing of a dead kangaroo on the front steps just as the first customers were arriving. The issue of eating kangaroo was certainly controversial in the early eighties but by this time the heat had mostly gone out of the argument as more and more evidence showed that it made a lot of sense to use properly processed kangaroo meat. In any case, although the police turned up, they remained quietly on the sidelines. We removed the carcass and the protesters drifted away.

A more dramatic and potentially life-threatening incident involved a woman arriving in the restaurant in a hansom cab. The horse-drawn cab ride had been a planned treat for the woman from her daughters – a grand way to arrive at a historic mansion for a special dinner. Presumably no-one in the family knew that the woman was dangerously allergic to horses. By the time she arrived she was in a state of collapse. Christoph, our senior barman at the time, carried her inside, her daughters sobbed, we rang an ambulance and at the same time the evening's customers arrived and had to more or less step over the unfortunate woman, who, I am happy to say, survived.

Very early on in my restaurant business I became determined to celebrate the best produce we had in Australia and wherever possible to find and encourage small producers who could supply something special, even if sometimes it might mean buying a larger quantity than I needed to sustain the supplier. During the eighties I travelled to most Australian main cities and many regional areas and met some interesting characters. Many of those people were featured in my third book, *Stephanie's Australia*, which was eventually published in 1991.

In Darwin I encountered pearl meat and used it in a dinner. (The pearl oyster is huge compared with Sydney rock oysters or Pacific oysters, and the firm muscle where the meat attaches to the shell is cut away and sold as pearl meat. It is reminiscent of abalone. Sautéed or barbecued it is very delicious.) That dinner included wild barramundi wrapped in paperbark and cooked over coals in the back garden of the restaurant. On the same trip I was introduced to the nectar of one of our most beautiful grevilleas, *Grevillea pteridifolia*. My brother Christopher, a community advisor in Arnhem Land at the time, told me that Aboriginal children sucked the flowers as a treat, much the way I had sucked the flowers of honeysuckle when I was a child. I gathered and infused the blossoms to produce a haunting honey-like sorbet.

On a trip to the West I tasted freshwater marron for the first time and arranged to have them flown live to the restaurant on a weekly basis. I had no idea this was illegal until a wildlife inspector visited the restaurant a year or so later and we had to apply for a licence to import wildlife. Split, roasted, and served with apples and a browned cider butter, they became a very popular first course. This was also where I met my first rabbit farmer. Those huge white rabbits from Western Australia have never been matched since.

On one trip I met the entrepreneurial farmer Ian Milburn from the Mallee, who had taken on the challenge of rearing squab pigeon. I happily tested his first efforts and found them excellent. They remain the best I have tasted and will forever be a favourite.

A friend gathered marsh samphire from the inlet banks near Geelong, so I could steam it to serve with fish. I also incorporated a small quantity of roasted wattleseed in a classic blini recipe. I tried to love clove lillipilly berries and failed, finding the clove flavour

numbing and overpowering. It was a similar story with native pepper, but I enjoyed the flavour of lemon myrtle in tiny quantities and
roasted bunya nuts were delicious. I made an infusion containing
lemon-scented tea tree (*Leptospermum petersonii*) as the basis for
a *beurre blanc* to drizzle over Queensland slipper lobsters (also
known as long-tailed reef bugs).

Delightful Frenchman and grower Daniel Romaneix turned up
one day at the back door with salad greens to die for. Here were
the soft-leaved mignonettes, oakleaf and frisée leaves that I had
discovered travelling in France. He grew these baby salads in dirt
at his organic farm, not hydroponically as is more often the case
nowadays.

And then I tried my hand at 'farming' my own produce, inspired
by my hero Richard Olney's snail farming. In 1986 a highlight of
a European holiday with Maurice was an invitation to lunch with
Richard. When I first read his book, *The French Menu Cookbook*,
originally published in 1970 (although I don't think I discovered it
until the late seventies), I had that same feeling of instant rapport
as I had experienced walking into Alain Chapel's restaurant. Here
was a cook's cook, an original mind, a cook who was meticulous
about detail when it mattered but who could also write lyrically
or scathingly. I am surprised by how few cooks have read Olney's
books. It was in *The French Menu Cookbook* that I first read the
recipe for a twice-cooked soufflé which he called *Soufflé à la Suissesse*, now a standard preparation in many restaurants. (I wonder
how many chefs who make it realise that it probably first appeared
in print in 1970. I know that I made it for many years, with goat's
cheese, with crab or with sautéed zucchini, to name a few versions.)

I sent Olney a copy of my first book and asked if we could
meet. He agreed so Maurice and I travelled to the tiny village of
Solliès-Toucas, near Toulon in the south of France, to meet the

master. Richard was as shy as I was. He greeted us wearing baggy shorts and a flapping shirt. To put us at ease he produced a small sack of just-harvested broad beans and suggested we all combine to nick off the outer skin. Unlike most cooks, Richard preferred to remove the outer skin before cooking the bean, which is much harder to do. He proudly showed me his garden, one bed edged with a favourite herb of his – hyssop – and his kitchen. Richard cooked most of his food on a wood-fired range using a series of iron grills and grids. He also showed me the chicken incubator in his bathroom – alongside was a straw crib waiting to receive the new chicks. We spoke about snails and the difference between the huge and increasingly rare Burgundian vineyard snails and the garden snail, known as *petit gris*. He was up in a trice and returned with a metal bucket that had a simple 'lid' of chicken wire. Inside were garden snails, being purged with oatmeal to clean out their digestive tracts in case they had grazed on anything nasty. I was convinced I had to try this.

Back home I took to collecting and fattening my own garden snails and paid Holly's young friends to hunt them for me. We cleaned them and housed them in clean garbage bins to purge. There are startling photographs showing Annie Smithers up to her elbows in snails, twirling them out of their shells after they were cooked. We froze them in masses of small bubble ice trays. I created 'Snails on the grass', a dish of sautéed snails with puff pastry snail shells sitting on a garlic and parsley green sauce with tiny goat's cheese soufflés. We continued our snail farming operation for a time until the wonderful Irena Votavova developed her own snail farm. I don't think any of us were sorry to see the end of ours!

The repertoire at the restaurant ranged widely, influenced by where I had been, whom I had met, what I had been reading, and above all what was in season. Janni Kyritis introduced me to kataifi pastry, which almost immediately became 'nests' for sorbet-filled chocolate eggs. My trip to Hong Kong as a judge at the 1986 Hong Kong Food Festival had introduced me to bean curd skin, a wonderful wrapper for all sorts of things, and to jellyfish. I am still intrigued by the Chinese use of texture foods – the crunch of chicken feet or silver tree fungus, the chewiness of jellyfish, or the slipperiness of bean curd. In Japan I tasted and loved cold buckwheat noodles and was inspired to invent what became known as 'Autumn salad'.

Some of my ideas surprised those around me, such as deciding to stuff tripe, or to gather the youngest nettles in the spring to use for soup or to add to crepe batter. Others were about rediscovering techniques or dishes popular once upon a time. In this category would have fallen our rediscovery of junket (infused with one or two rose-geranium leaves), coddled eggs in their porcelain pots served as a dip for steamed asparagus, a suet-crusted steak-and-kidney pudding steamed in a basin, hot water crust pies, bread sauce to accompany those fantastic pheasants, and everyone's favourite – bread-and-butter pudding.

Influenced possibly by the limpid, barely set vegetable jellies at Alain Chapel, I first discussed my idea for creating a dish that represented a rock pool with Janni in 1980. Our first version was based on a clarified shellfish consommé spooned over upturned oyster shells (the 'rocks') so that the jelly broke and shimmered as it caught the light. Among the rocks were prawns, small squid and even a small fish. Later versions varied. There were always oysters, sometimes there was bright-green sea lettuce seaweed, sometimes an opened sea urchin, and eventually I preferred to make the jelly from a clarified stock based on a Szechuan hot and sour soup recipe.

The sharpness of the rice vinegar and the zing of the chilli seemed to lift the experience of spooning the jelly, which had started to seem a bit too much like a real rock pool to me!

It is overwhelming to contemplate the number of menus I devised over the seventeen years of the restaurant's life in Hawthorn. But themes did emerge. I had a strong preference for clear broth versus creamy sauces. I enjoyed offering a trio of tastes that varied in texture but were in some way thematically linked. I developed an interest in first courses that blended salad leaves with vegetables and in the rediscovery and re-examination of classic preparations. We created stand-out dinners to celebrate a return from travel, maybe after a judging stint in Hong Kong or a holiday in Italy. My profile was further boosted by teaching sessions in various cooking schools, and requests for public appearances or to judge all manner of competitions.

While being a judge in Hong Kong in 1986, I enjoyed the company of the charming Robert Carrier, who was at the height of his fame as a cookbook author. We judges were treated to a meal at the Lung Wah restaurant in the New Territories, famous throughout Hong Kong and beyond for its sensational pigeons. I wanted to find out how these were prepared.

I was escorted into the kitchen, tucked myself into a corner as neatly as possible and watched in wonder. The woks were heated by diesel and each wok station was well insulated with firebrick as the flames roared, surged and glowed like an ironworker's furnace. Flames shot high as the woks were flipped. The cooks worked unconcerned in singlet and shorts, frequently with lit cigarettes in their mouths.

Alongside were the huge cauldrons of master stock. Spice bags dangled in the bubbling brew as dozens of pigeons swam desperately (or so it seemed, as they all still had heads intact). Another nonchalant cook was in charge here, poking, prodding and skimming the oil from the surface. Once they were cooked, after about fifteen minutes, the birds were swished into a bath of soy and put to rest until ordered. Then they were deep-fried in that unbelievable heat for three or four minutes before being rushed to the table to be enjoyed with salt spiced with roasted Szechuan peppercorns, light soy and chilli sauce. Diners then tore at the birds, relishing the crisp skin, crunchy neck, splintery beak (and, if you are really Chinese, brains) before getting to the juicy, rich flesh.

Over the years I and many other cooks have attempted this twice-cooking of pigeons, quail and chickens. Our efforts are not bad but I do not think we can reproduce the astonishing heat of those diesel-fired woks that I saw in Hong Kong. The Lung Wah version is still the best I have tasted.

I was often invited to host promotions at hotels or in other restaurants. I was always pleased to be asked and usually agreed, but as every appearance drew closer I always experienced conflicting emotions. I wanted to be sure that I gave of my best, which seemed to mean going over and over what I was to do, which was exhausting and often quite unnecessary. And I always felt anxious until I felt that my preparation was absolutely complete.

Another highlight was my winning menu created for a Gastronomic Competition, sponsored by the Hyatt Hotel Group in 1989. The menu was designed to celebrate the outstanding pheasants I bought from one of our suppliers. My supplier never knew how many she had, as she free-ranged the birds among tall grasses. These birds had a layer of succulent fat and when roasted the skin would crackle and burst with juice as one sliced the breast from the ribcage. They were extraordinary.

I called my menu 'A Feast of Pheasant'. It started with the neck, which I stuffed and served as a small crisp sausage settled on a corn griddle cake, to suggest the bird's last meal. It continued with a consommé made from the bones in which floated a ravioli stuffed with the liver and giblets of the bird. Next came the rare-roasted breast then the slowly braised legs on a green salad. The finale was a chocolate egg, with streaked markings to suggest a pheasant egg, filled with a nougat ice-cream and a mango yolk. The egg sat on a nest made of shredded kataifi pastry. I was very proud of this menu.

The prize was a trip to London and the opportunity to cook a dinner while there. I think it was the very same year I accepted an invitation to do a week-long promotion at a London Park Lane hotel called Inn on the Park. Together with two of my own staff we cooked from early in the morning until late at night to keep up with the greater than expected demand for our roasted Moreton Bay bugs, mussel soup, boned and stuffed rabbit, boned and stuffed pigs' trotters and passionfruit pavlovas. All labour-intensive stuff, designed to show off rather than with a thought to workload.

One lunchtime during this promotion, I was being interviewed for a magazine when out of the corner of my eye I saw a stately woman with a faintly familiar profile and white upswept hair being escorted from the dining room by two solicitous companions. I was aghast! This was my lifelong hero and inspiration, Elizabeth David. The queen of food writers had chosen to come to lunch to taste my mussel soup, my boned and stuffed rabbit and I was trapped, having to answer some pretty mundane questions and missing the opportunity of . . . what? I have often asked myself, what would I have done? Stammered some sort of thanks for a lifetime of inspiration? To this day a few paragraphs from any one of her early books, opened at random, acts as a tonic for me. Her prose is at one and the same time captivating, intelligent, sensual, and reveals the essence of a dish or an experience.

I had rather hopefully sent Elizabeth David a copy of my first book and to my delight she had replied with a warm letter saying how much she had enjoyed it. This precious letter went missing in some subsequent clean-out of filing drawers – one of the tragedies of my life!

Stephanie's Restaurant won many awards, both locally, and nationally. Claudia Roden judged the 1988 *Australian Gourmet* restaurant awards and Stephanie's Restaurant was the winner. I was overseas at the time of the announcement and was delighted and excited when my staff called to tell us of our success. I was also very disappointed to have missed meeting one of my literary heroes. As for many others, *The New Book of Middle Eastern Cookery* by Claudia Roden was a treasured tome and still is. I did meet her the following year during my guest week in Park Lane, and she agreed to write the foreword to my forthcoming book, *Stephanie's Seasons*. In it she remembered her visit to the restaurant.

> I will never forget my enchantment. The meal was a thrilling experience, full of surprises. Each dish combined a variety of elements with different textures, colours, flavours and aromas, all in perfect harmony. Each was exquisite and a joy to look at. I remember especially a bowl of delicately flavoured jellied consommé full of delicious sea creatures – huge oysters, sea urchins, crayfish, the tentacles of tiny baby squid, giant prawns in their shells – with a sprinkling of caviar and a garnish of seaweed and tree fungus. The dishes were in a way familiar, with echoes from various countries and cultures, but at the same time uniquely original. They reflected the changes that have been happening in Australia. Australian cooks have cast off the shackles of Anglo-Saxon cooking traditions. They have absorbed the influences of their immigrant communities, are looking at the great cuisines of the world for inspiration and expertise, and are making the most of their resources.

13

Snips, Snails & Tails

The Symposium of Gastronomy and Meeting Maggie

While there was a continued increase in celebratory eating in Australian restaurants during the eighties, there was also a more cerebral interest in food and foodways being explored. A small group of five or six serious food enthusiasts, which included academics and a couple of cooks, planned a gathering of like-minded people. This gathering was modelled on the Oxford Symposium on Food & Cookery, convened as an annual forum for people interested in all manner of food topics, and would become the Symposium of Australian Gastronomy. Sociologist Michael Symons was the driving force in its establishment.

The first symposium was held in Adelaide in 1984, and was called 'The Upstart Cuisine'. There were about fifty of us. The venue has moved around the eastern and southern states ever since and the symposium is held approximately every eighteen months. It was very different from anything I had experienced since long-ago university days and at the beginning I often felt inadequate and awkward listening to very academic papers on some unusual topics.

The philosophy of Jean Anthelme Brillat-Savarin, as expressed in his book *La Physiologie du Goût* (*The Physiology of Taste*), was to be the subject of the first gathering. Gastronomy is defined by Brillat-Savarin as 'the reasoned comprehension of everything connected to the nourishment of man'. Over twenty-five years, the attendees did address an extremely wide range of topics pertaining to the nourishment of man (and woman), of the body and the spirit and of the environment in which we find ourselves.

There have been some astonishing ideas discussed, some brilliant presentations (and some very dull presentations), but there has always been at least one paper that made each meeting memorable. Almost without exception the food served has been exciting and delicious. Each symposium is held over two-and-a-half days and the papers are punctuated with extraordinary meals and well-chosen wine. Every attendee meets some old friends and makes new ones.

Rereading the published papers from the various symposia has been fruitful and revelatory. Papers that had been read too fast by nervous presenters, stumbled over or maybe presented in rooms with dubious acoustics, suddenly made sense. Occasionally I even had a Eureka moment of sudden understanding and wished that I had grasped the point when it was originally presented.

Over and over again we wrangled with the question 'What is Australian cuisine?' Our culinary diversity seemed to me to be such an obvious answer. We also explored the question 'What constitutes true gastronomic writing?', the speaker suggesting that there was little of it. I bristled during this discussion, finding it far too dismissive, believing that I had contributed at least some writing that could be so described. By 1984 I was a regular contributor to *Epicurean* magazine and *Home Beautiful*, wrote occasional pieces for newspapers and had already established a discursive style of food writing that went beyond just writing a recipe.

'Should the symposium become some sort of action group with a constitution?' was another question we grappled with. This discussion caused serious splits between original convenors. Most attendees decided that they preferred to have their brains tickled and their palates delighted but had no interest in formalising the gatherings or becoming lobbyists for change.

Highlights over the years have been many – too many really to single out more than a handful. Two separate presentations by anthropologist Betty Meehan describing Indigenous food preparation and traditions in Arnhem Land added a reminder that the original Australians have much to contribute to any understanding of Australian cuisine. Michael Symons argued that Australia was saddled with an industrial cuisine due to the fact that it had never had an agrarian past.

Brilliant speaker and philosophy student Anthony Corones spoke convincingly of the value of 'multiculinarism' at the third symposium in 1987. 'The more deeply we open ourselves to other cuisines the greater our understanding of food,' he said. Another speaker, the former Premier of South Australia, the late Don Dunstan, identified greed as the greatest world problem.

The food at all of the Australian symposia has been delicious and carefully conceived. One of the differences between the Oxford and Australian Symposia was that from the very beginning the Australian group included some professional cooks. From our very first meal where attendees were asked to bring a loaf of bread to remind us of the earliest days of white settlement when Governor Phillip asked guests to bring bread, the meals usually had meaning beyond mere sustenance.

The final banquet at the first symposium is legendary. Prepared by a young Adelaide chef Phillip Searle, working with another outstanding and imaginative chef Cheong Liew, it was out of this world, fanciful, fantastic, breathtaking and delicious. We were beckoned to the dining space by white-faced clowns who appeared and disappeared from behind bushes and trees, one of whom was a young Geoffrey Rush. It was a performance piece as much as a meal. Phillip and Cheong set the bar very high and most would admit that this banquet has never been surpassed. The menu alone can never communicate the excitement and creativity that we experienced.

'Jellied seascape' was a fish tank full of exquisitely flavoured crab consommé in which many sea creatures seemed to float. As it was ladled into cups by the white-faced clowns, I could not help thinking of the rock pool dish that Janni and I so enjoyed making four years before in 1980. It was really a jellied seascape in miniature!

This was the menu. Each dish was astonishing.

Jellied seascape
Goose galantine
Consommé
Sand crab custard
Goose liverwurst
Steamed lambs' brains

Suckling pig
Quails *en vessie*
A basket of goose and venison
Snapper with rice wine

Mount of pigeons
Raspberry and vanilla ice-cream
Blackberry trifle

And so it was with some trepidation that I agreed to cook the final banquet for the third symposium in Melbourne three years later in 1987. I titled the evening 'Snips, Snails and Tails'. I wanted to create a witty dinner that would surprise, taste delicious and include some very homely ingredients – in this case nettles, garden snails (my dish inspired by a delicious snail, parsley and garlic combination I had enjoyed at a famous Burgundian restaurant), pigs' ears and tails, oxtails, a calves' foot jelly and a rose-geranium junket. Among the salad leaves were lemon-scented marigold petals and a dish of absolutely perfect home-grown vegetables – beans, carrots, turnips and garlic – all tender, small and impossible to find in the marketplace.

My very special suppliers has searched out and supplied these baby vegetables, as pretty as jewels, if not quite as costly. The meal was a success and reflected my growing interest in home-grown seasonal produce.

Maggie Beer and I met at the first Symposium of Gastronomy. In 1978 Maggie and her husband Colin travelled on a Churchill Fellowship to research the breeding of game birds. They were already breeding and selling pheasants to customers but wanted to know more and to expand their operations. In Scotland they visited farm shops where customers could find out how to cook the birds they were buying. Maggie returned convinced that she needed to show customers what to do with the pheasants. In 1979 they opened the Pheasant Farmshop, aiming to do just that. Responding to demand, within a year she and Colin transformed the Farmshop into the Pheasant Farm Restaurant; neither had restaurant experience, but both had tons of determination and energy. When we met, Maggie was feeling overwhelmed by the task she had set herself and had begun to wonder whether she had bitten off more than she could chew. We found we had a lot in common: we were both learning on the job; we both had energy to burn; we both truly loved good food; and we both loved above all to give pleasure to others. Maggie came and spent a few days with my team at Stephanie's and returned home with new ideas and renewed conviction that what she was doing was worthwhile.

Maggie's star has soared since those days. She is now a household name both for her range of high-quality food products and as a result of a four-year television series *The Cook and the Chef* she made with Simon Bryant. She is a natural performer, radiating an enviable zest for life.

Over more than twenty-five years Maggie has been a marvellous friend. Locked into small businesses, we both understood, as none of my other friends could, the relentless pressure of dealing with cashflow, bank interest rates, wage demands, budgets, machinery breakdowns, managing people, and yet maintaining enthusiasm and creativity and the all-important ability to inspire others to maintain the vision, not to mention finding time for family and friends.

At different times one or other of us felt we were sinking. Crises seemed to be part of small business. With each other we could let it all out, discuss possible solutions and find some solace in a beautiful meal one or the other cooked. Colin was solid as a rock, supporting Maggie in all she did.

These days we are both somewhat less stressed; restaurants are behind us, our families have grown up, we have new interests. Nevertheless Maggie maintains a punishing schedule. We still love nothing more than spending a weekend together, talking, eating and drinking several glasses of lovely wine. Maggie has a special love of aged riesling.

14

A Spode Tea Set & a Loaf of Bread

Loss and Starting to Write 1980–7

The eighties were the best of times for the restaurant. In other ways they were the worst of times.

In July of 1980 Kathy Wright's husband, Bruce, died suddenly after suffering an aneurism while playing squash. It was a deep shock to all his friends. Bruce Wright and John Tinney had been the best of friends and had shared many adventures. Bruce was so young, so full of energy and such a devoted dad to his three young daughters. He had been a champion of my various dealings with the National Australia Bank and always an interested friend. Bruce's death and the public opening of the second Stephanie's Restaurant were days apart. Kathy came to the celebration of the opening night and remembers sitting next to my father. That is true friendship.

There was more sadness to come. A few months later, still in 1980, Monty told me that he was going to have a few tests in hospital because he was feeling breathless. I have always been terrified of serious illness. A cold, a sore toe, a sprained ankle I could deal with, but something unknown and to do with life-threatening things such as spurting blood and exposed guts or distressed breathing or, worst of all, vomiting, left me wanting to run away from the situation.

I blame it all on my youngest brother, Christopher, and his asthma. I have only to close my eyes to see once again his heaving chest, blue-rimmed lips and terrified eyes. He would trail through the house clutching the strings of his favourite pillowcase, wanting to join the rest of us, but giving in and sinking onto a couch coughing and coughing, fighting for each breath. I was sure every breath would be his last. As soon as I hear someone wheezing or looking green I want to put the maximum space between them and me. I am scared. I am frightened. I am terrified.

I was no help to Lisa, who was fourteen years old. I was so frightened myself. Simon, Lisa's brother, was just five. Monty's partner said the fear was that Monty had lymphoma. I was participating at another of the Great Chefs' dinners at the Rothbury Estate in the Hunter Valley in New South Wales and Maurice and I were on our way to the dinner when I was called back to answer the phone. It was Monty's partner to say that Monty's body scan had shown he was 'riddled with cancer'. I can remember the moment but not really what I felt other than shock and numbness. I rang my friend Helen and asked her to speak to Lisa. She quite rightly told me that this was my job but that she would be there to give me support. What an emotional coward I was.

The next day, on my return, I sat with Lisa on the couch with Helen in a chair nearby. I held Lisa's hand and told her it was unlikely Monty would recover from this illness. She fell into my arms and I held her, overwhelmed by my inadequacy to make it better.

Monty was in hospital. It was nearly Christmas. I remember that I worried that Lisa would not be looked after in Monty's will. This worry seemed very important and I think I hung onto it as it appeared to be one thing I could do something about. I attempted to query the terms of his will and then had to deal with the angry visit of his partner, who accused me of acting inappropriately. I was shocked and hurt and realised that I did not know how to react. Perhaps my timing was dreadful but I still think it would have been a good idea for Monty to have discussed much earlier how he meant to provide for Lisa. Of course he had no warning that he needed to put his affairs in order. And the reality was it was many years before it was all sorted out.

At some point I came to my senses and went with Lisa to visit Monty in hospital. He was tender to me and we kissed each other. Lisa sat on the far side of the bed and just stared at him, her eyes brimming with tears and wide as saucers. I have no memory of any conversation at all. What did we do or say?

At the time this took place we were actually in the middle of a summer holiday, having rented a house at Barwon Heads with Helen and Jim Murray and their three children, as we often had done before, and both families had already moved in. Lisa and I drove back to the city again when we heard that Monty's condition had worsened. I asked her whether I should drive her straight to the hospital and she replied that she didn't want to go. I should have insisted. Instead we went to the restaurant and stayed there, where I was rung by Monty's partner an hour later to say that he had just died. I told Lisa, who sobbed. I hugged and kissed her and tucked her into bed. I also gave her a sedative, thinking she would sleep. I now realise that this was a stupid thing to do and an example of my fear when faced with physical collapse and my fear also of confronting deep trauma. Dur-é showed greater empathy and held Lisa while she cried.

We returned to Barwon Heads and I had my own wake that evening by sitting with Helen and drinking a lot and crying a lot. Later that night Lisa slept in my room and she tells me that she listened to me sobbing but pretended to be asleep. It seems neither of us felt that we could claim comfort from the other.

My memories of the very sad funeral are of little Simon trailing a teddy bear as he walked from the church and Lisa crying by herself until I folded her in my arms. I also wept into the chest of Malcolm Good.

I think of Monty a lot these days, maybe because Lisa looks very like him, and I wonder whether we could have done better with each other had we not been under so much pressure. Monty found it very difficult to have a wife who needed to confront emotional issues head on. I needed to talk about the issues, to be 'heard' and to resolve the problem. He preferred life to flow smoothly and to curve gracefully around any rocks rather than have to deal with any obstacles, whereas I always wanted to get out the crowbar, remove the rock and examine it.

As I have mentioned earlier, in the early eighties I was finding that writing about food and food-related topics was something I was increasingly enjoying. I wrote regular columns from 1980 onwards as well as occasional commissioned pieces for other papers and journals. Writing came easily to me and I felt very close to my readers as I poured out my thoughts or discoveries. I also wrote quite fast, which was just as well as my time for writing was restricted to days off or sometimes early in the morning. And as the interest in eating out and restaurants in Australia and overseas became more and more widespread there were plenty of outlets for my early work. My literary hero was Elizabeth David, whose writing sustained me in moments of gloom and inspired me all of the time.

My first commissioned piece of journalism was for *Home Beautiful* magazine in 1980. The late Tony Hitchin was the editor at the time and he went on to edit material I later wrote for *The Epicurean*. He was an excellent editor, very well read, and an enthusiastic gourmet. He understood that good writing about food was as important as good writing about any other special interest and was always encouraging.

Most editors wanted food writers to write a recipe or three recipes with a minimum of text. Space was always the issue. But I certainly was not interested in just writing recipes. Often what I wanted to communicate were thoughts that had some connection with my life. In commenting on the weather, or what was happening in the garden, or something fascinating or, indeed, something horrifying in the world, I believed I was adding depth and shape to what can otherwise be a very one-dimensional account of how to cook a particular dish. It certainly helped the reader get a sense of what was important to me and as my public profile grew I tried to use words responsibly.

I do have opinions, and I see no particular virtue in being neutral as far as the big issues of the day are concerned. Odd, really, because I am so shy and would be very hesitant to stand and speak out at a public meeting, having no confidence in my debating skills. However, I am content to present strong views to a wider audience of readers.

I went on to write for the 'Good Weekend' under several editors; I had a regular piece for many years in *The Age* 'Epicure' section; and I wrote columns for the *Sunday Age* and many, many other one-off pieces. My good friend Angela Clemens meticulously filed most of my stories, the printed version together with the original for easy reference. It is a pity that so few of these stories are dated – a bad habit of mine.

These short pieces span almost thirty years. Reading them now I cringe at the severe tone I sometimes adopted, sounding more like a strict maiden aunt than the encouraging friend I would have preferred.

I did allow my life to invade the pieces. In about 1982 I wrote about Holly's restricted food choices, the article headed 'Holly had a little lamb'. She protested about this but really rather enjoyed the brief notoriety. Reader feedback was almost always complimentary and was very encouraging.

My columns gave me a great platform from which to champion special producers and unusual ingredients. If I tasted some lamb wrapped in saltbush and loved it, I was quick to report on it so that others would be encouraged to try it. When Daniel Romaneix arrived on the food scene with bunches of French tarragon and chervil, both herbs very difficult to grow in quantity and unavailable commercially until this time, I wanted all chefs to know so that we could ensure he stayed in business. After tasting extra virgin olive oils from some of the first Australian-grown olive groves I was quick to note how good they were and how much fresher than oil that had travelled for months before appearing on shop shelves. I hoped that the freshness factor would counteract the difference in price between the local artisan production and the subsidised lower price of imported oils of mysterious provenance.

During the eighties and nineties the food media seemed to expand by the month. Every paper, magazine and supplement wanted a food column, it seemed, and more and more frequently they would seek my opinion about all manner of culinary matters. Regularly I was asked what became *the* question of the eighties: is there an Australian cuisine? The media preoccupation with national culinary identity would not go away.

In 1984 my first book, *Stephanie's Menus for Food Lovers*, went to the printers, to be published the following year. I had collected twenty menus from the Stephanie's Restaurant repertoire, describing why I had put one dish with another and the stories behind each dish. I wrote the recipes in what was becoming my own style – meticulously detailed so as to leave no confusion, with a personal introduction to the recipe. By now I wrote each recipe in an encouraging voice.

My father was very disappointed that I did not write under my maiden name. He was proud of the collective Burchett writings, including pamphlets that both he and his father had written in the 1930s, his own recent and well-regarded history of East Melbourne, Mum's cookery book and of course the many books written by his brother Wilfred. And in retrospect maybe I should have done so. Having been variously named Burchett, Montague and Alexander I felt a little foolish contemplating reverting to Burchett, especially as I had already established my reputation as a restaurateur as Stephanie Alexander.

My parents had decided to move to a retirement village in Mornington sometime in 1982 – very reluctantly, it should be said, on my mother's part. They had already had one move from their big East Melbourne home to a smaller but still spacious apartment in East Melbourne, on the first floor. My father, who always believed in anticipating change rather than having it forced upon him, had formed the opinion that my mother was finding it more difficult to manage stairs and that the East Melbourne establishment was too big for easy maintenance. He was also attracted to the idea of moving back to the Mornington Peninsula, where they had been very happy and still had friends. Typically, once he had made the decision and convinced Mum, they moved within months.

Both my brothers had been settled in the Northern Territory for more than ten years, and the prohibitive cost of travel from the Territory meant that Christopher, John and their wives and young families visited the southern states very rarely. John now worked in the Northern Territory Education Department as a senior public servant. He and his wife, Maria, had two children,

Ben and Amy. Christopher was employed as an advisor in Aboriginal Tourism and he and his wife, Catherine, also had two children, Caleb and Lillian.

In 1986 my parents took a holiday to visit both families. My mother developed a bad cold and racking cough the day before she was due to return. By the time the plane touched down after the first leg in Adelaide she was experiencing breathing difficulties. From my sister's house, at Keilor, close to Melbourne airport, she rang me and explained her surprising symptoms. 'I'm perfectly fine,' she told me, 'until I try and move about and then my breathing feels just as constricted as the boys' used to.' She was well and truly familiar with all the symptoms of asthma. They called into the restaurant en route for Mornington. I went out to the car park for a chat so Mum did not have to get out of the car. She seemed happy and excited at having seen her interstate grandchildren. They continued on to Mornington, where she collapsed. Dad rang me weeping to say she was very bad and he was waiting for the ambulance. Diana and I drove as fast as we could to Mornington, detouring to the hospital. She was not there. Diana rang Dad to find out where she had been transferred to and was told that she had died before the ambulance arrived. She was seventy-two.

No real cause of death was ever determined. My mother had decided, as had my father, to donate her body to the University of Melbourne, so other than the attending ambulance officer surmising a blood clot, we knew nothing more. My own hypothesis many years later was that maybe she had suffered an undiagnosed case of deep vein thrombosis.

I had never seen a dead body before I saw my mother lying on the floor covered with a light blanket. It made me so very, very sad. I said goodbye, stroked her cheek and kissed her cold face. My mother's principal pleasure in life had been the planning and preparation of lovely food. Perhaps unsurprisingly she had steadily put on a little bit of weight in each of the last twenty-five years. She and I had had endless telephone discussions as she despaired of losing these extra kilos. As I gazed at her body I can remember thinking what a terrible waste all the guilt and denial had been, how it all meant nothing. One died anyway, struck down unfairly as it seemed in her case.

Diana and I stayed with Dad that night and it was a terrible night for all of us.

More than a shock, it was totally devastating for my father. Theirs had been a lifelong love affair and a devoted partnership. My siblings and I grieved in our own ways but Dad quickly slid under a blanket of depression such as he had not suffered for ten years. He needed to be cared for, taken to psychiatrists, listened to for hours and hours ('If only I hadn't insisted we fly home that day . . .'), cooked for, hugged. For a time there really needed to be someone sleeping in the house as he would wake shuddering, weeping and needing to talk, but Mornington was an hour and a quarter from the restaurant. I willingly took on this role, however, waiting and hoping for the day when the newly prescribed anti-depressants would start to help, but knowing it was likely to take weeks. I taught him to make bread and this did become a serious interest for him over the next few years. The travelling to and from Mornington added a new pressure to my life, but it was one I accepted without question. One morning Dad rang and said that the cloud had started to lift. It was an enormous relief.

So when *Stephanie's Menus for Food Lovers* was published in 1985 and we celebrated with a party at the restaurant, it was a bittersweet moment for me. My father was present with his movie camera but Mum should have been there! My mother,

Mary Burchett, deserves more recognition as one of Australia's earliest food writers. Her way of describing dishes has strongly influenced my own style. Her book was published in 1960 and her short pieces were mostly commissioned for the original *Australian Gourmet* magazine, commencing in the mid-sixties. Her published work was a source of great pride for her. The tiny cheques she received (fifteen dollars per thousand words) she carefully deposited into a special account and when a sufficient sum was saved she bought a bone china Spode tea set. The cups are cream with a delicate rose transfer pattern. I love this tea set and have it in my own kitchen, always on display, often used, and a tangible reminder of my mother.

Stephanie's Menus for Food Lovers pioneered the path for other books by Australian chefs, a trickle that has become a flood. I have kept the considerable correspondence from readers, especially that I received after I wrote in my column about my mother's death and the death of my very dear friend Josephine Pignolet. Josephine was a delightful young woman and an exceptionally talented cook. She wanted to cook in the tradition of *les mères lyonnaises*: women who in the nineteenth century established simple restaurants in Lyons that aimed at honest cooking using local and seasonal top-quality ingredients for local people. Josephine did not want to be compared with those who aimed for the stars, but, given her talent and that of her husband Damien, their tiny restaurant Claude's soon became one of the stars of the Sydney food scene. They both talked about a *cuisine correcte*, where no step was ignored and no effort was ever too great.

I have a happy memory of Josephine and me preparing a dinner for about fifteen people in John and Jean Tinney's apartment in Paris in 1983. I remember it as an Indian summer of brilliantly clear blue skies and golden afternoons. We shopped in the expensive food shops of Passy and cooked a superb meal of which I only remember that the main course was Bresse chicken.

Four years after this supremely happy holiday Josephine died in a car accident, in 1987. Damien's subsequent cooking career would have to continue without his partner, confidante and muse.

15

New Season's Olive Oil

Family Life, Travel and the Road to Recession 1987–9

By 1981 Lisa was already an experienced traveller, having been to Canada and Jamaica with her father in 1975 and again in 1978, and having met the large extended and scattered Montague family. Both were very happy holidays. Her friendship with her cousin Ken in Toronto deepened on each visit. And in mid-1981 Jenny Little invited Lisa, then aged fifteen, to visit her and Graham in the United States, where they were living while he spent a sabbatical year at the University in California, Berkeley. By this time the Littles had a daughter, Jessica. Jenny's generous invitation was very important for Lisa, and was especially meaningful after her months of sadness since the death of her father. Lisa was delirious with excitement. Jenny was a wonderful 'aunt' and escorted Lisa to see all the Hollywood sights: the movie sets, Disneyland (Lisa's second visit), the homes of the stars, and all the magical things Lisa had dreamed of doing. Her highlight was attending a taping of our favourite family show, *Happy Days*, and actually meeting Chachi and the Fonz. Five-year-old Jessica went on these exciting excursions too.

Lisa's next big trip was to Paris with Kathy Wright and her three daughters at the end of her secondary schooling in 1983. They all stayed with the ever-welcoming Tinneys. Lisa and Catherine Tinney were already good friends. I rang Lisa with her final results, which guaranteed she could enrol at La Trobe University. The Wrights and Lisa moved onto the United States and spent time with Helen and Jim Murray and their three children in New Jersey.

Lisa was back home when my mother died in 1984 and grieved deeply. I believe she felt abandoned all over again by another who had given her unconditional love.

From 1985 until 1988 Lisa was at La Trobe University majoring in Latin American studies and furthering her talent for languages. She travelled to South America in 1985 with a fellow student, doing the four-day walk into Machu Picchu, polishing her Spanish, and sent home very cheerful and interesting letters. She had developed into a delightful and mature young woman, with good friends, an active social life and an enduring interest in all forms of media. Admittedly she seemed to hold back from easy expressions of affection towards any family member other than Holly. Her stepmother had left for the United Kingdom years before and there had been almost no contact with her brother, which made her sad. Soon after her return from South America Lisa set up house with Catherine Tinney in a Carlton terrace, coincidentally in the same street as my first house.

Meanwhile Monty's former business partner Jim Vlassopoulos had decided to reopen a Jamaica House, at yet another location in Lygon Street. (At different times the restaurant operated at four different sites in Lygon Street.) In many ways Jim Vlassopoulos was like a second father to Lisa. Jamaica House represented a connection to her father and to Jamaica and was very important to her. Both Lisa and Catherine waitressed in this new establishment on a casual basis.

Holly and I had been desolate when the Murrays left for two years in the States in late 1982. But on the family's return to

Melbourne, the children simply picked up their friendships where they had left off. Jim Murray was a great friend, compassionate and supportive in my darkest days, and has always made me laugh. It was a great shock when Jim and Helen divorced in 1991. (Helen married Bruce Lagay, an American academic, in 1992.)

By 1987 our finances had improved and it seemed that Holly would benefit from a more academic environment than appeared to be on offer at the local high school. We made the decision that she should go to Wesley College, where she settled in well and met lifelong friends. Perhaps not surprisingly, Holly showed an early interest in the French language. She and William Evans, a charming waiter at the restaurant, exchanged little bursts of French conversation most afternoons, which I found very entertaining. (Holly's interest in all things French continued and she had two periods of living in France, once in 1993 as an exchange student and later to complete her degree at Jean Moulin University in Lyons in 1997.)

Holly loved school and did well. She started to write stories while she was still at primary school. I have a treasured copy of a 'magazine', *The Voice*, entirely planned, written and set by Holly, in which she interspersed stories, news items, letters to the editor, a recipe, advertisements, an agony column, even a cartoon. It is very entertaining and clearly shows imaginative flair and literary ability.

On at least three occasions during the late eighties we had great holidays as a family in North Queensland. We always rented a house so that I could cook and we could spread out. And as always I recorded highlights in a notebook.

There is a banana plant outside our door . . . I bought a 2.7 kilo barramundi (caught that morning) and stuffed it with coriander leaves, spring onions and pieces of shredded lime zest. I dipped the banana leaf in hot water to soften, oiled it and wrapped the fish first in the leaves and then in foil. It took nearly forty minutes on the barbecue. On more banana leaves I baked a panful of sweet potato and pumpkin tossed with basil leaves until beautifully crusty. While the fish baked I pounded a sambal of hot chilli, preserved lemon, coriander and spring onions.

The Murray children – Fiona, Virginia and Angus – were Holly's preferred playmates, and we had years of shared family holidays. The Murray children and Holly would amuse themselves very creatively all day long. They produced plays, dressed up, read stories, built ambitious castles on the beach, and were very entertaining.

Sometimes the Murray daughters came with us on one of our Queensland family holidays. The memory of the Incident of the Glass-topped Table of 1987 still makes me shiver. Holly was twelve at the time, Virginia eleven and Fiona thirteen. That evening Maurice and I were invited to a friend's house not very far away. The girls had the prospect of some favourite food for dinner and knew we would be home not too late. They decided to re-enact a scene from the popular television show *Young Talent Time*, which frequently included views of the dancers' feet filmed from below. Holly and Fiona were to dance *on* the glass-topped table and Virginia, the younger Murray daughter, would lie on the floor underneath to take the pictures. You can imagine the rest. The glass shattered. The children were all cut, Virginia worst of all. Their screams brought the next-door neighbours, who must have thought a murder had taken place. Glass and blood were everywhere. Someone ran to get us. We spent most of the night in the local doctor's surgery – he came quickly in his board shorts and bright shirt, and sewed them up. Virginia had more than forty stitches. Fiona and Holly's cuts were relatively minor but it did put a big dampener on the final day of the holiday! I had the unenviable task of telephoning Jim and Helen and telling them of their daughters' injuries. No swimming or sunning was possible with those heavy bandages. It was a very subdued group that got off the plane in Melbourne.

Just as my parents imbued in me a fascination for travel and other cultures, I seemed to have passed on the travel bug to both my daughters. And travel was so important to Maurice and me too, not only as time out, but also so we could be friends again. France and Italy always energised and refreshed me. I would leave Australia feeling drained of inspiration and exhausted. Each new immersion in the smells and tastes of wonderful, everyday food revived me for the next dive back in. Market visiting was always a high priority, as was having the opportunity to cook some of the lovely food. Travelling through the lush countryside and spending time in small villages reinforced the primal connection between landscape, agriculture and good, locally produced food.

Our friends Jean and John Tinney were posted to Paris in 1982, where John was Senior Trade Commissioner, and remained in the grand Australian Embassy building on Rue Jean Rey until late 1985.

They were then posted to Rome from 1986 to 1990. When we travelled Maurice and I usually stayed at simple *auberges* or *pensiones*, but we always looked forward to the mod cons as well as great company at the beginning and end of each trip with a visit to the Tinneys. These dear friends had many visits from Australians during their years in Europe.

Paris is always enchanting. It has so much to offer but visitors do have to put in. These days my knees complain after fifty Metro ascents and descents. I still haven't conquered the bus system, and without a good sense of direction I am likely to take the bus going in the wrong direction. And besides, I love taking the Metro and listening to the language all around me, catching some of it, missing a lot more, soaking up the insouciance of the youth of the world, looking on, observing, reflecting. Some things have changed. In my very first days in Paris so many years ago I remember being struck by a notice that appeared in every Metro carriage: '*Pas plus d'un litre par jour*', a public plea to restrict alcohol intake to less than a litre per person per day!

Whenever I visited Paris Jean and I would stroll the avenues and the covered passages. We both lacked the courage to actually go into the *haute couture* boutiques but we did a lot of window-shopping (or 'window-licking' as they say in French!). And an hour's café-sitting and people-watching was always rewarding – pity most French coffee is so bad. I am reminded of a splendid scene I watched while sitting with Jean one day. It was mid-morning in the Place des Vosges, perhaps my favourite Parisian square. A notice instructed us to stay off the grass, '*Pelouse au repos*' (The lawn is resting). I admired a woman, probably in her eighties, with severely cropped white hair, an ebony-topped cane, wearing a narrow-cut long black dress with a stunning white coat, white-framed sunglasses, leaning on the arm of a young woman, perhaps her granddaughter, as they strolled the arcades. So stylish.

There have been many times in my travels when I have chosen a place to visit or a restaurant to experience after reading an especially evocative passage in a book.

I was drawn to Le Grand Véfour, in the Palais-Royal, by reading a biography of Colette and asked a friend to join me there for lunch. Colette loved food and much of her writing details meals enjoyed, described in mouth-watering detail.

Colette had a great friendship with Raymond Oliver, the chef at Le Grand Véfour for many years, and she lived her last days in an apartment whose windows overlooked the Palais-Royal gardens. I own a much-used copy of Raymond Oliver's exhaustive tome

La Cuisine, my reference for the finer points of how to dissect any beast or bird. At the end of her life Colette was racked with arthritis and practically unable to move, so Chef Oliver sent treats to her, or arranged for her to be carried to the restaurant for a special meal. On 3 August 1954, he sent her a vegetable broth. It was her last meal.

So, sitting in what has to be one of the grandest and most beautiful dining rooms in Paris, there were ghosts present. With its painted panelling and curtains held back with embroidered sashes the restaurant reeks of time past and *la belle époque*, but why not experience a moment of grandeur? And the lunch was absolutely delicious.

The rollcall of restaurants we visited on our French *séjours* includes many that have disappeared, changed owners or changed beyond recognition. During the eighties almost all of these restaurants had three or two Michelin stars. We were determined to continue to sample the best that Paris had to offer. I collected so many menus they spill from their folder. A sample would include Taillevent, Le Pré Catelan, Guy Savoy, Georges Blanc, Lucas Carton, Au Trou Gascon, Jamin, Lous Landès, Les Prés d'Eugénie, Le Carré des Feuillants, l'Ambroisie and Beauvilliers. There were many more.

In 1987, once Holly was well settled in Wesley College, Maurice and I planned a longish holiday to Rome, Verona and on to Ithaca, where my friend Melita Vlassopoulos was to spend summer with her elderly parents.

Betsy Bradshaw (who had married my first boyfriend, Malcolm Good, in 1983) offered to move in along with Malcolm to look after the girls once again in our absence. There was genuine affection between Betsy and both girls and I think they really looked forward to our departure. Back in 1983 when Betsy and Malcolm first looked after the girls they had a wonderful time, despite – or rather because of – the Jane Fonda Chandelier Incident. Betsy had always been interested in keeping fit and as a shared fun activity suggested following a Jane Fonda video, to 'feel the burn' – or the pain or whatever they were exhorted to do. Unfortunately they did this just as the evening's guests were arriving in the restaurant downstairs and being shown to their seats by the ever-suave Christoph. His calm was sorely tested when one of the large, round etched-glass lightshades bounced from its heavy brass support, narrowly missing a customer and Christoph himself. Fortunately it did not break. Christoph must have taken the stairs four at a time to stop the exercise class. He was suitably outraged and all three girls were chastened, but I am sure had the giggles afterwards.

So with the opportunity for the girls to be 'safely' in Betsy and Malcolm's hands again, and with the Tinneys based in Rome, Italy came further up our travel agenda, and having a column to write for *The Age* gave me a focus for these trips. The Italian holidays were marvellous and the sights and tastes stimulated wonderful menus upon our return. I also developed a deeper and deeper understanding of the connection between landscape and produce, of the necessary difference between sustaining and inexpensive peasant dishes, and those dishes that were more refined. And I was beginning to truly appreciate simplicity, Italian-style.

In Tuscany my first experience of just-pressed new season's extra virgin olive oil was a revelation. In a *fattoria* in Lucca I watched the oil flow in a golden river and joined the mill workers in grilling a slice of saltless bread over the nearby coal fire, rubbing it briefly with garlic and then pressing it into the stream for a sensational snack. I had never tasted olive oil like this. It was addictive.

So often a restaurant describes its offerings as simple. It is such a cliché, but to produce genuinely simple food is so hard to get right. It is almost impossible to achieve in a restaurant unless one has a garden nearby. Just-picked zucchini, a truly fresh fish (not really possible without having caught it yourself), a garden-ripened non-refrigerated tomato, a ripe peach, delicate salad leaves grown in soil, really ripe strawberries, properly stored and richly flavoured olive oil – how many diners will notice or care? I experienced such dishes in Italy more often than I had done in France, which I found interesting. In France the vegetables were frequently over-worked and even sometimes over-cooked, and rarely had the same central place in a menu as they had in Italy.

Together with the Tinneys we had some good eating adventures in and around Rome, memorably at a simple trattoria near the Ponte Milvio that we dubbed Il Frantico, where the speed and flourish of the waiters had to be admired even if it did not induce a feeling of relaxation. And another night, sitting at an 'outside table' in some backstreet, we laughed at the Italian ability to overlook traffic and exhaust fumes less than a metre from one's chair, and allow the restaurant to claim it had an 'outdoor' eating space. It could also correctly claim to serve brilliant, crisp, stuffed zucchini blossoms and tissue-paper-thin ravioli with a herb and ricotta stuffing bathed in a red-gold sauce of sweet, sweet tomato. It was almost worth the traffic fumes.

I think back over all of my Italian experiences and I cannot remember it ever raining. Of course I chose to travel outside of winter but the sun was *always* shining. And every city I visited seemed to have its own mood: sombre, beautiful Florence; chaotic Palermo; exciting Rome; silent, watery Venice (in late autumn without too many tourists); grey, monumental Milan; elegant Torino and Urbino. As always, my most memorable times have been not when I was just passing through, but when I have had a comfortable base from where I can cook and reflect on what I have seen or tasted.

Part of the pleasure of Italy is the contrast between the excitement and chaotic pressure of life in the congested cities, the almost universal good humour and exuberance of the population that is irresistible and contagious, and the continued existence of places where life seems untouched by the city pressures. Here you can be still and reflective or view wonderful art in surprising places, admire the glorious scenery or feel almost at home in welcoming small villages. And then of course there is the food and the respect it is given.

In preparation for this Italian holiday one of the waiters at Stephanie's, William Evans, had lent me the wonderful novel *The Birds of America* by Mary McCarthy. I absolutely loved this book and read it several times.

The young hero, an art student, suggests tactics to ensure the best visit to Michelangelo's frescoes in the Sistine Chapel. He counsels that on entering the chapel the trick was to wait calmly. Once full with tour groups, the throng would soon move all at once into the Stanze di Raffaello, permitting perhaps ten minutes of near solitude to gaze undisturbed before the next wave arrived. During this period of relative calm he would lie on the floor and, using a mirror, admire the panels on the ceiling. He also revealed this discovery:

> He knew another secret passage, which he had found on his own, in the Stanze di Raffaello. You walked through a door marked 'Leo X' in the wall beneath the 'Incendio del Borgo' and discovered nice clean toilets.

We didn't dare try for the toilets, but we did walk hurriedly to the chapel and had a few moments before the first crowd pressed in and lingered as suggested after the first wave moved on. The frescoes had just been cleaned and the effect was startling. My imperfect memory of an earlier visit when Holly was a baby had been of sombre figures in a muted background. Now the colours were startlingly bright, the cloak of one figure a brilliant mint-green, of another a rich rose.

I returned to Italy in 1989 to attend a cooking workshop of just six students hosted by Marcella and Victor Hazan at their home in Venice. Like many others I had always consulted one of Marcella's books if I wanted a clear explanation of an Italian technique or a clarification of any confusion. Her work is clear, authoritative and comprehensive. I was fortunate that Marcella and Victor had passed through Melbourne on a book promotion and had come to Stephanie's Restaurant for lunch. On the menu that day was a long-simmered dish of tripe with tomatoes, wine and lots of herbs. It was sticky and delicious and they were full of praise. My reward for having delighted the Hazans was a place at the cooking workshop.

It was in Marcella's kitchen that I first understood how to peel sweet peppers while they were raw, using an asparagus peeler (often known as a speed peeler), as opposed to roasting and peeling them as we do for salads and *antipasti*, and appreciated the possibilities of the difference in texture. I learnt from Marcella how to make gnocchi without using eggs. And I listened to her explain that pasta hates the cold as she kneaded her pasta dough on a wooden board rather than the marble bench. Victor showed us a different *salumi* and a different bread each day and offered us tutored tastings of Italian wines.

The Hazans introduced me to Mara and Maurizio Zanetti, the owners of Da Fiore, a seafood restaurant in Venice, which at the time was unknown to tourists but is now considered one of the finest restaurants in the city. It had the smallest, barely visible sign, and the restaurant itself was down the very narrow Calle del scaleter. Inside it was brilliantly lit and the menu was uncompromisingly Italian. Here one ordered fish or shellfish and mostly it came unadorned save for lemons, olive oil and maybe pepper or a touch of chilli. At Da Fiore I tasted my first razorshell clams, minute cuttlefish and *canocce*, a speciality from the Venetian lagoon.

One of the glamorous new dining rooms at Stephanie's in Hawthorn in 1980.

'Karawau', the premises of the second Stephanie's Restaurant in Hawthorn.

Judging at the Hong Kong Food Festival in 1986.

Me with Janni at the staff party after the opening night in 1980.

The original staff at Hawthorn.

Showing off one of the spacious dining rooms in the Hawthorn restaurant.

The front-of-house team at the second Stephanie's.

Annie Smithers and Mary-Rose tackle the snails.

The kitchen team a few years after opening.

photo: Viva Jillian Gibb

Me and teenage Lisa.

Cooking for school children, long before the Kitchen Garden Foundation.

In London during a promotion at a Park Lane hotel, in 1989.

Holly and Lisa with a coconut on a Queensland holiday, in about 1981.

Always inspired by Paris.

With Jean Tinney in Brasserie Lipp, Paris, in 1984.

Joyce and Malcolm Good Senior. Joyce inspired me to appreciate beauty in everyday life.

A happy time with Holly and Maurice, in about 1986.

Always more relaxed on holidays.

Mum and Dad, comfortable in their retirement in East Melbourne.

Malcolm Good and Betsy Bradshaw were married at the restaurant in Hawthorn in 1983.

Me, Maurice and Dur-é celebrating our success at *The Age Good Food Guide* awards night in 1989.

Claudia Roden was a guest at the Seventh Symposium of Gastronomy in Canberra in 1993.

photo: Mark Chew

I was always most comfortable in the kitchen, tucked away from the public.

My annual Boxing Day party is eagerly anticipated.

Duffy Clemens and Graham Little, at one of my Boxing Day parties.

Simon Griffiths sets up for a shot in our rented house in Lavalade, south-west France, in 1998.

Good friends Holly, Fiona Murray, Lisa and Virginia Murray.

Dinner at Lavalade. Clockwise from front left: Anna Dollard, Colin Beer, me, Duffy Clemens, Angela Clemens and Maggie Beer.

Lunchtime at Lavalade: Maggie and Colin Beer, Duffy and Angela Clemens (in background), and publisher Julie Gibbs.

Tony Tan dresses up for a farewell party in Hanoi, during our trip to Vietnam in 1998.

John and Jean Tinney at a café in France.

The photographer had great fun with this shot.

A favourite shot of the two girls and me with our much-loved dog, Rosie.

Me with two of my favourite men,
Graham Little and my father, in 1995.

With my sister Diana at a book launch.

Dad loved to fish for flathead in Port Phillip Bay.

Jenny Little, Jean Tinney and me at my
sixtieth birthday party.

Malcolm Good and me on a New Year's Eve boat
trip to Southgate in 2000.

photo: Simon Griffiths

Picking salad greens with students
at Collingwood College.

Jamie Oliver came to see what we were doing with
the Kitchen Garden project in 2006.

photo: Newspix/Ellen Smith

In the kitchen with students at Collingwood College
in 2011.

photo: Andrew Craig

This picture was used on the cover of the Victorian White Pages in 2008–9.

I do love working in my kitchen.

To me, the vegetables are as attractive as the flowering plants in my garden.

These days I have vegetables and herbs in the front garden.

On the set of *MasterChef Australia* in 2010.

Maggie's friendship over many years has been very special to me.

Angela Clemens and me – friends for life.

Each cupcake for my seventieth birthday was topped with a small edible sculpture of something personal and memorable.

My daughters and me at my seventieth birthday party in 2010.

The front covers of my books.

My girls and me.

We had so many adventures. It might seem that I was rarely at home but not so − few holidays were longer than three weeks and several of the trips were concentrated in less time.

I have to acknowledge, perhaps with a hint of regret, that although I love it I am a timid traveller. I read with some interest or incredulity the accounts of intrepid adventures in remote places, of freezing nights on mountainsides, of wading through leech-infested rivers, or climbing for days along glaciers, and marvel at other people's endurance, courage or sense of adventure. And yet in the rare moments when I have allowed myself to creep outside my comfort zone I have been thrilled.

Many years ago, around 1989, while researching my third book, *Stephanie's Australia*, I travelled with my brother Christopher and with Indigenous guide Bill Harney west of Katherine along the Victoria River to better understand the land of the Lightning Brothers, Jabiringi and Yagdjagbula, ancestral beings who, in the Dreamtime, helped shape the traditional land of the Wardaman people. This was my first contact with the extraordinary rock art of this country, much of it far older than the pyramids. In France I have visited the caves in Lascaux that reproduce the world-famous rock art of that region − the originals, now closed to the public, are twenty thousand years old. I find it astonishing that by contrast visitors in Australia can still walk right up to original Aboriginal paintings in Kakadu National Park that are just as ancient.

Here in the bush I slept under the stars for the first time. There were six of us. Each bed was a framed mattress of galvanised chain mesh suspended from four poles rammed deep into the ground and secured with a cement of crushed termite mound. Snug in my oilcloth swag I was mesmerised by the night sky. It was brilliant, thick with stars such as one never sees in a city. And then in the morning, for nearly an hour I watched the sun gild the treetops, hearing the rush of feathers as the birds started the day. The crackle of dried gum twigs and a whiff of eucalyptus smoke told me that the billy was about to boil for tea.

I am comfortable being anonymous in the sheltered cocoon of a plane, but on the ground it is more difficult. The solitary traveller balances loneliness and introspection with keen observation and the occasional solitary pleasure. But it can be hard to avoid melancholia.

When I am away I dream a lot about my other life – I compost the problems seeking solutions via the subconscious. I cannot control it. The upside is that distance sometimes lends a bit of perspective.

When I look back at my close to two hundred spiral-bound notebooks, I am fascinated and somewhat appalled at the endless lists that appear. Lists, lists, more lists, and then more lists. Always stuff to do, mixed in with notes to buy milk and washing powder. No time to waste, something else to fit in somehow, another lead to be chased, someone else to contact, an idea to share. And then another list.

I have to conclude that I needed to drive myself at an amazing pace – wanting to be across everything, wanting also to fit in time with my daughters and my friends. Since the start of my restaurant life I had almost forgotten how to read for pleasure. I still tend to read fast, without full comprehension or reflection. Often I finish a book and start it again in order to savour the experience more slowly the second time. Unallotted time is a concept I am unfamiliar with. Once the frenetic pace stops I am confused and anxious. It takes time to settle into a slower routine.

In among all the lists in the notebooks just sometimes there is a sentence reflecting sadness or despondency: 'At least once a day I feel utter despair at the enormity of the task and the impossibility of achieving perfection.' Why did I think perfection was ever achievable or necessary? This relentless quest for the unattainable meant that I too easily overlooked the joy and delight in the present moment.

Looking back, I have to admit that I made some very bad decisions. I always believed I could do it all and have it all. A restaurant and a baby – no problems. A restaurant and two young children – easy. A restaurant, a regular column, writing a book and two children – no problem at all. It's significant perhaps that the 'marriage' is not up there in importance with the restaurant. I do not believe it was arrogance, I think it was an unthinking hope that the marriage would look after itself while I forged ahead creating, doing, writing, carousing. Of course I punished my body with little rest, little exercise, too much wine, too much food (or too little during the Jamaica House days). I was impatient, easily irritated, highly critical of myself and others, constantly striving for that elusive perfection, accepted invitations to do extra events when commonsense would say 'enough is enough', rejected any advice that did not endorse this drive onwards at any price. But I always loved my girls. And I am so proud of the beautiful, intelligent women they have become.

My marriage to Maurice took ten years to unravel. I think we did each other considerable damage and maybe the end should have come sooner. It took me far too long to learn that I was able to manage on my own and still achieve my dream. And that I did not need to feel angry and resentful, as often as I did.

Maurice still had to learn that to react angrily to every financial hurdle solved nothing, had unwished-for consequences and just added to the shared torment. Probably our pleasurable holidays fooled us and allowed both of us to think that things were improving. Back home the camaraderie and enjoyment of our time away together quickly collapsed under everyday stresses.

I am very aware that this is my story, not Maurice's. It is horrifying to read my saved notes, the notebook entries of this period, the record of therapy sessions. Years passed as we fought each other, each crippled by low self-esteem and exhaustion and determined to take out our frustrations, disappointments and anger on each other. We both yearned for trust and support and neither gave it to the other. We had bitten off more than we could chew with our relentless and enormous business; it really needed management skills that neither of us had. We needed professional help with financial planning, computer technology and personnel management. Instead we tried to do most things ourselves or allowed amateurs to have a go. They frequently did more damage than good and resulted in further harm to our relationship along the way.

In the early eighties I sometimes ran away for a few days, often to the home of my friend Damien Pignolet and his wife, Josephine. As restaurant owners they were fully aware of the pressures of restaurant life. Even though it appeared there were no solutions to my predicament, I was able to pour out my woes and be offered wholehearted sympathy and understanding.

The pattern repeated itself time and time again. Away from the restaurant, either at our newly constructed beach house at Barwon Heads from 1982 onwards, or at a holiday destination anywhere at all, we behaved much better, enjoying pleasurable time together. Maurice enjoyed being with the various children who shared our summer holidays, participating fully and energetically in their games of beach cricket or efforts with surfboards or windsailing, and he always investigated and appreciated the best of a new place.

The girls coped as well as they could with our scratchy relationship. Maurice and I indulged in a great deal of undermining behaviour, which was hard for Lisa and Holly to endure. Family mealtimes were often silent or accusatory. Lisa and Holly often retreated to the television. I retreated to 'my' kitchen.

Maurice had an ambivalent relationship with the restaurant. While he enjoyed the prestige it gave him, and he could be a charmingly urbane host, I felt he was very jealous of the friendship I had developed with Dur-é, who had the responsibility for directing all matters pertaining to the front of house. He also appeared to resent the cheerful camaraderie in the kitchen, where he felt excluded. In contrast, I felt wonderfully valued by my colleagues: they did not shout at me or suggest that I was wantonly extravagant and ignorant of financial matters, as he did. In turn I would accuse Maurice of failing to understand the cost of quality. The truth is that I *was* ignorant of financial matters, but it was also true that I had an intuitive understanding of how to balance an expensive item with others that were more reasonable. When I tried to get Maurice to talk about an emotional issue his reply was about a financial or business issue.

In retrospect I also have to admit that the planned elegance of Stephanie's, with its well-spaced tables arranged over several rooms, certainly permitted easy conversation and added to comfort, but it required more staff to service. Nowadays the same number of diners would be accommodated in one-third of the space, with a corresponding decrease in labour costs and increase in noise. Labour costs were far more important than the food costs in the big picture.

Dur-é had consolidated her position from that of casual waiter in the late seventies to front of house manager in the Hawthorn establishment in the eighties. She was highly skilled in engaging with both staff and customers and once her attention was focused on someone they felt supremely important. She was the recipient of many confidences and always knew who was feeling bad, who had an unresolved personal crisis or who had a fascinating story in their past. We became good friends and I saw her as a confidante and ally in my miserable battles with my husband. She would listen, always gratifyingly endorsing my position. We often ate together in the restaurant at the end of the regular service or in many other restaurants. She was very amusing and could entertain with stories of her own childhood in Malaysia and later escapades since her arrival in Australia as a teenager. Dur-é, by her own admission, was a survivor and permitted no criticism of her manner or motives. She needed to feel indispensable to others and she just about achieved this at Stephanie's.

Whether I had a deep interest in financial matters or not I was soon forced to take notice. By the mid-eighties interest rates were rising fast. We had significant borrowings, including interest-only loans, and once the rates started to climb from eleven per cent at the beginning of 1985, to fifteen per cent in 1987, and then the all-time high of seventeen per cent in 1989, Maurice became convinced that there would be an economic crash. He was correct.

The developing economic crisis did not prevent the Federal and State governments celebrating the Bicentennial Year in 1988, marking two hundred years since white settlement (or white occupation, whichever way you wanted to look at it). I was approached to join a committee charged with the task of creating a public event that would capture the imagination and celebrate Victoria's place as the foodie state of the nation. I persuaded the Victorian Bicentennial Committee to stage an event to be known as the Harvest Picnic.

Initially this was conceived of as a one-off event; its continued success was unexpected. The event has continued, although the categories of participation seem to have been broadened to include public entertainment and quite a deal of space for large sponsors to advertise their products or services. It still attracts thousands of people.

The idea was very similar to the philosophy that underlies the present-day farmers' markets – to invite specialist growers and producers to meet the public, sell their produce and offer information so that food lovers could learn more about their produce, as well as have an enjoyable picnic. Junk food and processed foods were to be outlawed. From my constant contacts with farmers and specialist producers, I was more and more aware of their frustrations. Quality costs more but rarely were the producers able to talk to the consumers, and too often there were middle-men who obscured the message. It was also fair to say that many producers understood very little about how their food would be prepared or served. In meeting and sharing thoughts there were benefits for both groups.

The first Harvest Picnic held at Yarra Park attracted more than three thousand people. It was so successful that I needed help the following year. I called in my friend Yvonne Smith, who for the next two years managed the event. Event management was not one of my skills, even if I could always be counted on for a good idea.

Back at the restaurant, to add to Maurice's concerns I was airing various crazy schemes whereby I would open a second business with Dur-é as a partner. My motives can only be described as very confused. I suppose I wanted to put some space between my husband and me, to try something different, to prove I could manage on my own, or probably a mix of all three. It was a ludicrous idea. Maurice was very fearful of my plans and obsessed with the state of the economy, but he allowed himself to be convinced that a more creative solution would be to invite Dur-é to become a one-third partner in Stephanie's, to find a nearby house for us to live in and to expand the restaurant operations by renovating the upper floor where we presently lived. He worked out the fine detail himself, as I would have been incapable of doing. The legal machinery was put into place, the bank consulted, the business sold to the newly created company, partnership documents signed in April 1989 and the Alexander family moved to a lovely house in Hawthorn with renovations starting again, just in time for the full impact of 'the recession we had to have' to take effect.

Maurice's worry was legitimate but his response to it was devastating – it broke his health for the next three years. Dur-é and I appointed a mutual friend, John Smith, as manager to oversee the financial side of the business. Maurice and I officially separated in October 1989. Holly, like Lisa, now had to cope with an absent father, in her case for three years rather than forever. She was fifteen. During this time Maurice seemed unable to sustain their relationship, which had been a close and happy one. These days Maurice and Holly have re-established much of their former camaraderie.

16

Crabapple Tart &
a Squeeze of Calamansi

High Expectations in the Nineties

In the nineties I had to operate on many levels and develop some new skills. I had to deal with a sick and absent husband, a serious recession and my eventual divorce in 1992. Although Maurice and I were living apart from late 1989 I still had to cope with the impact of his absence on Holly and the repercussions of the changes in ownership of the restaurant. And that was just the first two years! I also had to try to get my head around complicated financial concepts and for the first time try to understand balance sheets.

With Maurice unable to participate in the operation of the business, his share was sold to Dur-é and me. He was removed from any responsibility for debt repayments or other obligations of the business. I hoped that having the source of extreme financial anxiety lifted from his shoulders would help Maurice make a full recovery. I think it did but it took time.

I had to be a mother to both my girls without assistance. I had to care for my ageing father who by this time had developed diabetes. I had to maintain momentum, creative energy and morale at the restaurant. I had to maintain and promote the public persona that attracted attention and comment and brought customers to

Stephanie's. Yet despite the fact that so many problems loomed I still had an inexhaustible drive to push myself towards that elusive idea of perfection. Frequently I acknowledged that I was falling short of this impossible ideal, which brought on feelings of failure or inadequacy. I also needed to find some time for myself.

Most restaurants in the nineties faced steep financial challenges. The recession hit at discretionary spending. The Fringe Benefits Tax Act of 1986 had drastically reduced the lunch trade of city restaurants that depended on the big spenders of the eighties. They disappeared almost overnight and in came lunch specials, the 'two course and glass of wine' offer, as a way of tempting custom. As Stephanie's was in the suburbs, we had never had a significant lunch trade, so this was one worry we did not have, but certainly there were fewer grand parties, fewer corporate promotional evenings and our regular customers dined out less frequently. The upstairs expansion had been justified mostly by the reality that we had been full every night during the eighties and had turned away plenty of private dinners. It was this custom we now hoped to service.

In my predictable need to do everything as well as possible (in hindsight I might say as extravagantly as possible) I had insisted on installing a complete second kitchen in the upstairs makeover, with a service lift that cost so much money I blush to remember it. Most restaurateurs would have expected wait staff to run up and down stairs with all food coming from a central point, but not me. A second team of cooks and waiters operated the upstairs section of the restaurant, still with elegantly spaced tables ensuring privacy and comfort – at a *huge* cost to the establishment. At capacity, serving a maximum of one hundred and forty diners at a single sitting every night, we would have employed a team of twelve to fourteen cooks and kitchenhands over both kitchens, and I cannot remember how many bar and wait staff – at least fifteen. Wages were killing us.

The original downstairs refit in 1980 had concentrated on opening as soon as possible and attracted little attention from the authorities. Nine years later, when the expansion was planned, Stephanie's Restaurant had achieved a nationwide reputation and all at once we found that we were required to employ an architectural historian to do paint scrapings of the upstairs rooms to discover original colours (all at our expense, of course). This insane work took weeks, if not months, and resulted in colour schemes that were startling, complicated and very expensive to apply. We had added three new dining rooms: the Cato room, named for the original owners (once our family sitting room); the Burchett room, a small private room named for my parents, which was used a great deal (formerly Maurice's office); and a smaller room, the Hawthorn room, which had marvellous views over the city. (This last room had been the family TV room. Imprinted on my mind is the image of dear little Holly sitting at her yellow painted table, on her little yellow painted chair, thumb in mouth, staring at the television, for several years after she had really outgrown this baby furniture.) What had once been our bedroom became the new kitchen.

At some point a customer advised us that Wesley College owned a significant collection of early Australian paintings that it stored in a vault. The artworks had been a gift to the college from a member of the Cato family. We were persuaded that it would be a coup to display some of these works on the walls. What we hadn't bargained on was the cost of insuring these beautiful paintings. For a few years we had works by Arthur Streeton, Norman Lindsay, Penleigh Boyd and others on the walls. It took us too long to decide that this was a luxury we could absolutely not afford. They were beautiful though.

The reality was that we were hopelessly overcapitalised. We could never hope to recoup these massive expenses. Understandably Dur-é had hoped to see swift return on her investment.

One decision I made was to sell the building and to lease it back from the new owner so Dur-é and I would then be truly equal partners. As a result of this decision I was able to repay my father his substantial investment in my dreams, which was a great relief to me (and no doubt to him).

At the sixth Symposium of Australian Gastronomy, in 1991, I gave a paper entitled 'Towards a sensual food life'. This paper preceded my work in establishing the Kitchen Garden Foundation by more than ten years so it is interesting and strangely comforting for me to read what I was thinking even then:

> I would like to see more of us making connections between food and the earth. Growing some food, be it only a pot of parsley, or a tub of cherry tomatoes, seems to very quickly stimulate meaningful awareness of soil, weather and human endeavour. We should ensure that our children dig and plant and help us pick, or at the very least watch others doing so.

At this time I was just starting to grow some of my own food at home. I grew a wide range of herbs and, in the summer, one or two tomato plants to accompany the basil and a small plot of soft-leaved salads.

My travels during the early and mid-nineties were enjoyable escapes from a troubled and confused reality. A holiday in England, France and Italy with both daughters in 1990 is remembered by the three of us as significant and very special. Holly was suffering with Maurice's absence, Lisa was experiencing her own identity crisis, I needed time out with the girls away from restaurant pressure, and we had a wonderful, wonderful time together.

I had a friend, Ian Atkins, whom I had known since my far-off Coburg Library days. Since the late seventies Ian had been living with his mother in a lovely stone house with a walled garden in the village of Midford, just outside Bath. We had always shared a love of good food and, since the eighties, whenever I visited Britain, Ian would collect me at Heathrow and off we would go, driving from one splendid restaurant to another. In these early trips we visited Gravetye Manor; ate with Rick Stein at Padstow in Cornwall (my first ever turbot); visited Elizabeth David's favourite country restaurant, the Walnut Tree in Wales, where we ate Lady Llanover's salt duck served with pickled damsons (a kind of plum); visited Joyce Molyneux's The Carved Angel in Dartmouth; and many more. We also visited country houses and country markets. (I have a note reminding me of a visit to a Women's Institute market at the hall in Freshford, a village in Somerset, where I sampled a delicious cake stuffed with currants and crusted with icing sugar – surely I meant an Eccles cake?)

Ian had also introduced me to some very special country pubs. Not since the sixties, on my very first visit to England, had I experienced smoke-blackened, cosy dining rooms with log fires burning and locals in tweeds and caps enjoying honest, local fare. Maybe such places were more numerous in the West Country.

On this holiday Ian was a splendid host to the three of us. I wanted Lisa and Holly to experience an English stately house. We lunched at Woolley Grange near Bath and it was an extraordinary experience. I had two outstanding dishes: grouse with a wild blackberry and juniper sauce, and a marvellous *tarte tatin* of John Downie crabapples.

On an earlier visit to England my cousin Rainer and his wife had taken me to see Hatfield House in Hertfordshire, the home of the Marchioness of Salisbury, where I had been overwhelmed by the beauty of the avenue of John Downie crabapples with surprisingly large fruits splashed in red and gold. At the time I was determined to have one in my own garden. I now have five John Downie crabapple trees myself and every year I make a similar tart in memory of Woolley Grange. The crabapples cook to a delightful bronze-pink colour and retain their sharpness, which makes a lovely contrast with the caramel.

Each year my dear friend Annie Smithers also comes to spend an evening with me, and she gets out the ladder and picks most of the crop to make her incomparable crabapple jelly. Annie, who owns Annie Smithers' Bistrot in Kyneton and a more informal business in nearby Trentham, was once an apprentice of mine and we always have plenty to talk about.

After spending time with Ian in the United Kingdom the girls and I moved on to Paris, where after a few days we arranged to collect a hire car and drive out of the city. Neither Lisa nor I slept much the last night in Paris, anticipating everything that could go wrong with driving out of the city. It was actually trouble-free and once we left the *périphérique* and took our first minor road we all relaxed. Lisa did all the driving as I was too timid and Holly was just sixteen. We drove via Burgundy and into the south where we stayed for a week. We picnicked beneath Mont Saint-Victoire, enjoying an absolutely delicious *tielle sétoise* (squid pie) and a *fougasse aux grattons* (bread studded with pieces of bacon) bought from a market stall while trying to recall Cézanne's paintings of this mountain seen so recently in the Musée d'Orsay. I certainly retained the memory of the squid pie and it became a favourite dish for some special occasions in the restaurant. We then sat up all night on a train to Venice, not something I will ever do again.

My notes tell of visiting the Accademia Gallery. It was so wonderful for me to visit these galleries with the girls, who really wanted me to offer explanations and set the work in a historical context. Wonderful, but my memory was severely taxed. (I had flashbacks to those confused fine arts lectures so long ago.) I was also aware of my lack of a Christian upbringing. I was simply unable to explain the finer points of why a head or a breast was on a plate, or why St Sébastien was full of arrows.

This year marked a watershed in Lisa's life. She reconnected with her stepmother and brother Simon in England, and she visited Jamaica and wondered if that was where her future lay. I acknowledged her need to consider this option but in my heart I dreaded that she would decide to stay. I wondered whether she felt closer to her father's memory in Jamaica than anywhere else. She has told me that during this trip she developed even closer ties with her Jamaican and Canadian cousins and aunts and uncles. On the tenth anniversary of Monty's death Lisa, together with her Aunt Lee, the wife of Monty's brother Mervyn, visited the family memorial to her father in the quiet countryside of his childhood. And she decided that she couldn't feel comfortable living in Jamaica – she was too Australian. Soon after this realisation she rang and said she was coming home. I was delighted and relieved.

Lisa was able to return to Australia secure in the knowledge that there would always be a welcome for her in Jamaica and in Canada. However, at this stage in her life, Jamaica still represented deep loss. It would be twelve years before she returned.

The nineties was proving to be a very significant and jam-packed decade for all of us. The Australian Tourism Commission planned three dinners in the United States in 1992 to promote the diversity and richness of Australia as a culinary destination. They had decided that my recently published food travelogue *Stephanie's Australia* would be a focus for these dinners. It was the first Australian food book to concentrate on some of our pioneer food suppliers, highlighting the issues they faced as well as their triumphs. So much has changed since that time. This book is now out of print and many of those championed have moved on or are no more, and yet it still tells an important story.

I was asked to execute dinners in New York, Los Angeles and San Francisco and I planned the detail with my then head chef, Geoff Lindsay. I wrote about these dinners in detail in *Stephanie's Seasons*, a diary of my culinary year, including that as our plane circled Los Angeles airport we saw fires burning. We touched down to be told that the city was rioting as an all-white jury had just acquitted four policemen of charges relating to the bashing of a young Black man Rodney King. The dinner in New York went well; however, due to the rioting in those cities the dinners in Los Angeles and San Francisco were less well attended.

Geoff and I took advantage of being on that side of the world to visit some wonderful restaurants. San Francisco's Zuni was high on our list and we loved it, ordering its famous wood-fired oven-roasted chicken with a bread salad. I must say I find irresistible the combination of a butter- or oil-rubbed free-range chicken stuffed with lemon and herbs, roasted on a thick slice of bread that absorbs the juices and becomes a crunchy and sticky delectable crouton. We also visited Alice Waters' Chez Panisse in Berkeley, which I had visited with Maurice once before and described to my friends and staff. Chez Panisse was a successful example of all that I believed central to a fine restaurant. The brilliant and beautiful still life of fruit and flowers as one entered the dining room sets the tone, promising that all the senses would be engaged by the experience. And so it proved.

The menu at Chez Panisse offered diners exceptional raw materials. There was respect for those who produced or grew this food, thoughtful combinations of ingredients, simplicity of presentation and culinary precision all coming together in absolutely delicious dishes. Alice came and sat and talked, bringing with her a plate of fragile wild strawberries for a final and memorable taste for the evening.

In 1992 came a sad but momentous milestone. Elizabeth David, my literary inspiration, died. I wrote about this in my second book, *Stephanie's Feasts & Stories*:

> I was once so impressed by a few paragraphs in *Italian Food* extolling the delights of the rich and savoury fish soups of the Adriatic as she had experienced them near Ravenna in 1954, that I trekked to the same spot by bus and on foot on a grey rainy day, foolishly and romantically hoping to find the same joyful dish more than twenty years later. Although the restaurant still existed (complete with modernised aluminium windows) the fish soup was not on the menu that day. Still I will always remember Ravenna because of this experience (and I did after all spend part of the day marvelling at the Byzantine mosaics at San Vitale) and I am sure that Elizabeth David would have understood.

Elizabeth David's recipes were different. They coloured in the background, put in the people, even suggested the weather, described the journey, and I remembered all of this whenever I prepared a dish she had described, or one close to it. It may seem presumptuous to claim likeness with Elizabeth David but I recognise in myself the same need to add personality to my recipes. Like her I sometimes distance myself from other people, especially if 'other' people in fact means a noisy crowd. And I work hard and sometimes play too hard. I think she did too.

In her unauthorised biography of Elizabeth David, Lisa Chaney claims David was often insensitive in her responses to others. I have been accused of this many times. What I think of as clear and direct communication can be received as highly critical and hurtful. I also read that she had an excellent memory and that she kept notebooks. As I have said, much of the reminiscence that fills these pages has been assisted by the nearly two hundred notebooks I have kept over the last thirty years. I also feel in tune with the way Elizabeth David drew on her travel experiences to record authentic dishes, more of them emanating from ordinary households and daily life than recipes passed on from restaurant kitchens. And I feel another link in our need to surround ourselves with the tools of our trade that are not just functional but are also aesthetically pleasing. Her knowledge of the provincial cuisine of all of France and the regional food of Italy has never left me wondering. She is on her own in her power to communicate the essence of a dish, to create an instant need to get to the kitchen and start cooking. Elizabeth David inspired my mother, who introduced me to her work, and it is a rare week that I do not dip into one of the works of this extraordinary writer.

Claudia Roden, another fine food writer, was the special guest at the seventh Symposium of Australian Gastronomy, held in Canberra in 1993. We have met several times since, in London, where she cooked dinner for me, and in Tunisia, on an olive oil tour. I think it was in Tunisia that she showed me how to make kohl for lining the eyes with a burnt matchstick!

This symposium coincided with a major exhibition of Surrealist art. Once again we had a final banquet that was a performance piece as well as a meal. These final banquets were becoming very competitive. This one was designed by convenor Gay Bilson and crafted with the considerable help of Janni Kyritsis. The menu was not presented until the end of the evening. It read:

Stomach

Egg

Flesh

Bone

Skin

Blood

Heart

Milk

Fruit

Virgins' breasts

Dead men's bones

No-one present will ever forget the 'stomach' element – a tablecloth of cleaned but unbleached tripe in colours of 'dirty beige, muddy brown and brindled black', as described by convenor Barbara Santich. Or the bandaged waiters. Or the piles of marrow bones, a single bone wrapped in gold leaf in each pile (a reference, it was said, to a line from John Donne – 'a bracelet of bright hair about the bone'), to spread on toast to accompany a very fine consommé. Or the blindfolding of every diner. Or the child rising from a centrepiece of figs and grapes.

Much more down to earth but very, very delicious was the 'Poverty Lunch' prepared and presented by Sean Moran at the ninth symposium in 1996. It took place in the sandstone buildings of East Sydney TAFE, which was once Darlinghurst Gaol. We offered our bowls like Oliver Twist to receive our portion of corned hogget and pease pudding, accompanied by absolutely delicious brussels sprouts slow-cooked with onion. (Brussels sprouts had been the least favourite vegetable of my childhood and to find them to be remarkable was a triumph.) On our table we had dripping flavoured with rosemary and garlic to spread on our bread.

I attended one of the Oxford Food Symposiums in the mid-nineties, 'Going Today – Gone Tomorrow', intrigued to experience what had been the catalyst for the Australian gatherings. People from all corners of the globe and very different walks of life descended on Oxford for this annual conference.

The best papers were marvellous and I will never forget the presentation by Irishwoman and food historian Regina Sexton on the food of County Cork. I can still see her flashing dark eyes as she talked with relish of *drisheen*, the blood sausage of Cork, and of 'a pig that died with a smile on its face'. She spoke of *crubeens* – pigs' feet, fresh and salted. Six or seven dozen *crubeens* would be bought and boiled to satisfy the guests at the 'afters' of a wedding. Saltiness led to increased thirst and it was not unknown to wake up after a party with your lips stuck together (and a hangover). Knuckle bones were given to babies as we might give them a dummy! Cooked salted pigs' tails wrapped in cones of newspaper were frequently carried by children on the streets as they played at games. The image of babies in their strollers sucking on knuckle bones rather than dummies is unforgettable!

I have long been fascinated by tripe – both its culinary possibilities and the polarising effect it has on different people. So I was delighted to listen to a Mr Shipperbottom giving a dissertation on the vanished tripe halls of Manchester. There were two hundred and sixty specialist tripe shops in Manchester in 1906; in 1994 there were none. In 1917 a tripe restaurant opened in Wigan, seating three hundred, with panelled walls, palm trees and a ladies' orchestra and called the Tripe de Luxe Restaurant and Tea Room! How could one not be delighted with such dissertations. The memory still makes me smile – a bit like the pig!

During the nineties the International Olive Council and the Boston not-for-profit group Oldways Preservation Trust sponsored visits to various olive-oil-producing countries. The thrust of these meetings was to promulgate the health benefits of extra virgin olive oil and to enjoy the traditional offerings of the countries visited. These meetings included seminars and discussions but the organisers also included memorable experiences not usually available to a casual traveller. And always emphasis was given to the local food. In 1993 it was Tunisia.

The breakfast buffet served in our hotel was fascinating: a porridge made from sorghum mixed with fresh dates; chick pea and semolina shortbread biscuits; marinated fish; platters of halva; a bowl of pomegranate seeds, delicate sheep's milk ricotta cheese, hummus, plates of tomatoes and of course olive oil; quince paste and pale, creamy butter. Not a cornflake in sight.

I loved the street food, the *briks* made from tissue-fine pastry, the light-as-a-feather beignets fried in olive oil, the coiled breads balanced on trays held aloft by small boys, the snails sizzled on a charcoal brazier. (Back home I made my version of the delicious chick pea soup I had loved in the market known as *lab labi* with chunks of bread, harissa, crushed spices and a soft-boiled egg).

We ate sun-warmed dates in an oasis in the desert, walking on layers and layers of beautiful carpets thrown over the sand. We visited far-off Berber villages, built into the hillsides. We sat on roughly sewn-together pieces of carpet and lunched on a whole roasted goat we had to tear apart with our hands and freshly baked bread with olive oil and harissa. We visited the famous mosque at Kairouan, my first ever mosque so I was dumbstruck by the beauty of the blue and green tiles, the keyhole arches, the cream plaster sculpture resembling the finest embroidery – all whirling lines, circles, teardrops, diamonds.

Back home my beloved father was getting older. By the early nineties he was eighty-four and finding it harder to cope on his own at Mornington, and it was obvious to Diana and me that something would have to change. With everything else that was happening, my trips to Mornington had become fortnightly rather than weekly and both my brothers still lived interstate. I started looking for some sort of supported accommodation near me where I felt he could be happy and where he could still keep his books, music and some other cherished possessions. It was not easy.

He was initially very apprehensive but admitted that he would prefer to be nearer his daughters. In 1994 he moved to supported accommodation in Hawthorn, a fifteen-minute walk from my house although a three-quarter-hour drive for Diana. For the next eight years I took the major role in his care, organising frequent appointments with dentists, skin specialists, eye doctors, neurologists and general practitioners.

Preston Reid, a friend of Dad's from Essendon days, was also widowed and in need of extra care. Preston moved into the same establishment and for several years these old friends shared a whisky together after dinner and listened to some beautiful music, chosen by Dad. They were both pretty deaf and worried in case the volume of the music was offending other residents. I bought them both fancy headphones so they could sit and sip and listen in peace.

This happy time ended when Dad had a fall and minor stroke in 1998. It was decided that he needed to move to a nursing home. Diana and I did some investigations and found a brand-new facility that seemed to offer every comfort and whose advertised care left nothing to be desired. It was a private nursing home and all four of us needed to make contributions to meet the monthly fees. It started well. Diana and her daughter Penny visited Dad regularly, my brothers wrote and telephoned. I visited twice a week. Lisa and Holly came as often as they could. Dad continued to read widely until his eyesight deteriorated. I then brought him large-print books as well as videos. The works of Shakespeare were perennial favourites. Happily he owned a lovely well-spaced edition with each play in a single volume that he could manage. He designed short programs of classical music from his extensive collection of CDs and offered a weekly music program to the other residents. By this time he needed a wheelchair.

In my eighth book, *Stephanie's Journal*, I wrote of this time:

> At eighty-eight Dad is writing down his memories of the latter part of his life and he spends a lot of time reviewing videos he has made of the travels he enjoyed with Mum. Yesterday he asked me for an atlas to better follow the images. Today it was their trip through the Brenner Pass and into northern Italy. I think he is communing with Mum as much as anything else, and I find him wistful and melancholy. Old age is not great. Saddest of all is that the world has shrunk to become not much bigger than his room . . . For one formerly passionate about world politics and to whom we all turned for the big picture to help us better understand every territorial conflict, he now admits to skimming the newspaper and finding most of it irrelevant . . . He is just so lonely.

As in many other nursing homes, staffing was a major issue. The use of casual staff was necessary but it meant that there was very little continuity and no possibility of friendships between staff and residents. In the relatively short time my father was there, senior management changed every few months. I spent a considerable amount of nervous energy raging and railing against the lack of service, the indignities he suffered, the appalling lack of consistency, the terrible food, and a thousand other small and large problems that he poured out at every visit. Aged care is difficult and the very old can be cranky and opinionated. My father was both of these things but he had all his mental faculties and could not understand how a polite request to, for example, please close his door so that the fluorescent light did not shine in his eyes all night, could be repeatedly ignored. Or why a nurse assisting him to shower would leave him naked on a chair with the door to the passageway open so she could shout to a colleague. Or why his necessary hearing aids were not put in correctly day after day. I was making him meal-sized portions of delicious soft chicken or veal braises until I was told in no uncertain terms that it was against health regulations for nursing home staff to serve 'outside food' to residents. So it was back to unchewable meat, stale frozen fish, scoops of lumpy mash, and unripe fruit. Oh dear, I could go on and on and I feel my temperature rising even writing it down.

The girls and I had by now moved to our new house, still in Hawthorn and very close to the restaurant. Maurice was living not too far away so that he and Holly could still meet. Our divorce was finalised in 1992 and Maurice then took over the ownership of the Barwon Heads house. He loved the ocean and I think the security of a mortgage-free piece of real estate also helped him recover.

I decided that one thing I could do for Holly was accede to her request to get a dog. And so Rosie came into our lives. She was a chocolate-brown fluffy ball when we got her – a miniature poodle that stole our hearts (and frequently the napkins from our laps, if she felt she was being ignored). She was bright and mischievous, endlessly entertaining. I am sure many mothers will sympathise when I say that although Rosie was Holly's dog, the responsibilities of ownership eventually came to me when Holly left to spend an exchange year in France in 1993, and later to complete her degree with a semester at university in France.

In 1993 as the time drew near for Holly's year-long absence I felt increasing dread. At the airport, Lisa and I were concentrating on keeping brave faces, until Holly had us both completely undone by turning back from the doors at Immigration, rushing back, her small fingers white to the knuckles as she dug in, sobbing, for one last hug that had to sustain us both for ten long months.

Holly had a mixed experience in her exchange year in France. Her first host 'family' was an elderly woman with adult sons no longer living at home. The house was in a remote village in Brittany and nowhere near any recreational facilities. Holly went to and from her school by the school bus and then had little to do for the rest of the evening but share a two-seater couch with Madame and listen to her making racist comments about the immigrants she blamed for all social ills in France. (Plus she was fed packet mashed potato – she had been hoping for the delights of *cuisine bourgeoise*!)

I was horrified and it took too long to extricate Holly from this situation. Her second 'family' was a complete contrast and a wonderful choice. With them Holly went hiking, explored historic places, experienced real French food (it was from one of their meals together that she sent me a photo of her eating snails with gusto), dramatically improved her French, and she kept up the friendship for several years after returning home.

Holly was an excellent correspondent and she wrote long letters home. (*Letters* in those days, rather than short emails!) Lisa was now living with Catherine Tinney and I missed having my girls around me. Rosie was pretty good company but it was not the same. Over the fifteen years of Rosie's life Holly was often absent and I was the loving stepmother.

As co-owners of Stephanie's Restaurant Dur-é and I made sure that one or the other was at the restaurant at most times, although we left the responsibility of closing each night to our trusted staff, which meant that very late nights were now quite rare. Both of us took short holidays several times a year, negotiating with each other and again with our wonderful senior staff. We had many more quiet 'services' in the first part of this decade, and frequently could sit and enjoy a meal in the dining room ourselves, invite friends to join us, or take an evening off. I also worried a lot about the financial health of the business.

My own creativity was sustained and challenged by travel, by the excitement and anxiety of creating new menus, and by writing about it all. By the nineties I had settled into the routine of a seasonal change of menu at Stephanie's Restaurant with only minor changes if a product was no longer available. I was always excited and fascinated to discover someone who grew or produced something edible and delicious, be it sour cherries, marsh samphire, new varieties of waxy potato, or fresh peppercorns from Queensland.

I had a collection of shoeboxes in a tall cupboard in my study (I still do). They were the initial repository for torn clippings, sometimes a thought, sometimes a recipe I thought I might like to try, sometimes an article that I found fascinating. Over the years the shoeboxes filled to overflowing. But one day I would ask myself where had I seen the idea of lamb shanks cooked with lemons but without liquid in a sealed clay pot and I would go tunnelling through the paper until I found this 'recipe' torn from a travel article written by someone travelling in Crete. And then I would try it, make adjustments and decide if it had a future in my repertoire or not. My notebooks from these years are full of new dishes, including sketches of how the dish might be presented. A random sampling mentions:

cured duck breast ham with pickled cherries. (These small bandaged parcels hung from broomsticks in the cellar until deemed ready to slice) . . . Salad of duck confit, duck cracklings and pig's ear with a cumquat vinaigrette . . . black silky chickens served with purple congo potatoes with a ragout of sweetbreads and oyster mushrooms . . . cold-smoked kangaroo with a salad of braised leaf chicory . . . terrine of confit pigeon, with pigeon livers and baby turnips . . . duck breast grilled over rock salt in the manner of a *magret* . . . thin beef steaks with crushed fresh Queensland peppercorns . . . mussel, saffron and red mullet soup with its rouille and garlic croutons . . . candied angelica and honey tartlets . . . fruit poached in a syrup infused with orange blossom . . . freshly baked madeleines, served warm from the oven . . .

There were also special dinners to be planned for small or large groups, teaching commitments to be met at various Australian cooking schools, promotions to be organised that involved local or overseas travel, and the complications of arranging to export produce. We sent chilled Tasmanian Atlantic salmon and live marron to London for two different promotions, which necessitated employing a customs agent and learning about bills of lading and other paperwork I immediately forgot once the event was over, as well as meeting producers and achieving long to-do lists each week.

Over the years I had often discussed restaurant life with Graham Little, my brother-in-law. After a glass or two of wine Graham would indulge his fantasy of being the perfect host of some swanky club. We often spoke about food and about pleasure and anxiety, themes that featured over and over in my life and which were also important to Graham. At one point he was writing a chapter on gluttony for a book entitled *The Eleven Deadly Sins* to be edited by

Ross Fitzgerald. I lent him my bulging bouquets-and-brickbats file, which he found fascinating. It catalogued fifteen years of compliments and complaints (many more compliments than complaints!) and offered rich material for his investigation of public attitudes to restaurant dining.

By this time every customer arrived at Stephanie's Restaurant with very high expectations – sometimes seemingly that magic would happen. I could not guarantee magic and nor could Dur-é or any other member of our talented staff. I was too vulnerable to negative criticism (and I still am). Fifty smiling and happy customers were never sufficient to offset a negative remark from one surly person, or one unfortunate letter of complaint. Most of the wait staff had a more philosophical attitude and accepted that it was not possible to please everyone, although I suspect I believed the opposite.

In the early nineties Lisa had been working full-time in a university bookshop and also studying for a post-graduate qualification in Media and Public Relations. After graduating she transferred to a successful career in arts publicity. Holly had commenced an Arts degree and in 1997 returned to France to spend a semester at Jean Moulin University in Lyons to complete her degree.

On her way home to Australia Holly travelled via Canada, which is where she had her *Anne of Green Gables* experience; the book had been one of her favourites as a young child. Holly arrived in Halifax, looked at a map and decided to hire a car and drive to Prince Edward Island to visit the famous house. Like her father would have done in similar circumstances, she wanted to travel the most scenic route, ignoring the fact that it would take longer. She estimated the drive would take a couple of hours but the scenic route, coupled with the fact that it started to snow, made it several hours longer. She had never driven in snow, was unsure whether she should have chains on the car, and it was getting dark. She arrived at the Anne of Green Gables house at five past five and, despite her pleas about having come all the way from Australia, she was refused entry. She still has pictures of the exterior!

Around 1995 my partnership with Dur-é was becoming frayed around the edges. There were no profits to share, just mounting debts. I started to wonder whether it might be a good idea for me to open another, more informal business. Would customer expectations be more realistic? Dur-é already had interests in other restaurants and spent a lot of time advising her distant staff by telephone. Strangely she was not at all pleased when I expressed interest in investing in another business myself.

Dur-é and I tried to be creative and plan an exit strategy, and in mid-1996 called for expressions of interest in Stephanie's Restaurant. However, there was no response. No-one wanted to step into what I had to acknowledge were pretty big shoes. The public interpreted our announcement as meaning that the restaurant was about to close and they came in droves. Effectively the misreading of the announcement helped us limp through hard times. We owed too much money to ever contemplate closing unless we had an excellent offer, so the message to both of us was 'Keep going'. But underneath our brave faces there was growing tension.

I enjoyed two other marvellous holidays tucked into the difficult nineties, to Japan and to Vietnam. As it was for my parents, 'taking a holiday' always seemed like a good idea when I was faced with a difficult decision or with the need to chart a new course. I could never ignore the many problems surrounding me at this time, but I could push them away for a time. Both trips left me with wonderful memories and much to think about. And sometimes the subconscious mind threw up possible solutions to problems.

I gratefully accepted the invitation of Professor Richard Hosking to visit him in Hiroshima for a week. Having met Richard at the

1996 Symposium of Australian Gastronomy, I knew that he spoke fluent Japanese and was deeply interested in the food and social customs of this country. And of course I had my mother's memoirs to remind me how much she had loved her time in Japan. There was also another important family connection.

The city of Hiroshima has ghastly significance for the whole world and for my family in particular as it was here that my uncle Wilfred Burchett reported on what he saw immediately after the dropping of the atom bomb in 1945. He was the first Western journalist to enter the city and his headline appeared in the *Daily Express* in London on 6 September 1945:

THE ATOMIC PLAGUE:
'I Write This As A Warning To The World'
DOCTORS FALL AS THEY WORK
Poison gas fear: All wear masks

I was four years old at the time of this headline but its importance and Wilfred's scoop has been periodically reviewed and remembered over the intervening sixty-plus years. (I write this in 2011 as the world looks on aghast at the tragedy unfolding in Japan in the aftermath of the earthquake, tsunami and nuclear plant breakdown.)

My mother's interests had been in art and landscape and of course food. My interests were similar, with the bonus of having helpful interpretation of sights, tastes and customs from Richard and his Japanese friends. These friends made sure I did not leave their country without seeing the best of its culture, be it culinary, religious, architectural or theatrical.

At the market in Kyoto I bought a lump of cured, air-dried bonito called *katsuobushi*. Without prior knowledge no Westerner would recognise this as fish: it feels like and looks like a lump of wood although it still has a faintly pungent smell. In the market women stood to buy small packets of bright pink shavings as they curled off the special cutting tool, like a large carpenter's plane. (Just as Italian women stand patiently in the *salumeria* to have their prosciutto sliced.)

When I asked my mother's cousin Betty what she remembered of her Japanese holiday with my mother in 1937 she mentioned the tea ceremony at once. My mother wrote about the experience:

> In a Teahouse built away from everyday living it is easier to feel tranquil and surrounded by beautiful things; it is easier to think uplifting thoughts. When every eventuality has been foreseen and behaviour proscribed the mind is free to reflect, and surrounded by elegant simplicity every guest learns to appreciate the beauty that owes nothing to cost.
>
> Water from a mountain spring is esteemed above that from a tap and the perfect tea kettle is a simple black iron one. The tea bowls are not made of beautiful porcelain but of heavy handmade pottery and they are valued for the texture of the glaze or for their homely shape.

I am especially pleased that I have my mother's Japanese iron tea kettle. It has gained extra significance now that I realise how much she loved it.

My visit to Vietnam was as part of a group tour organised by my friend, chef Tony Tan. Our tour started in Hanoi. As always a visit to the market was a highlight and some of the sights were challenging. Freshness is vital in such a steamy city so there was no room for sentiment. Live paddyfield crabs were pushed into hand-cranked mincers, their legs waving feebly as they were crunched up to be sold quickly as crab paste to melt into soup. Legs were ripped off live frogs, and eels were beheaded and skinned alive. All shellfish and fish were sold alive.

There was plenty of fascinating food ready to go – shredded unripe papaya, shredded banana flower, peeled garlic, bean sprouts with tail removed, a wall of bananas (green, ripe, red) and a coconut stall with freshly grated coconut and freshly squeezed milk. Our market guide stressed precise combinations of salad leaves and herbs to accompany or be cooked with specific dishes. This leaf (*rau rút*) and this root were to be used for cooking crabs, this herb was to be used when braising eels with fermented rice and beer, perilla leaves were a vital ingredient when cooking freshwater snails with green banana and turmeric, wild betel leaf was used for wrapping morsels of seasoned beef before grilling, sawtooth coriander was to be sliced into *pho* and so on and so on.

Such specific knowledge is essential in preparing the many delicious and subtle flavours I experienced. It is also what prevents me from trying to cook most Asian dishes. I do not have this knowledge and although I am interested to observe and delighted to taste, I am very happy to let Tony or a Vietnamese chef prepare my dinner.

A few days later in the south, we explored part of the Mekong delta in small flat boats. We visited communities on tiny islands (once the impenetrable stronghold of the Vietcong) where families made sweets from coconut, or where they harvested honey and served us tea sweetened with the honey and sharpened with a squeeze of calamansi (a kind of citrus).

The gentle charm of the Vietnamese people, the beauty of their countryside, and the freshness of their food impressed everyone in our little group. I will return. Until I do, the food in Victoria Street, Abbotsford, is an accessible reminder.

17

A is for Apple

The Cook's Companion 1992–6

I needed to write. My short pieces appeared mostly in the 'Epicure' section of *The Age*. These impressionistic articles were written while I was travelling somewhere, either within Australia with a focus on sourcing great suppliers or simply recharging the batteries, or overseas visiting restaurants or enjoying food experiences or rural idylls. My editors appreciated this style in the eighties and nineties and so did the readers. Sadly it seems there is less and less space for this sort of discursive writing and nowadays most editors want it short and snappy with a big food-on-plate picture and a recipe.

I wrote six books in the nineties, including the life-changing *Cook's Companion*. Less ambitious works had preceded it. My first book, *Menus for Food Lovers* was published in 1985. I discovered that I loved explaining and encouraging, and the response from the public was that they appreciated having techniques explained in simple language.

The next was *Stephanie's Feasts and Stories*, published in 1988, which drew on many of the travel experiences I had written about in my columns. The reader moved with me from Venice to Hong Kong to Verona to Greece, to Bali to Burgundy and the south of France and places in between. I tried to link the dishes described to the location and to explain why I had been inspired by the experience. Sometimes this 'taste memory' included a glimpse of scenery – a herb-scented picnic spot, a bustling marketplace, a roadside mushroom stall. Sometimes I was reminded of a warm evening and a sea breeze. Sometimes I remembered an explanation of an important detail – the round 'female' fennel bulbs are sweeter and less stringy than the flatter 'male' bulbs, said the man in the marketplace in Verona. And often the recipe reflected my pleasure in a shared experience.

The first of two diaries, *Stephanie's Seasons*, appeared in 1993. It included an account of a month spent in 1992 in a farmhouse in flood-torn Provence and the trials of running a restaurant during a recession.

These descriptive books sold well but spectacular success had to wait for the next big project. Perhaps it took me too long to realise that my greatest talent was the power to inspire by example, with words as well as actions, drawing upon my considerable reserves of real-life experience and commonsense. Also important was my ability to hear the concerns and anxieties of real people – people who worked hard, wanted to live well, loved their children and their friends and actually changed their behaviour because of what I said. Often I overheard friends or strangers expressing doubt at their ability to make this or that, or I would look with dismay at the contents of trolleys in the supermarket queues, packed with mixes, frozen meals, instant noodles, packets of powdered soup, or some preparation that just needed the cook to add water or an egg. I did not believe that the reconstitution of these products would bring joy to the cook, nor would it fill the kitchen with enticing smells, nor would it offer an opportunity for Mum or Dad to involve their children in mixing or stirring or rolling. I just knew that I was able to lessen anxiety and raise expectations of what could be achieved in the average family kitchen. I have always known that a bit of my enthusiasm and relaxed attitude in the kitchen rubs off on anyone, young or old, male or female, who spends time at the kitchen bench next to me. After all, this is exactly what I had been doing for many years, working alongside young apprentices and kitchenhands. And I also knew that I could do it without belittling anyone and, even better, with humour.

Many years before and as a first-time author in the early eighties I had asked my friend Diana Gribble to help me interpret my very first publishing contract. Di and her friend Hilary McPhee had established the iconic McPhee Gribble Publishing house several years before. Di said she thought I should 'write a book with everything you know about cooking'. At the time I ignored this advice and continued with my more descriptive titles. History would show that her instincts were, as usual, correct.

By 1992 my first thoughts of writing an alphabetical guide to ingredients started to move beyond just thoughts and became a slim file on my computer. I fiddled with the structure for some time until the shape of this book began to declare itself. I was pretty excited and kept the project under wraps for many months. As I reread each section I had a growing sense that something really different was being created as my fingers flew over the keyboard. I seemed powerless to keep the word count under control. Once I had identified the major varieties of an ingredient, I knew that the reader or cook also needed to know what to look for in the shop. They would also appreciate knowing how to handle the item once they brought it home. And then they needed to know how to cook it, how it was cooked in other cultures and what flavours married especially well with it.

It was then that I hit on one of the most popular design features of the book. Sometimes a cook has just a few minutes and wants simply to combine a bit of leftover cooked lamb with something to make a quick snack or a simple salad. I included quick ideas that became the 'marginal recipes'. I meet many people who tell me that they mostly use the recipes in the margins.

Writing this book began to fill up all my leisure time, and I would be at the computer by six in the morning and eagerly dash back to it at ten o'clock, at the end of a busy service at the restaurant, for another hour or two. The pile of printed copy grew and grew.

The pattern at Stephanie's Restaurant was to note down recipes on system cards; a new version would be written on a different card. I still have my original and very precious cards and when I open the drawer to check for an early version of something the faint biscuity smell of cooked flour wafts out. There are recipes written in so many different hands – here is one from Geoff, here Robert, here Simone, here David, here Annie, here Janni, here Tansy – nearly thirty years of trial and error in a few filing drawers.

In some way *The Cook's Companion* grew from this compilation of experience, the hints it contains, what the French call a *truc*, derived from genuine discoveries, the selection of one version rather than another, a considered preference or quite simply the best version we had tried. I initially thought that an alphabetical guide to ingredients with a few words of advice on choosing and storing them, as well as a few recipes ranging from the simple and straightforward to the more adventurous, would result in a thickish paperback. Once I started, my need to be precise, to ensure that I had covered all known anxieties, to reassure and inspire with effortless dishes, to include all the standard dishes a new cook would want to find in a single volume – well, it just grew and grew.

By the time I had completed the entries in the letter 'A' and was well into the letter 'B' I had to have a 'true confession' session with Julie Gibbs, my friend and publisher. She probably did a double-take when I pointed to the impressive pile of printed copy and told her that it represented just the beginnings of something I thought was going to be very special. My memory is that she was visibly startled, laughed out loud, gathered up the copy and went off to read it. She recalls going to Bob Sessions, then Publishing Director, who said very swiftly, 'Tell her to cut it.' Julie did not tell me this and I can only imagine that she must have been very persuasive. It was years later that Bob confessed his initial response to me.

I am grateful to dozens of industry experts who checked the copy and offered insights and understandings that greatly enriched the text and added to its authority.

Many of the recipes are from friends and colleagues, all of whom are acknowledged. This follows the tradition of the notebooks and recipe journals many of us have inherited from our mothers and grandmothers. So many of those recipes are annotated and as such are records of important friendships. My maternal grandmother's cookery book records the source of almost every recipe. I can read that Chocolate Walnut Bar is from Melba, and that Date Loaf came from Eunice. I wanted to record my friendships too. Some recipes are from the published works of friends and colleagues. Every one of them gave permission for their work to appear.

I was so fortunate to have such a supportive publisher. This monumental and brilliantly designed manuscript was never cut and the sales have vindicated the trust Penguin had in me. Julie Gibbs has been not just a good friend (and was endlessly encouraging during the bleak days when I was stuck on the letter 'C'), but is a publisher of rare skill and élan. She has never been afraid of a challenge, she recognises publishing gold, but she is also respectful of the author's words and intent. Her authors are fortunate to have her.

Design work went on at the same time as the all-important editing process. Sandy Cull produced the brilliant design that allowed the book to be accessible despite its load of text. (And how many other cookery books appeared after its publication that were straight-out copies of her elegant and excellent design, especially the placement of the marginal recipes and the breaking-up of the text!)

One of the hallmarks of the wonderful relationship I have forged with Penguin has been their investment in creative and intelligent editors and great designers. I worked wonderfully well with principal editor Caroline Pizzey. Daily bundles of a few pages flew between my home, the Penguin offices in Ringwood and the country town two hundred kilometres away where Caroline lived. Caroline and I would check our diaries and organise two- and three-day sessions at my home, where we laboured over these ever-growing piles of paper. Caroline was brilliant at ensuring that every entry was consistent with others and would gently force me to alter, amend, re-examine, re-measure and rephrase. I was often frustrated and scratchy when now and then an alternative for a precious word or phrase was suggested but Caroline was almost always right.

It is interesting to remember that although I had written the original manuscript as a Word document the editing process was entirely done with a paper copy. We shuffled mountains of paper. Was it because of its complexity, I wonder, with the need to go back and forth between entries constantly to check consistency? My more recent books have all been edited electronically, which is possibly more efficient, but obviously not as tactile.

There was a day, nearly three years from the one I had first started, when we declared ourselves finished. It had been a highly creative and deeply exhausting process, but both Caroline and I felt triumphant. Now it was up to others. It was published in October 1996, the culmination of four years' work.

Not a day goes by without someone coming up to me and confiding that they use the book every day. 'In fact it's my bible' most of them tell me. And they confide their favourite recipe. Rarely have two readers had the same favourite recipe. There can be no greater thrill for the author of a cookery book than to know that it is actually being used by so many people on a daily basis.

I also know that for many Australian cooks I have become part of the family. Again I hear over and over that when there is a dispute or indecision over how something is prepared, or when someone is short of an idea, they say 'Let's see what Stephanie says'. What a wonderful compliment that is.

The Cook's Companion was considered a huge gamble by Penguin. Eight hundred pages long and without any food-on-plate pictures, it crept onto the market. Both the publishers and the booksellers held their breath. Would the public spend the then considerable sum of seventy-five dollars on such a huge book? I think the initial print run was ten thousand copies. To the delight of all concerned it quickly became a publishing phenomenon.

The sales took everyone by surprise. I was whipped around the country on a book tour and heard over and over again funny stories from the small independent booksellers who had carefully looked at their budgets for Christmas ordering and had ordered maybe five copies. To their astonishment everyone wanted one. One of the largest supermarket chains had made a huge initial order and was selling the book at a significant discount as a loss leader. Various independent booksellers told me the same story. They went with a trolley and bought stock from this retailer, cutting their profit margin to almost nothing just so that their best customers had their copy before Christmas.

It was reprinted twice before Christmas 1996, and then, due to the annual shutdown of the printing firm in China, no more copies could be obtained until February. I was pessimistically certain that we would miss the thwarted Christmas trade, but in February, booksellers reported that the books were walking out the door. I was incredulous. I had written a smash hit!

The financial bonanza enabled me to pay off all debt to the banks, to buy out Dur-é so that I was the sole owner of Stephanie's Restaurant and to make sure that Maurice had a secure financial future. For the first time in five or six years I was looking at blue skies.

The book won several awards, including Best Food Book at the Gourmand World Cookbook Awards in 2004 and at the World Food Media Awards in 2005. And it was listed by UK magazine *Waitrose Food Illustrated* as tenth in a list of most useful cookery books ever.

The book was reprinted in a larger, revised edition in 2004, eight years after its initial publication, and more than ten years since the original research. At first a revised edition seemed to be a simple matter but a closer look revealed that much of the original text needed revision; new ingredients were available in our markets, which required whole new sections to be written; and the very popular marginal recipes needed to be expanded and, most importantly, indexed. By the time I was satisfied with this new work it had acquired three hundred and fifty new pages, twelve new entries (several of them expanded in scope), more than three hundred new recipes and about five hundred new marginal entries.

Julie Gibbs and the design team at Penguin understood that while many (including me!) had become strongly emotionally attached to the orange book, we needed to be seduced by the look and feel of this new model. The orange book became the stripy book with a striking cover, a reproduction of a painting by contemporary artist Matthew Johnson. Happily for my ongoing financial independence the book continues to sell steadily. It is consistently among the top ten cookbooks sold in Australia, fifteen years after it was first published.

My task with the revised edition was to retain the proven *Cook's Companion* tone. Maintaining a light touch, a softly-softly approach with more than a touch of whimsy and humour was important. The revision took two years.

Having been a librarian in an earlier life, the need to organise information has always been part of my style. As my father instructed us, I have always 'looked it up in the index'. These days I may Google the information that I'm after, but not without checking my own tried-and-true reference tomes. I do like to have a fact confirmed beyond reasonable doubt and I am intolerant of sloppy writing that ignores this step. And anyway it is part of the fun of writing to chase down a clue, see where it leads, and now and then make marvellous new connections. Another consequence of my library training is the attention given in both editions to meticulous cross-referencing. This is so often ignored in recipe books. A good index is a wonderful thing but cross-referencing is even better!

A new feature of the revised edition is a longish essay that attempts to set down my thinking about the food issues of the day: gene technology, aquaculture, hydroponics, advertising of junk food, organics, plant diversity and the food future for the next generation – serious issues for serious times. The response to the first edition has made me very aware of the responsibility that goes with becoming an authority on any subject.

Overwhelmingly, my main aim has been to remove anxiety from what should be a joyful part of life, to clear up mysteries and make cooking accessible to all. I don't think I can improve on the last lines of the introduction.

My commitment to *The Cook's Companion* continues to be central to my life. It will all have been worthwhile if this book encourages young people to start cooking and experienced cooks to enjoy cooking more.

18

Elderflower Fritters

Tuscany, Richmond Hill and the Last Big Bash

I have to jump back at this point to explain why I decided to set up house in Tuscany with more than thirty strangers and many friends for two whole months. In 1995 I had a memorable Italian holiday, this time in Umbria. Both my daughters were with me, as was Maggie and her husband, Colin, and later my publisher, Julie Gibbs. It was here that Maggie Beer and I planned our future Tuscan cooking schools.

We rented a hilltop villa at Monte Corona. Our nearest village was Umbertide and our nearest sizeable town was Perugia. Higher up, at the top of our mountain, was a monastery where the monks had taken a vow of silence. The ascent was steep but climbers were rewarded by a vista of a green and isolated world, unfolding as far as the eye could see. The deeply rutted track was edged by hawthorn, wild rose, elder trees, scrub-oaks, olives, prolific blackberries, flowering grasses and, in one very special spot, a carpet of delicate wild cyclamen. The elder trees were in flower and I mused about elderflower fritters, which are often written about and always sound very romantic. The flower sprays, or panicles, are picked and dipped into very light batter (which is best with a few drops of orange-flower water added), fried in olive oil and served dusted with sugar. It is not often noted that the blossom must be picked and used within twenty-four hours or the delicate honeyed fragrance and flavour disappears and you are left with a tasteless lump of batter. Also not often mentioned is the difficulty of picking these blossoms from a tree that might be ten metres tall.

The villa had a magnificent fig tree. We enjoyed paper-thin prosciutto with fresh figs, and a delicious sauté of potatoes, onions, garlic, rosemary and figs. Maggie had figs with yoghurt for breakfast. As there seemed to be no birds in Italy, the fig tree had not been violated. From our balcony we looked down on the unreachable top of the tree and could see figs that had split, displaying their ripe rosy interior. In Australia half the fruit would have been pecked over by this stage or the tree would have to have been netted.

Giovanna Garzoni, an artist of the late Renaissance, captured the seductive charms of a ripe fig in several of her luminous paintings, many of which I have seen in the Pitti Palace in Florence. I was reminded of them as I gazed at the fruit of our Tuscan fig tree. Her works are remarkable and reproductions of them are always nearby me as I work. (They were also the inspiration for the still-life photographs in my *Kitchen Garden Companion*, many years later.) You can almost taste and smell the blossoms and fruits set out on rustic family platters displaying the chips and cracks of daily usage.

I wrote my first entry in the notebook after dinner:

A pale full moon watched over us on our first evening. We had dinner on the terrace and all retired early to our respective rooms, to beds fluffy with feather quilts, swathed in froths of mosquito net, in rooms with stone floors, chestnut beams, creaky wooden doors and flickering uncertain lights. I slept with windows open and shutters wide and woke with the dawn. The villa floated above veils of cloud, the sky changed from pink to a watery blue.

Days passed easily with walking, talking, reading, and when we needed extra stimulation, driving to one of the nearby hill towns to explore and be delighted, shopping for food and other things, cooking and eating and drinking.

My mother had also enjoyed at least one holiday near this area of Italy and kept her own travel notebook as well as a sketchbook. I have two of her watercolours painted in the Tuscan town of Arezzo, one of which depicts a mushroom seller. She wrote:

Arezzo . . .
Because it was autumn it was funghi season and each day at the beginning of the *passeggiata* (the promenade hour) the funghi sellers came in from the surrounding countryside and squatted at the corner of Garibaldi Street and the Corso Italia with their boxes and baskets of what to us resembled strange, poisonous-looking mushrooms. Some were pale violet and fan-shaped but most were cinnamon brown on top and yellow underneath.

The funghi were sold by weight that was decided on old-fashioned brass balances, but no serious buyer would order even half a kilo without minute inspection. Each mushroom was selected with love and care before the buyer indicated that a particular mushroom could be added to those he or she had already selected.

I was interested in Arezzo firstly because I wanted to tread where my mother had trodden. Imagine the thrill of finding a man selling mushrooms at the corner of Via Garibaldi and the Corso Italia sixteen years after my mother had been intrigued by the same scene! Arezzo is also memorable for the brilliant paintings by Piero della Francesca in the Church of San Francesco depicting the *Legend of the True Cross*. I wrote:

> Italy is so mind-bogglingly rich in splendid works of art that one can soon feel overwhelmed. Overwhelmed as much by what one has not been able to see as by the extraordinary works that abound not only in famous palaces and galleries but tucked away in rarely visited villages. Not another church, I am horrified to catch myself thinking! Not another Pinturicchio! There is such a thing as sensory overload, not to mention sore feet!

We all adored the marvellous poultry bought in the marketplace in Umbertide. Guinea fowl, chickens, quail and pigeon were often on the menu. The flavour of these birds was outstanding. Maggie and Colin were sure that the dry hand-plucking made a difference to final flavour. In Australia almost all producers immerse birds in hot water before placing them in a plucking machine. The skin loses its tautness, some of its fat and probably also much of its flavour. And we were sure that these birds were farm-reared, probably on small farms and fed good things – certainly not pellets. I closely inspected the seeds and grains in the crop of the pigeons as I cleaned them and can definitely vouch for them.

We were enchanted by our Umbrian holiday and as we lazed in hammocks or relaxed after a lunch on our sunny terrace, conversation often turned to how we could return to this enchanting country for a longer period. Maggie and I started considering a residential cooking school that might take place towards the end of 1997, by which time, I assumed, the restaurant would have been sold and I would be somewhat more carefree. We were sure that we could communicate our enthusiasm to other Australian food lovers. Our idea was to seek to interpret the Italian repertoire in our own ways, paying full respect to local, seasonal ingredients and methods. We did lots of sums and even Colin started to take us seriously. Of course, we would need to find a suitable villa. How many students would we take? Who could we ask to help in this adventure? Where would it be? What would we cook? Julie Gibbs joined in the discussions and suggested a book might result from this plan.

Back in Australia I was involved in a new venture that brought me a lot of joy. I had located an ideal building in Bridge Road, Richmond, for a relaxed café and cheese room. A new consortium entered into the planning of this venture with excitement and plenty of energy. The original partners were Will Studd, my daughter Lisa and my friend Angela Clemens. Will is an Englishman who has become Australia's acknowledged cheese expert, with a special interest in high-quality European cheese. He also led the campaign in Australia to change regulations to permit the importation of cheeses made with raw milk and to allow local specialist cheese makers to use raw milk in their own production. This issue is still controversial and far from resolved but Will has never backed away from a fight.

I loved the space I found on Bridge Road. The building has so much character, with its huge, curved windows overlooking one of Melbourne's busiest retail strips. Richmond Hill Café & Larder was to be its name. I insisted on the old-fashioned word 'larder', as it had all the subliminal messages I wanted to convey – somewhere cool and well-ordered, with cream-coloured and yellow whole cheeses, mounds of butter, marble slabs, wooden scrubbed shelves, quality preserves and a few beautiful handcrafted objects.

We discussed setting up a cheerful, sunny café that would include a temperature-controlled and humidified cheese room modelled on the business we both knew well in London, Neal's Yard Dairy, owned by Randolph Hodgson, who had successfully championed the cause of traditional cheese makers in the British Isles. The shelves at Neal's Yard were laden with brilliant cheeses from all over Britain and Ireland, many made from unpasteurised milk. We planned a Cheese Club, also modelled on Neal's Yard Dairy.

In April 1997 Richmond Hill Café & Larder opened for business. It was soon obvious that the customers had pretty high expectations here too! Its instant success took us all by surprise. We were full in half an hour. Day one saw queues of people trailing out the door and down Bridge Road. At no time did I consider being more than a menu advisor and it was just as well, as the pace of service and the numbers kept the young staff almost running. Not to mention that I was still responsible for keeping up morale and standards at Stephanie's Restaurant across town.

Anna Dollard came into my life in 1997, just as the magnitude of these two businesses threatened to crush me. I was still working hard at Stephanie's Restaurant but the overwhelming public response to this less formal business in Richmond was astonishing. We had no office, few staff, a brand-new kitchen, few systems in place and still in poured the customers. Julie Gibbs came to have a look and stayed for a cup of tea. I related my woes, essentially saying I could not cope. Julie flicked open her phone and said, 'I believe Anna Dollard has just returned from Europe and doesn't yet have a job.' (Anna had worked as Julie's editorial and personal assistant at Allen & Unwin before Julie moved to Penguin.) And so it proved and Anna came into my life.

On her first day Anna came to the café and organised trestles for desks, set about sorting paperwork into useful piles, and I cannot remember what else. She radiated calm and purposefulness, and there was a collective sigh of relief.

Soon she moved into the office in my home at Hawthorn and set about ordering my life. With her background in publishing and a broad interest in the arts Anna was the perfect assistant for me. We both loved and respected words. Anna was far more punctilious than I am, and did not hesitate to pull me into line if I was about to put into print something she felt was inflammatory, or at least injudicious or, worse still, wrong. Her manner was always gentle but it could be firm. She also made me laugh often and we had many outings and adventures. Anna was the perfect accomplice.

As the date for the advertised Tuscan cooking schools drew closer, and without any serious offers for Stephanie's Restaurant, the Italian plan was starting to seem like insanity and the worst possible timing. By early 1997 we had secured deposits from many would-be students so Tuscany had to proceed. I had two months to shape up the systems at both establishments and to plan for my own two-month absence in Italy.

Fortunately the systems at Richmond Hill Café & Larder did not depend on my presence. I had several discussions with chef Nicky Reimer and the front-of-house team and felt satisfied that all would be well. At Stephanie's Restaurant Sonia Cooper and Valerie McLean would manage the front of house at the restaurant, Anna Dollard would manage all correspondence and requests for my time, Mark Bowdern would be in charge of accounts, Brian Wane would continue his calm management of the cellar and bar, and Jeff Wilson had a well-oiled team in the kitchen.

So I had to start packing.

It had taken us some time to find the right villa. We needed to accommodate seventeen people in comfort but not luxury and we needed a pretty good kitchen. It was inevitable that there would be compromises. When we finally located the Villa Corsano, a few kilometres from Siena, the fact that students would have to share rooms and bathrooms helped sort those who were probably least interested in cooking but more interested in a glamorous holiday with two well-known personalities, from those who loved to cook.

Strong friendships were forged. Maggie and I became deeply attached to our own support group. Tony was our major-domo, who kept our linen in impeccable order, created glorious flower arrangements and managed the refrigerators. Elena presided over the breakfasts for the guests, was creative and imaginative in her cooking, enchanted everyone and was indispensable in all classes. Careful and charming Peter Lortz did the driving and the inter-preting, guided the guests through wine tastings and looked after our mountainous stash of wine in the damp cellar. Later came our friend and photographer Simon Griffiths.

Maggie's extroverted and sunny nature shone and each group felt most warmly welcomed. I took longer to come out of my shell but hopefully after a day or so everyone felt pretty comfortable with everyone else.

The routine was that Elena and Tony would serve breakfast for the students in one of the two kitchens while Peter was out and about finding the day's ingredients. We then divided the group of twelve students into smaller groups and taught until around one-thirty, sharing tasks and utilising all the spaces in the villa and its gardens. Then Tony would set a magnificent table outside under the grapevines and lunch was enjoyed until around three-thirty. Time for a siesta and then we hoped that most of the students would be delighted to visit Siena for the *passeggiata* and dinner.

Maggie and I gave everything we could at these classes and sometimes by the evening we needed to be alone to debrief or simply relax. Sometimes we would take some sausages, a salad and a bottle of wine and escape to a shed by the pool. Tony or Peter would light a small fire and we would grill the sausages and eat our salad of radicchio, gorgonzola and toasted walnuts by firelight. The lights of Siena sparkled in the distance.

The three back-to-back schools took up nearly five of our eight weeks at the villa. The final three weeks were open house for friends and family. Colin Beer arrived, which brought an even wider smile to Maggie's face. Betsy Bradshaw arrived from Cambridge, where she and Malcolm were enjoying a sabbatical year. Lisa arrived from Melbourne, delighted to leave the madness of Richmond Hill Café & Larder for a short time. Angela Clemens and her husband, Duffy, came and as always brought good humour and fun. Holly came too, from Lyons. Julie Gibbs was there to share in the fun and to supervise the photography for the book.

The adventure is fully explored in *Stephanie Alexander and Maggie Beer's Tuscan Cookbook*, published in 1998. It also appears in *Stephanie's Journal*, my diary of 1997.

When I hear people say that they have loved every minute of their life, I cannot believe it. I certainly have not loved every minute of mine. Frequently I am asked whether I knew where I was heading, and I have to say I did not. I just wanted to go on. I suspect I did not dare to lift my head out of a difficult present to ponder how I might achieve a better or happier emotional life. The big picture usually seemed very foggy to me. I vented a lot to my close friends about how overwhelmed I felt and then just got on with it. When a specific problem loomed I worked to solve it. I did not ever consider admitting defeat if I really wanted something.

On the other hand, if I did not really care about something I could walk away without a second glance.

But I certainly loved travelling, experiencing new things and new tastes and being with kindred souls. The intimacy created by shared adventures has always delivered the most meaningful times of my life. I feel valued, cushioned and enriched by friends. Many of the travel stories in this book are also stories of friendships renewed and explored.

One date, 9 October 1997, was life-changing for me. I had arrived in Italy several weeks earlier extremely tense, my head bursting with various options for ways to resolve the financial and personal difficulties back home. I felt guilty about what I had left behind; my stomach was in knots; sleep was elusive. I could not see a way forward. And then, seemingly miraculously, under the influence of true friendship and empathy, overnight I dreamt of a different existence. The way forward suddenly seemed obvious. I wrote in my notebook and in *Stephanie's Journal*:

It is time to move on (from Stephanie's Restaurant) . . . Fate is extraordinary. To have come to this huge decision just at a time when I am in the company of someone who has made a similar one not so long ago in her own life would seem to have been planned. It was certainly not planned but there is no question that Maggie is the perfect sounding board. She understood the gravity of the decision and its implications that will affect my life from now on . . . distance has been important in coming to this conclusion. Away from the necessity of dealing with the daily grind I have been able to appreciate how rich life can be.

Here in Italy I have eaten under the stars, and in sunny gardens, walked in leafy woods, laughed and read books and had real conversations about meaningful things . . . and I want to do more of these things.

Maggie and I talked long and late about my decision. Six years before, in 1993, she had closed her hugely popular Pheasant Farm Restaurant. She was emphatic and confident that as one door closed many more would swing open. After a couple of glasses of Brunello di Montepulciano I became quite philosophical and even a little tearful.

Thanks to the unprecedented success of *The Cook's Companion* I had been able to buy out Dur-é at Stephanie's Restaurant earlier in 1997, so that now I could make the decision to close the business on my own terms, and complete the final year on a high, surrounded as ever by loyal and marvellous staff. Again thanks to *The Cook's Companion* I paid every dollar I owed to anyone.

It is worth spending a moment reflecting on what a different future I would have faced without the financial windfall from this book. I would certainly have lost my home. And I shudder to even consider how I would have gone on.

Anna Dollard was my trusted confidante and supporter through this most difficult period. I have a folder full of fading handwritten letters I faxed to Anna from Tuscany, with more and more detail about how I thought the closure would have to be managed. Anna did a Herculean job of reassuring me, acting on my every suggestion to contact lawyers, business brokers and bankers, as well as gently offering considered opinions that helped me fully understand all the options. Anna confided in the restaurant manager Mark Bowdern, who fed through accurate financials, and together they conferred with the other professionals and plotted and pointed out the only way through the morass. Rereading this material I am astonished that I remember the post-cooking-school three weeks in Tuscany as so marvellous, when it does seem as if every second day I was sending or receiving long complicated faxes.

I returned to Melbourne in November, ready and willing to plunge into the detailed planning needed for this life-changing move. Once the decision to close Stephanie's Restaurant was made public the telephone went crazy. Every food lover in Melbourne and beyond wanted to come for one last meal. I designed a farewell menu that brought together many of our best dishes from the seventeen years we had operated in that location. We were fully booked, serving more than one hundred and thirty diners every night. I was interviewed about the future and admitted to mixed feelings of anticipation tempered with trepidation as to what might lie ahead. I received many, many lovely letters from the public thanking me for happy times.

I made the decision to put all the awards and significant photographs that related to the restaurant into the State Library of Victoria, together with as many menus as I could find. Perhaps one day someone might want to know more about what happened in the Melbourne restaurant scene between 1976 and 1997. I did lots of sorting of cupboards, and eventually started to work on a speech that I would give at the final party.

As the closing date came closer I made a decision to send Holly a plane ticket to come home for the occasion. She was in the middle of her semester of university in Lyons but so much of her life had been spent in the restaurant that it did not seem right for her to be absent on its last night.

Anna planned most of the stupendous final night and party. The more than one hundred guests were a mix of friends, family and loyal customers, and of course all the marvellous staff from over the years. Anna loved a creative project, whether it was organising details of the Last Big Bash – including a surprise memorial menu booklet with lovely farewell words from staff members that I will treasure forever – or something humdrum, such as the post-auction sorting of piles of unpromising and rather depressing stuff to sell at Camberwell Market. Everything she did was marked always with the slightly quirky or surprising Anna touch.

In the booklet Anna organised, many staff members from years gone by wrote about what the restaurant meant to them. Geoff Lindsay, who worked at the restaurant from 1987 to 1993, wrote:

> It took about six months for the knot in my stomach to ease due to the intensity of the activity in the kitchen and the concentration demanded by Stephanie, but what an experience it turned out to be . . . I believe that Stephanie redefined food in Australia, and it is her tireless search for ingredients and specialist growers ten years ago that is rewarding young chefs of today with produce unequalled anywhere in the world.

From Elena Bonnici, who worked at the restaurant on and off from 1990 to 1997, it was:

> I've risen from the dead several times over for Stephanie Alexander; and it's the same for me each time I walk through that back door by the outside coolroom. I'm an apprentice again, overwhelmed by the love and professionalism housed inside those walls. It is addictive and always emotional.

Neil Perry, who worked at the restaurant briefly in 1982, wrote:

> I stood out the back, washing lettuce, each component of the salad picked and lovingly washed, just as you had shown

me. It was that experience that reinforced the idea that every single thing in the menu must be of the best quality . . . It was these experiences, and listening to you talk philosophies on food and the cook's life, that made me realise it was a hard road to travel down, but if one accepted the challenge, it would be wonderfully rewarding.

Here is some of what I wrote about the farewell party in the final pages of *Stephanie's Journal*:

In the car park there are banks of flowers in buckets. The marquee is being erected. Gift bottles of bubbly are being slipped into frothy organza bags and tied with satin ribbon. Shimmering gold and cream balloons arrive.

In the kitchen one hundred quail have been boned and filled with a foie gras stuffing. Two kilos of caviar arrive. The entire kitchen team tackles the mud crab: we have forty kilos of live crab to cook, cool and pick for the freshest crab salad . . .

Lorrie Lawrence is finishing an absolutely spectacular floral extravaganza. Every table, every sideboard, every corner is bursting with flowers. There are roses everywhere, peachy and pink and yellow and cream, and every table has fresh peaches.

Anna handed me my crown for the night – a circlet of deep-red fragrant rosebuds and a Venetian mask adorned with the same scented rose petals, in case anything became too much! . . . The final bash was the party to end all parties.

It was a truly intoxicating night and I was drunk on emotion not wine. Surrounded by loving family and friends and loyal staff it seemed as if the night would go on forever. Part of me could not believe that this was the end. Jenny Little wrote a perfectly lovely account of the evening, which I still have, and in which she reminds me: 'With her voice of old gold, Maggie Beer talked of the glory that is Stephanie. "She is world class. And we are the lucky country – she is ours."' In my farewell speech I said:

> I have experienced love, pain, divorces, separations, births, deaths, accolades, axes, friendship, manipulation and greed. But I have not been bored for one minute of these twenty-one years. Depressed, exhausted, anxious, angry, exhilarated, excited, intoxicated – but never bored.

The worst part of closing this chapter of my life was the aftermath of the final auction of all furnishings and equipment. I could cope calmly with the sale of tables and chairs but I watched in horror as strangers levered panels of stainless steel from the kitchen walls, hacked at the coolroom, wrenched taps from the walls, gouged at benches, dismantled hot water systems. What had been a scrupulously scrubbed and clean kitchen stood violated and filthy with gaping holes in the walls, dripping water pipes and engrained grease marks in the floor where the stoves had stood for seventeen years.

Strangely I have no memory at all of walking from the building for the final time. Presumably I handed keys to somebody. Nor do I have any recollection of the time immediately afterwards. But I know that I said, along with Billie Holiday, 'So I say goodbye with no regrets.'

19

Jerk Pork & Duck Fat

Family and the New Millennium

The new millennium dawned full of hope, and for me it came with a sense of freedom. I had completed the project Stephanie's Restaurant after twenty-one years of full-time effort – wonderful years, difficult years, exciting years.

But almost at once tragedy struck. In February 2000 my brother-in-law and friend Graham Little died suddenly. It was devastating for his wife Jenny and daughter Jessica and a very great loss for his family and his many, many friends. As one of his closest friends wrote at the time: 'I feel as if I have been dipped in bleach – most of the colour seems to have drained from my soul.' That was just how I felt too.

Graham had the rare and lovable quality of being able to encourage lively conversation at many levels without rancour or bitterness, even among those with divergent views. And in his company one always felt 'heard'. I miss his talk, his humour and his intellect. We had such great conversations around the Littles' wooden dining table, ranging through literature, politics, sociology, fashion, travel reminiscences – and always accompanied by plenty of laughter, good food and wine.

The following paragraph from Graham's book *Friendship* was printed on the memorial service booklet:

> Friends love nothing better than 'a good talk'. They seem always looking for talk, investing time and energy in it, enjoying it as an end in itself, treating it as both work and play. Witty or earnest, disjointed or smooth, angry, troubling or pleasing, a patchwork of light and dark, of strong feelings and cool, sharp ideas, a conversation is life in a microcosm.

Graham does not tell us how to say goodbye to our friends. The emptiness continues.

At this time Lisa was seeing a young man who shared her passion for cinema. He had an extraordinary knowledge of film history and the history of popular music. As I knew little about either topic our first meetings left us both a bit tongue-tied. He was quite shy and reserved with me but seemed to glow in Lisa's company. After less than a year of courtship they surprised me by announcing their intention to marry. We organised a wonderful party. Lisa looked stunning in a fuschia-pink dress and she carried red roses. She was ecstatic that her Uncle Spurgeon and cousin Ken made the trip from Canada to Melbourne for the occasion, as had her cousin Sharyn, all the way from Jamaica.

Nine months later Lisa and her new husband set off to travel to Europe and on to Jamaica. For Lisa this trip was highly significant. She had such strong memories of her last visit to her island, when she had felt bereaved and alone, overwhelmed by memories of her father. This subsequent visit promised to be more joyful. She arranged to meet her brother, Simon Montague, now also known as 'Monty', who had flown in from London, and they connected properly for the first time. They became good friends and, importantly, they both acknowledged how much they enjoyed being in Jamaica. I was delighted to hear that she was having such fun there, and especially pleased that she and Simon were enjoying each other's company. The pictures she sent home showed both Simon and Lisa with huge smiles, tucking into jerk pork at roadside shacks and enjoying rum cocktails at a remarkable bar that floated in the sea.

But at the same time, Lisa was having early doubts about her new relationship. At one and the same time she was experiencing both joy and sadness. She remembers that joy triumphed. Lisa said nothing about her relationship problems, preferring to wait until she had had longer to reflect and was back home again. Lisa and her husband separated soon after this holiday and were divorced in 2005.

In late 2002 my wonderful father died. He had become very frail although his intellect was still intact. For the last year he had needed regular blood transfusions necessitating uncomfortable overnight stays in hospital, and it was his own decision to cease them. He discussed this with me and told me that he was tired and felt that his useful life was over. I think he may have been testing me when he proposed that the doctor should be informed of his decision. It was an awful moment. All I could do was clearly restate that the transfusions were keeping him alive and that he alone could make the decision to stop them. I dreaded the next step but realistically there had not been a lot of pleasure for him in his last few months.

He died peacefully in his own bed two days later with Lisa and me holding his hands and Holly holding me. Diana and Marcus and her children and grandchildren came to say goodbye too. For a few weeks my world seemed to stand still. I miss him very much. I miss his wisdom, his even-handedness in discussion, his huge understanding of world conflicts, his sense of humour, his love.

Almost to the last decade of his life he was called upon by each of his children to advise and assist with DIY projects – creating bookshelves, shoring up tottering walls, helping with renovations – you name it, he could do it. Enterprising, practical and creative, he also had a sensible approach to small business. He fixed an important lesson in my mind: be adventurous, follow your dreams, but don't sell the family farm! Time and time again I heard how he and a friend or business associate worked out a good deal for all parties – he never thought of working things to his own advantage. I have nearly come unstuck in business by assuming that everyone operates in this even-handed manner. Not so!

And I miss his deep interest in all of my projects. Without a partner to share and confide in, my father was often on the receiving end of my doubts and concerns, and he carefully stored newspaper or journal cuttings that mentioned my work. He had always been my most devoted fan.

I have his films, his photos, a copy of his autobiography and a smiling happy snap of him and Graham chatting together at one of my Boxing Day lunches. It is no substitute. The impact of personal tragedies and sadness never disappears. In time you adjust to a new reality. Life does go on.

The same year that my father died I published my ninth book, *Cooking & Travelling in South-West France*, of which I know my father would have been so proud. This book is dedicated to Graham Little, 'who came on the first adventure'. I had experienced the beautiful Dordogne in the south-west of France on at least two happy holidays with Maurice, one of these was the trip with Jenny and Graham Little when Holly was a baby. So my fascination with this part of France had existed for almost thirty-five years.

I wanted to investigate the region again in all seasons of the year. Julie Gibbs felt certain that a book on this area would be a success so we organised two research trips to take place in the summer of 2000 and the autumn of 2001 to complement the material I had already gathered during earlier spring and winter visits and my memories from long ago.

Julie and I rented a renovated barn in a tiny village, Mercadiol, far from any major towns. When Air France lost our luggage they presented us with a traveller's emergency pack each, which contained a pair of underpants, a toothbrush, a comb and – curiously, we thought – a condom! We set off in our hired car and were assured our luggage would be sent on. We had no other clothes and even though the temperature was in the high thirties we needed to wear something. Julie went to the nearest supermarket and found two cotton sarongs and two T-shirts. We did look rather odd in a tiny French village in our beachwear! Two days later a courier from Air France did miraculously manage to find our little barn and all was well.

The book we were researching was to be beautifully illustrated with photographs by our friend Simon Griffiths and would be made up of my now-familiar mix of landscape, social comment and food lore, and of course recipes. I hired a French photographer to take pictures during my winter research trip.

We persuaded Maggie and Colin, and Angela and Duffy Clemens, to join us for our autumn trip. Anna Dollard came too. Cheese expert Will Studd was happy to help for a few days. One of the restaurants that Julie and I discovered is featured in the book and the proprietor of Le Pont de l'Ouysse is still astonished by the steady stream of Australian and New Zealand visitors the restaurant welcomes.

Cooking & Travelling in South-West France won a French award, Le Prix La Mazille, for best foreign cookbook in 2002 as well as best French cuisine book in the Gourmand World Cookbook Awards. I was delighted with this recognition.

I decided to make a quick trip to France in early November 2002 to collect the latter prize, with Holly as my travelling companion. It was lovely to travel with her but I had forgotten that, like her father, she has a low tolerance for rich food. We were made much of in Périgueux and every meal included *foie gras*, truffles, duck and duck fat. Holly faced every new meal with increasing horror. She suffered a true *crise de foie* and we had to make excuses to not attend any more of these eight-course banquets.

We can laugh about it now but I blush when I remember the night we were telephoned in our hotel to say that our seats beside the Ambassador in the reception hall of the Hôtel de Ville were empty and where were we? In this case no invitation had ever been delivered and we were both in our pyjamas, having eaten a light soup at a local café and looking forward to television and an early night. Probably we have still not been forgiven for this perceived lapse in etiquette.

At the end of this trip we enjoyed a few days together in Paris. Our room was in the attic of a small hotel. From my bed I could just see the gilded statue on top of the column in the Place de la Bastille. It is Paris in the spring they write songs about but for me the city has special appeal in this mellow, misty late autumn.

A morning treat was a coffee macaron from Mr Mulot, one of the world's great tastes. In his window was a giant croquembouche of macarons: lemon, raspberry, coffee, chocolate, pistachio, hazelnut. I admired satin-smooth bitter chocolate tarts, and deep-crimson fruit jellies but left them for another day. And then we went for coffee in the Café de la Mairie on Place Saint-Sulpice. The wind had blown up and colourful woollen hats and scarves were much in evidence. The wind blew a whiff of pungent brown-paper Gauloises cigarettes – powerful but marvellously evocative and not too bad anyway when one is seated at the outside terrace

determined to enjoy the Parisian streetscape, even if the chill
factor was rising.

Penguin UK decided to distribute the new edition of *The Cook's
Companion* and in 2005 I was asked to attend a media launch
dinner in London.

A few months before I went, a friend had given me the dear little
book *The Whole Beast: Nose to Tail Eating* by Fergus Henderson,
the owner of St John Restaurant in Smithfield, London. This book
is a sheer delight, its irresistible language like none other, the food
at once startlingly different and yet starring familiar ingredients. On
shallots: 'roast until soft, sweet and giving'; on fixing a salad: 'toss so
all get to know the dressing'; and on browning a leg of mutton: 'you
want this to be a gentle buttery moment, not a ferocious burning
moment'. And in describing an eel, bacon and prune stew, Fergus
writes, 'the prunes should have swollen to delicious rich clouds'.
I blushed with pleasure to find my own name – Fergus included
my recipe for cornmeal dumplings to accompany salted duck's legs
and green beans.

I read the book while on holiday in Noosa Heads, reclining on a
cane lounge in T-shirt and shorts, temperature in the high twenties.
I had an instant desire to cook everything in the book, even though
many of the dishes were more suited to a cold English winter's day.

I decided that my celebration meal in London would have to
be at St John, and so it was. We enjoyed Fergus's signature starter
of bone marrow and parsley salad, followed by a guinea fowl and,
to finish, sublime Eccles cakes.

At about the same time as all this was happening I decided to
renovate my house. I wanted a larger and more spacious bedroom
and I wanted a dressing room. The architect and designer worked

well together and showed me an ingenious plan that would deliver the spaces I wanted. It did mean that the back half of the house would have to be rebuilt but I was up for it. I had to pack up several rooms, including my kitchen, and install a plug-in hotplate and microwave in the passageway, with a tiny bar fridge alongside. It was a bit like camping – for six months. The builders were charming and the result was absolutely worth the inconvenience. I love my new spacious bedroom and dressing room with its velvet pile carpet. I love my new sunny study that looks out onto the constantly laden lemon tree in the front garden.

Rosie the dog, now fifteen, had to move while the walls tumbled, and she spent a short but happy time living in Holly's house in Richmond. Sadly she did not live to experience the new spaces. Over the past year she had spent much time at the vet and had developed Addison's disease. Her sight and hearing had almost gone and she became sicker and sicker. The vet could do no more and Rosie was put down. Many tears were shed. There would be no more dogs for me while I was still away from home so often.

In preparation for the renovation works I had to sort the contents of drawers and cupboards so that as little extraneous stuff as possible was packed. I ditched early sets of pages of my books. There is no romance left in early manuscripts now that it is all done electronically – they bear few interesting little pencil marks or editor's notes, so into the recycling bin went huge bundles of paper. I also ditched an enormous number of holiday snaps – none of family and friends, but all of those artistic shots of churches and trees in blossom and old stone walls have gone.

There have been other moments in my life when I have had this same desire to reduce and clear what I see as no longer useful. Sometimes I have regretted it and have thrown away cards, letters, old menus and old scrapbooks. And I do value the past. Despite this ambivalence it can be exhilarating to know that with the start of each new chapter in my life – new restaurant, new house, new project – I am starting with a smooth, clear page.

20

Silverbeet & Salad Leaves

The Kitchen Garden Project 2001–

Stephanie's Restaurant was behind me. I enjoyed being a partner in Richmond Hill Café & Larder from 1997 onwards and it was trading strongly. As a shared responsibility it did not feel particularly onerous. *The Cook's Companion* was delighting new readers every day and delivering freedom from financial stress. Why did I decide to take on another huge challenge? Why not sit back and do all that reading I had promised myself for years? Or travel the world?

The answer is that I felt I could still make a contribution to a richer, more joyful food life for many more Australians, especially children. I had plenty of energy. I enjoyed feeling that what I was engaged in was of practical use to society. And I truly believed that to be culinarily literate was of central importance to personal independence and happiness.

In much the same way as I had felt impatient of the often repeated questions put to me during the eighties and nineties about Australian culinary identity, I felt similarly frustrated as I continued to read more and more articles in the press quoting rising levels of childhood obesity, bemoaning the eating habits of our children and foreshadowing astronomical public health costs when – not *if* – the consequences of these bad habits had to be tackled.

I was frustrated when the official response to these statistics was another pamphlet or set of guidelines, or endorsing a tick on certain grocery items. I could look back twenty years over a trail of similar initiatives and yet the numbers of overweight children had continued to rise. The cautionary and negative approach had failed.

I felt that while blaming a group is never very helpful, parents had to accept some responsibility for the state of things. It seemed to me that many families had lost any awareness of eating season-ally, were less likely to eat together regularly due to sporting and other commitments, and were doing less and less cooking from scratch and more and more opening of packets and jars or defrost-ing pre-prepared foods or buying takeaway meals, all in the name of speed. I suspected that these families were more likely to be of Anglo-Celtic descent than of Asian, European or Middle East heritage, where sharing home-made food around the table together is highly valued.

I was certain that if you offer a child the widest possible range of food from the earliest possible age in a loving environment, if you eat together as often as possible, and demonstrate your own enjoyment of flavour and texture and conviviality, that child will eat well forever, and will enjoy being with others around a table for the rest of his or her life. After all, that is the lesson of my own life.

I may not have achieved all of this all the time with my own children, but even allowing for the domestic ups and downs, not to mention living above a working restaurant, my children love to gather around the table with people they care for, and they are open to all culinary experiences. Holly was not always like this but I chose not to turn mealtimes into battlefields. Nor did I offer her alternatives when she did not like what was on offer. The deal

Holly and I struck before the girls and I had our big European adventure in 1990 was that she could choose anything at all from a menu but that she would then have to eat it. Holly tells me that during this trip, in a restaurant in Paris, she experienced a culinary epiphany – a perfectly cooked slender green bean – and at that moment she decided to open herself to every culinary experience that came her way. She has never looked back. Three years later, while on an exchange year in France, Holly sent me that photo of herself tucking into snails.

This approach to food was also important in the lives of my brothers, John and Christopher, and my sister, Diana. Each of my three siblings has a vegetable garden and a small or large orchard. Although there are considerable distances between our homes, we communicate about our crops and our preserving experiences, swap ideas for drying chillies or pickling olives, compare notes on how the beans are progressing, and discuss whether we will leave the eggplants in place for a second season rather than cut them down.

As I thought more about it and realised how many children were growing up without any pleasurable introduction to the wide and wonderful world of food, it seemed that an intervention during primary school was the best way of changing behaviour. And behaviour is much more likely to change if the alternative is seen as pleasurable and possible. Pleasure had to be paramount for this intervention to have any hope of success.

In the late nineties I read a great deal about Alice Waters and her Edible Schoolyard experiment at the Martin Luther King, Jr. Middle School in Berkeley, California, from 1995. Alice believes passionately in the importance of growing food sustainably and of sourcing food as locally as possible. I have had the pleasure of tasting such food on several occasions at her restaurant Chez Panisse in Berkeley. Alice pioneered the idea that children at school could

tend a vegetable garden and then gather to cook and eat what they
had grown. Her motives were to connect young people with the
natural world as well as to educate and broaden their food experiences. In 2005, after Cyclone Katrina, the Chez Panisse Foundation
established a 'sister' program in New Orleans. And since then the
foundation has announced plans to expand the program under
the new coordinating body, the Edible Schoolyard Project. Her
influence was seminal to my thinking. Both Anna Dollard and I
visited the Edible Schoolyard at different times around 2001–2.

Anna and I discussed my theories and tentative ideas for a way
forward. I started to think I could use the profile I had gained over
the last thirty years to start a kitchen garden program for children
not unlike the Edible Schoolyard Project in California. Someone
suggested I speak with Basil Natoli and visit the community gardens that he had helped promote in the public housing estate in
Collingwood. I did this in mid-2000 and was excited to see how
Turkish and Vietnamese neighbours were growing quite different
crops side by side, and sharing ideas and produce.

I was convinced that my project needed to take place in a primary school, believing that the younger the children are when they
start experiencing a kitchen garden program, the more successfully
it will be embedded in their future lives. Basil Natoli suggested I
approach Frances Laurino, then Principal of Collingwood College,
an inner-suburbs school in Melbourne.

I was introduced to Frances, an intelligent and practical woman
who had already taken her school down some innovative pathways.
She had introduced a Steiner stream within a government school,
and the Steiner parents were wonderful allies, believing that a
garden and food were important experiences for a young child. It
has always seemed very significant to me that Frances is Italian.
She has a backyard garden herself, she pickles olives, she makes

her own pasta and her own tomato sauce, she loves to gather with family and friends around a table. Frances was very supportive of my ideas to dig up part of the asphalt schoolyard in order to create an organic vegetable and herb garden, and to convert a little-used home-economics classroom into a lively and colourful kitchen and dining area.

Every student in Grades 3–6 would have a session in the garden each week and a double session in the kitchen. Specialist experts or enthusiasts in horticulture and cookery would need to be employed part-time to deliver the practical skills. The child's classroom teacher would also accompany the students to both the garden and kitchen classes and develop activities that built on concepts learnt in the garden and in the kitchen and could enrich the general curriculum.

In 2000, Basil worked for the Department of Human Services, which agreed to subsidise the cost of a gardener for the first two years of the project at Collingwood. This was very important initial support. It was left to the school to find the money to pay for the kitchen specialist.

So began our active involvement in the kitchen garden movement, all tactics and management emanating from the spare room of my house, with Anna and me becoming more absorbed in the work by the day. We both shovelled dirt for the garden at Collingwood College, she organised donations of a wide range of building materials and services, she wrote and collated brochures, she manned fundraising stalls, she drove hundreds of kilometres to support a second project at Yarrunga in Wangaratta, she designed graphic materials for our initial launch.

Almost as soon as the first classes started at Collingwood College in October 2001 we were besieged with enquiries from representatives of other schools wanting to know if they could visit Collingwood College and what advice we had for them if they wanted to go down the same path. We could offer nothing but encouragement, but behind the scenes the lobbying and politicking went on non-stop. I spoke about the philosophy behind this essentially practical project over and over again: to politicians, to bureaucrats, to service clubs, to parent groups, to health professionals, to philanthropic organisations, on radio and television, to anyone who would listen. Somehow the shyness that engulfs me in social situations disappears completely when I am on a public platform. I wrote letters to the paper, and generally made as much 'noise' as possible. Increasingly it seemed to me (and it still does) that here was a way to capitalise on my love of good, fresh food and the reputation I had forged over thirty-plus years for integrity, serious intent and single-mindedness in pursuing a dream.

Over the next few years Anna and I enlisted further help, including a legal firm, Arnold Bloch Leibler, which agreed to support us pro bono and facilitated our change of status to that of a charitable foundation. We transformed what had been a think-tank of two situated in my home into a foundation with a proper office, a board, a CEO and two project officers. (Our first 'office' was in one of the original nuns' cells in the fantastic Abbotsford Convent building, which had just been designated as a space for community groups. The convent spaces were rapidly filling up with artists and other interesting tenants. We remained there until our growth forced us out in 2010.)

Anna was absolutely indispensable in these early years. She supported me at all times, maintained scrupulous records, crossed every 't' and dotted every 'i'. She ensured that from the very beginning we would present ourselves as professional and responsible. She was also a lot of fun. We needed a sense of humour as every decision was protracted and every step forward seemed difficult.

The major stumbling block in getting what became the Stephanie Alexander Kitchen Garden program up and running was money and still is. We received some very welcome philanthropic support and were able to introduce the program in two additional schools, one in the country. And then we had a big breakthrough. I attracted the attention of the then Minister for Education Lynne Kosky in the Victorian State Government and invited her to visit the kitchen garden at Collingwood College. The students in Grade 4, aged around nine, gave her a guided tour of 'their' garden, pointing out the radicchio and kohlrabi, as well as the borage flowers to attract bees to the garden, and so on. They then invited her to lunch and chatted easily about all manner of things while they served up a risotto of fresh herbs and lemon, a cabbage and potato filo pie, and a salad of green leaves, grated carrots and beetroot. Lynne was genuinely astonished and went away convinced that here was a program with the potential to change the lives of children. Thanks to her lobbying the Treasury Department, the Victorian Government of the day decided to invest in our idea and from 2004 offered grants to forty schools over four years. Each school would still have to supplement the grant but it was a wonderful start.

At this point Anna and I decided that we needed to tell the full story of what we had done. It has been essential to emphasise continually that this program goes far beyond installing a garden in a primary school. There must be a teaching kitchen as well, the two areas must work together and there must be ways of incorporating the program into the curriculum.

Anna collated all the steps we had taken and I tried to turn this into a compelling narrative. Importantly I also wanted to include a significant number of recipes, all of which we could truthfully claim had been prepared and enjoyed by students of Collingwood College aged eight to eleven. The result was *Kitchen Garden Cooking with*

Kids, published in 2006. A copy of this book was given to every Victorian primary school by the Harold Mitchell Foundation.

Media attention was constant and now I found that at every interview I was being asked my hope for the future of this program. All I could say was that my dream was that it should be available to any interested Australian school, but in my heart I could not see how we were to achieve this. Yet increasingly when I visited schools parents would thank me for what I was doing for their child. Principals and teachers would say there were no words to express what an impact this program was having, not just on the children, but on the school community. I dared not voice it, but somewhere deep down I knew that I was creating a small revolution that had the potential to carry all before it.

For more than eight years Anna continued as a positive, practical and creative force as the Stephanie Alexander Kitchen Garden Foundation we had created grew to a new national level. By this time Anna had a young son who was needing more of her time and regular travel to Italy had also become part of her life. She decided to move on.

I was very, very sad to see her go, and experienced that special pang when you know that the show must go on, even though it feels as if your right arm has been torn off.

By the beginning of 2005 there was also change in the air at Richmond Hill Café & Larder. Lisa had already resigned from her position as its promotion and marketing manager and had now returned to working as an arts publicist. The remaining partners had started negotiations with would-be buyers. I was becoming more and more involved in the kitchen garden project with its newly established 'foundation' status. By now nobody in the kitchen at Richmond Hill Café & Larder had any history with me and this made my job of being an in-and-out consultant and mentor rather difficult.

The analogy that springs to mind is of the relay race and the changing of the baton. Many of the initial staff at this café had been with me at Stephanie's Restaurant. For more than twenty-five years the baton had always changed from someone who had worked with me for quite a long time to another younger hopeful, and so it had gone on. Little *trucs*, preferences and prejudices had been understood and passed on while allowing room for change and difference. Until suddenly the baton was dropped completely. All the runners disappeared and it was left tumbling until it was finally picked up by someone who had no connection with those who had run on.

My role had to change too. It was then that the full reality of my own passing years was apparent. I no longer had the energy, stamina or desire to power through a ten-hour day, or hurtle up and down those stairs. Sad, but a reality. All of this turmoil brought up lots of feelings about the end of the active cooking stage in my life.

In 2007 the foundation had its second major breakthrough, thanks to our lobbying and to the power of the wonderful model at Collingwood College. The Australian Government, through its Department of Health and Ageing, added its support to our efforts, offering to fund infrastructure for up to one hundred and ninety schools over four years. At the time of writing there are more than two hundred and fifty primary schools around Australia with Stephanie Alexander Kitchen Garden programs. An amazing achievement, since Collingwood College commenced its program only in 2001.

I am often asked to speak on increasingly varied topics. In one week: 'Why are we poisoning our children?'; a panel discussion elsewhere on whether philanthropy reinforces the gap between the haves and have-nots; and another panel discussion on community health and wellbeing through multi-sectoral partnerships. I rather wish I could clone myself as each of these events requires thought and quite a bit of preparation.

As I write we have small schools, large schools, schools in cities and schools in the country. We also have schools in remote places such as Coober Pedy, Flinders Island, Bourke and a school in the Punmu Community in the Pilbara, and schools for children with special needs. We have developed a network of project officers and a vibrant website that gets better and better, and we have staff members dedicated to developing fun and meaningful units of work so that classroom teachers can make the best possible use of their time in the gardens and the kitchens.

We still believe that the model we developed for Collingwood College offers the optimum pleasurable food education. And every class needs volunteers as the work is done in small groups. The grant monies on offer represent a part of the cost of developing these new spaces in a school. The school must then hold a community meeting to elicit support for the work. Every school tells us that this program really appeals to its community and that they have made new friends along the way. At foundation level we are discussing ways forward that may assist schools that do not qualify for a grant to start their own pleasurable food education journey.

It is fascinating and very satisfying because we see that this program works. Children show willingness to try a new food if they have had something to do with growing that broad bean or that silverbeet. Their self-esteem soars. Parents report that the child shows much greater interest in what goes on in the kitchen and into the family shopping basket. Gardens are planted at home. For those of us who observe the children it just seems like a no-brainer: make it happen everywhere and solve the problem of poor eating among children! If only it were that easy to convince those who hold the purse strings. Money upfront now will head off what we are told on a daily basis will be a public health crisis later on.

It is too easy to use up all one's energy lobbying, or in the many vital administrative tasks including applying for grants. You also need to be re-energised by the children themselves. I am always greeted by young kitchen gardeners, faces beaming, who all want to show me the garden and point out what they have been doing. I then get to meet the chickens and to inspect the worm farm, and only then am I escorted into the bright and buzzing kitchen where more busy children are chopping, stirring or setting tables with posies of flowers and herbs.

When Jamie Oliver first visited Collingwood College in 2006 he was amazed by the skills of the young students. Jamie has worked hard to promote several initiatives in the United Kingdom all aimed at improving the food choices of children and the general community. To date he has not had the sort of government support we have had. He returned to Australia a few years later and I escorted his manager Louise Holland to visit Westgarth Primary School in autumn. The children cooked and served potato gnocchi in a basil and pine nut sauce, accompanied by a leafy salad with red cabbage, and another salad of fresh figs and grapes drizzled with honey. I don't have to say anything on these occasions; the children say it all. The garden looked glorious with rambling pumpkin vines and tomato plants laden with fruit. We are in constant communication with Jamie Oliver's office and anticipate working more closely together in the future.

On a flying trip to launch the program at Alawa Primary School in Darwin it was so exciting to experience first hand the differences between a school sited in the tropics and those I knew well in the southern states. The children at Alawa showed me their tropical garden. I admired hanging bunches of bananas and dangling pawpaw and jackfruit, examined patches of sweet potato, okra, rosella, and noticed flashes of scarlet from the prolific bird's-eye chilli bushes.

The lunch menu was certainly different. Honey-seared crocodile (donated by a local crocodile farm) with a ripe rose pawpaw and avocado salad; a crunchy green pawpaw salad, a banana flower salad with grated cucumber; rice paper rolls; and a roast pumpkin and basil salad with sunflower seeds. It was all delicious and a perfect example of what we always hope to see – home-grown seasonal food reflecting its environment.

The program is integrated into the curriculum of the school and offers endless ways of improving literacy and numeracy. Children design a frog pond, measuring the perimeter and area of the space and calculating how much water will be needed. They discuss the nature of aquatic plants and what will be needed to make this pond a happy home for frogs. They use their wood-fired pizza oven to create special events for their parents and friends of the school. The students develop a database, print out flyers, calculate and order ingredients, write a business plan working out their expenses and likely profit, and best of all get to make the pizzas and sell them at a special highly anticipated evening twice a term. Another teacher conducts her classes in Italian, leading to much fun and a serious discussion of the difficulties faced by new arrivals to this country. And there are hundreds of other activities in action in classrooms around the country.

The original kitchen at Collingwood College has been demolished and we now have a brand-new beautiful purpose-built facility. This is now known as the Kitchen Garden Learning Centre at Collingwood College. Half the week it delivers classes to the students and the rest of the time it is available for training days.

I went along to a training day for sixty-five kitchen and garden specialists from schools all over Victoria and some from interstate.

They came together to network and to practise skills with about ten invited experts. The sessions included keeping chickens in schools, making compost, building supporting structures, espaliering fruit trees and collecting seed. In the kitchen others were learning how to pickle olives and other vegetables, make unusual pasta shapes, make potsticker dumplings and wontons, make simple cheeses, make and link sausages, and understand spices. And then everyone sat down to lunch at tables groaning with samples of everything they had made, augmented with platters of the freshest salad leaves picked just moments before. It was inspiring for all the participants, and for me: it brought out goosebumps and tears in the eyes as I realised the breadth of what was being learnt, all of which would be passed on to the students.

I continue to lobby at the highest political level. The findings in the recently published evaluation of some of the Victorian kitchen garden schools undertaken by researchers from Melbourne University and Deakin University were extremely positive, showing that children in the program schools were much more likely to try new foods than children in schools without the program and that the program itself was highly valued by the students.

I have never doubted that this was happening but in order to lobby government and to have any realistic hope of driving or changing policy, it was essential that we have empirical evidence. And now we have it. At the evaluation launch held in the garden at Westgarth Primary School the children performed magnificently, digging up impressive clumps of Jerusalem artichokes and, just as proudly, a bit later on, offering wood-fire-cooked chapati with red lentil dhal, a cabbage coleslaw and a leafy green salad, and a platter of roasted vegetables including the Jerusalem artichokes.

Journalists often ask me if I think the incredibly popular television series *MasterChef Australia* will have any long-lasting impact on families at home and the health of our children. I am unsure what to reply. Certainly many families are watching young amateur cooks turn piles of fresh food into appealing dishes. This can only be a good thing. My friend Kathy's grandchildren now play 'MasterChef' as often as they play the old standards of 'school' or 'mothers and fathers'. And Maggie Beer tells me that after she appeared on one episode cooking the superior chickens sold by her daughter Saskia, retailers ran out of the item in the next few days. But I cannot help asking whether this interest in best-quality food will be sustained. And with the show's emphasis on fancy food and challenging dishes, whether it will encourage or discourage children and families who wish to cook family-friendly food and would not want to cook under such pressure.

For me the last ten years have fostered new friendships. Board member Kate Doyle brought initial business skills to the organisation and she is now a very good friend. The foundation's CEO, Ange Barry, is also a very good friend and she directs all activities at the foundation with energy, good humour and impressive strategic thinking. Her background is with not-for-profit foundations and she is a tireless advocate for social change. There are some wonderfully creative people working for the foundation and I greatly enjoy the time I spend with them. They are all much, much younger than I am and that is a pleasure in itself. I cannot help but gain insight into younger ways of thinking, not to mention the young person's nimble mind with its ability to cope with all manner of technology.

I can always be counted on for a good idea. But I have acknowledged the difficulty I have with visualising the big picture, or perhaps more accurately, with anticipating the necessary steps and strategies needed to make an idea a reality. My understanding of finance is pretty basic – I have to rely on others, and I do. In considering the big projects in my life (and I mean here the non-writing ones) – Jamaica House, Stephanie's Restaurant, the Harvest Picnic, Richmond Hill Café & Larder, the Tuscan cooking schools and now the Stephanie Alexander Kitchen Garden Foundation – I acknowledge that managing finance has always loomed large, and that expert guidance has always been needed to turn good ideas into sustainable reality. I admit to impatience that those who say they care about the health of our children do not follow through with sufficient funds to make a difference for all Australian children.

On the wall at home I have a larger-than-life portrait of myself by Melbourne artist David Disher. I am wearing red gumboots and leaning on a spade. Around me is a garden that is lusher than any earthly garden could ever be, with a glorious blossoming fruit tree. In the far background is a fence and behind it are tiny figures associated with junk food organisations, all reduced to insignificance by the vibrancy and power exuded by this verdant garden. The expression on my face is one of contentment and happiness. It feels right.

21

Pinned Fish and Yabbie & Yalka Wontons

Brain Food, Bush Food and the New Gastronomy

Although I am spending more and more of my days thinking about children and food I am still aware of what is going on in the world of professional cooking as well as keeping a critical eye on all the messages regarding food choices being transmitted to the community. I will continue to spread the word about the pleasure to be had from good food that follows the seasons. I still love to give pleasure at the table. I quite like the adrenalin rush of the professional kitchen but the point for me has always been the food. I have never been interested in being a performance artist. I have always responded most deeply to sound, good cooking that is firmly grounded or springs from traditional knowledge.

The message was reinforced at the Fourteenth Symposium of Australian Gastronomy entitled 'Preservation or Change?', held at Beechworth in country Victoria in 2005. Chef Stefano Manfredi prepared a meal at the nearby former migrant reception centre at Bonegilla with a powerful message. When he arrived in Australia from northern Italy with his parents in 1961, they were taken to Bonegilla. Stefano shared an early memory:

The first meal that I remember, I can remember it as a smell more than a meal. It was the smell of boiled mutton and it was accompanied by little pastel cubes of vegetables floating in bain-marie water and there was gravy, of course. And then for dessert we had junket and Two Fruits. And this would've been okay but we had it day after day after day after day after day.

Stefano proceeded to use the same ingredients and show how they ought to be cooked. We had spoon-tender, sticky slow-roasted lamb shoulder (or was it perhaps hogget?), caramelised roasted root vegetables, all served with the roasting pan juices. The junket and Two Fruits reappeared as a buttermilk pannacotta with quinces poached in Rutherglen muscat.

The story of the migrant experience is always humbling and often harrowing.

The final banquet at this same symposium was also notable. We were all staying at the former mental asylum at Beechworth and the banquet was prepared in the old catering kitchen. The chef was Melbournian Andrew McConnell, one of the country's finest. The artistry and technical brilliance of his first course was breathtaking. We were instructed to wear flat shoes and dress warmly.

Andrew has always been interested in traditional ways of preserving food, and an example of this is present on almost every one of his menus. He made a short statement to this effect before we entered the first room.

We were in the dishwashing area of the old catering kitchen. On its stainless-steel tray was mounted the granddaddy of all iceblocks, glistening and glittering, which had had small hollows chiselled or drilled at regular intervals. Each little hole held a frond of seaweed-like greenery and a freshly opened oyster. There were also smoked mussels. We served ourselves with the proffered toothpicks.

We moved into another room where our feet crunched on a carpet of rock salt. The air was chilly as if we were entering an ice cave. On the walls were specimen boards and on each board was pinned perfectly cut slivers of fish, variously smoked, cured and pickled. Each species was identified with its scientific name exquisitely written in copperplate script. We were in a museum, or so it seemed. The fish might have been pinned butterflies. After a short moment of amazed admiration we helped ourselves to the samples and they were, of course, piquant and delicious. I loved this course, for its wit and precision, and then its flavours.

The Symposium of Gastronomy has to be seen as a fascinating and somewhat eccentric club. Its members are so diverse, it now has almost no connection with the food industry, perhaps a little more with the wine industry. It has quite properly outlawed any relationship with sponsors, so is beholden to no-one. The symposium may have originally claimed that it was open to both academics and practitioners but for the last few years the only room for practitioners is if they are asked to contribute their creativity and labour to prepare a meal. Otherwise it has moved towards academia.

During the first fifteen or so years of Stephanie's Restaurant I consciously sought to identify, encourage and support those who were engaged in growing or producing high-quality produce, be it cheese, salad greens, milk-fed lamb or wild mushrooms. Other restaurateurs followed suit. It may be one of those special characteristics of the oft-discussed 'Australian cuisine' that much of the gastronomic education of the general public was led by the restaurant fraternity. We were able to keep those suppliers in business and we made sure that they and their produce became well known so they could be more widely supported.

By 1996 I had become convinced that such suppliers would make a fascinating topic for a television series. I could see that combining cooking, storytelling, great scenery and fascinating characters would appeal to the general public as well as food lovers. I pitched my idea to the ABC and it was accepted. *A Shared Table*, both the television series and the book that accompanied it, appeared in 1998–9.

Anna was involved in all of the planning and travelling for this series. We criss-crossed the country, learning from enthusiastic growers and producers, from apiarists to crabbers, observing how to harvest cockles with one's toes, understanding biodynamic wine production, watching in horrified amazement as women pulled mangrove worms on a beach in the Tiwi Islands, meeting sardine fishermen and buffalo farmers and oyster farmers and cheese makers. I looked sadly onto orange groves laden with fruit that no-one wanted to pick. I explored the banks of the Murray at Barmah with artist the late Ian Abdulla and gazed in horror at the choked Murray mouth. I walked through muddy water-chestnut ponds fearful of what lurked in the slime oozing between my toes. I baked wild barramundi caught by my brother John in Darwin, and returned home after each adventure more and more in awe of the size, the diversity and the impossibility of generalising about this extraordinary continent and its people.

Many other television series followed with more or less the same aim in mind – to follow a presenter as he or she 'discovered' and interacted with the growing number of wonderful characters producing more and more interesting produce. There appeared to be an insatiable demand for food shows on television, and most were moving out of the studio.

The story of Australia's indigenous foods has been much more difficult to present to a wide audience. Most city dwellers understand little if anything of these foods, and need to be reminded that they have sustained populations for thousands and thousands of years. However, other than native fish and shellfish, most bush foods are hard to find and can be challenging to use. So more than a decade after my television series and book, I was delighted to be asked to judge the 2008 Bush Food and Wild Food Festival to be held in Alice Springs. I looked forward to learning a great deal.

Like many city slickers from the south my acquaintance with bush foods had been limited by availability. In my restaurant days I had wrapped barramundi in paperbark and used wattleseed in blini and *Grevillea pteridifolia* flowers in a sorbet. And I was thrilled with a dish I tasted recently at Melbourne restaurant Vue de Monde where chef Shannon Bennett presented a dish of wallaby smoked with scarlet bottlebrush (the still-smoking flower on the plate wafted an intense smell of the bush), sprinkled with Tasmanian mountain pepper. But in Alice Springs I learnt how fleeting and elusive many of our bush foods are.

I renewed my acquaintance with quandongs, the lovely rose-pink fruit often called a native peach. These were combined with a small quantity of one of the lilly pilly family, the clove-scented riberry, to make a pie filling for the final banquet by Raylene Brown, one of Alice Springs' busiest caterers. Raylene told me that as a young girl she had travelled with her mother, who cooked for the teams that built the road from Alice Springs to Darwin. So she knew how to cook for a crowd without fuss, using bush foods as well as the standard dishes needed to feed hungry workers.

For the festival awards there was a professional section and an amateur section. In the professional section I ate plenty of kangaroo, a delicate camel carpaccio, and a clever dessert called 'Bushlava', a baklava with a filling of local dates and wattleseed steeped in a red-gum honey syrup.

But it was the amateurs who showed dazzling originality and extraordinary talent. Among the foods I tasted for the first time were dried bush raisins, also known as bush tomato before they are dried. Chutney is made from the ripe fruit and it can be used like pea eggplant in curries. Its smoky roasted raisin character develops once the fruit is dried. I also identified roundleaf saltbush (*Atriplex nummularia*) called 'old man saltbush' and wild passionfruit (in bud and as unripe berries). In Arrernte language the wild passionfruit is known as *arrutnenge* and is picked when the skin becomes orange.

'Everyone likes it,' I was told by a local woman. 'It is sweet like mango. You don't eat the skin – it's bitter – but you can eat the seeds.'

Other firsts for me were wild orange (*Capparis mitchellii*), and lerps, the crystallised honeydew produced by leaf scale found on river red gums.

One of the talented amateur cooks was Ange Vincent, a research analyst employed at the Alice Springs Desert Knowledge Centre, where much research is done not only into bush foods but into many other aspects of desert life. Ange had several entries in the competition: her gravlax with desert lime and saltbush was stunning, and her wild passionfruit tart was a completely new flavour to me. The wild passionfruit is *Capparis spinosa* ssp. *nummularia*, which is very closely related to the plant from which European capers and caperberries are collected. Ange had picked and pickled the unripe buds and unripe fruits, and used them to garnish her gravlax dish. The fruit change from hard green ovals to orange and split open when fully ripe; she used the ripe flesh for the tart filling. Desert limes were made into a syrup and both the flesh and the syrup were used in the dish.

My astonishment increased as amazing dish after amazing dish was offered for tasting. Yabbie and *yalka* (bush onion) wontons introduced me to the delicious tiny water-chestnut-like bush onions. These tiny bulbs grow on the river banks, and Raylene says as children they roasted them.

The overall winning dish was titled 'Kalkardi Mignonnes', entered by Anna Szava. The mignonnes (meaning 'small and dainty') were delectable chocolates filled with a marzipan made from roasted, coarsely crushed wattleseed, bush honey and hazelnuts. (Kalkardi is the Arrernte name for the seed of Acacia colei, one of the wattleseed family.) They were dipped in seventy-percent-cocoa dark chocolate mixed with a judicious quantity of mountain pepper. On top of each chocolate was a pair of lerps or 'fairy wings'. Anna worked as a community advisor for many years in a remote community and had been introduced to the lerps by the children. She told me that she couldn't get the kids to listen to her as they were all up a gumtree shaking the branches so they could eat the lerps.

This dish was truly astonishing. Two Indigenous women at the dinner told me that if I look on the ground under a tree that has these lerps there will be a pile of the honeydew where it has slid from the leaves. The very next morning on my walk I looked and there it was. A procession of ants was engaged in dragging this sugary substance to their nest and they had it piled like a lace collar around the entrance. I scraped the flakes from several leaves into my hand and ate them. They dissolved on the tongue like icing sugar. I didn't want to think too much about it but assume the scale is created by the larvae of some insect that later emerges to munch on the gum leaves.

(Just for the record I can say that a couple of weeks later I found this scale on gumtrees along the banks of the Yarra River in Toorak. I ate some and it didn't seem as sweet as in the desert. All in the mind, perhaps?)

Other than wattleseed, which does exist in readily collectable commercial quantities, and probably quandongs, many of the other foods I tasted are found in only small quantities and over a vast distance. They are also seasonally susceptible – it was so dry in Alice Springs and the surrounding countryside in that year that there had been no appreciable harvest of bush raisins. And then in 2010 the area was flooded.

Raylene would like to see Alice Springs declare itself the centre of bush foods in Australia, giving the town a true point of difference for the visitor. This makes a lot of sense. Interested visitors could come and experience what is ready to eat right at that moment.

I spoke with one man who had spent eight years working with remote communities gaining the trust and friendship of Indigenous gatherers of bush foods. He was the first to say that attempting to create a business from bush foods is fraught with very real problems, human as well as financial, not to mention a scarcity of supply. 'Foraging' has become a buzzword for some of our young chefs. I hope that some of them are inspired to ask Indigenous Australians for advice on what is available where they live. And from my experience during these few days, once I started to do a bit of foraging for myself (lerps and saltbush) I did start to see the landscape differently. I had to conclude that I had been privileged to attend an extraordinary event. It is unlikely that similar dishes will ever be experienced by many people. In their own way such dishes are as extraordinary and as esoteric as the creations prepared in the most lauded temples of gastronomy.

As an Australian attempting to appreciate where we have come from and what we now have, it is both puzzling and fascinating to consider the vast distance between the bush foods of Central

Australia, and the 'new gastronomy', originally from Spain, now influencing our most renowned chefs. For a food-curious observer and practitioner, both were equally intriguing, and after my exposure to these amazing tastes from this ancient culture, I could not help musing on the likely longevity of the new gastronomy I first experienced in 2001.

Every foodie has read plenty of commentary on the fantastic dishes served at the now-closed elBulli, at Roses, some distance from Barcelona, created by the brilliant Ferran Adrià. I did attend an extraordinary demonstration he gave with his colleague Juan Arzak several years ago at Tasting Australia in Adelaide. Over the course of an hour or so he showed just a few of the startling and revolutionary techniques he was working with at the time. The audience was spellbound and you could have heard the proverbial pin drop. The man is universally described as a genius. Alas, I never went there. Descriptions of some dishes he presented at elBulli sound delicious, many more seem incomprehensible but all are very intriguing. Adrià's restaurant may be closed but his influence has spread. This new gastronomy, sometimes described as 'molecular gastronomy', has changed the world of high-end restaurant food and I needed to experience it for myself.

In many ways the trip I took to Spain in 2001 with Lisa echoed my voyage of discovery in France in the eighties during the heyday of *nouvelle cuisine*. Given Lisa's proficiency with Spanish, her love of good food and her enthusiasm for travel, she was the perfect companion for this Spanish adventure. Experiencing the new gastronomy was just one of the motives for the holiday. The itinerary gave us one week in Barcelona to admire the works of Antoni Gaudí, taste traditional food and relax, before a serious food week in San Sebastián. We booked meals at three renowned restaurants all close to San Sebastián.

In Barcelona we visited the Pasteleria Escribà on La Rambla for elevenses and ordered the hot chocolate, which was shiny and nearly black, scalding hot and quite wonderful. It was bittersweet and rich but not cloying. And with it came delicious sugared pastries with toasted pine nuts scattered on top. You could buy long sticks of chocolate for melting, which resembled a twist of licorice until you had a good sniff.

As it was a holiday weekend the crowds were out and we followed them to Port Olimpic. One of the highlights was watching two Spanish families eating together at nearby tables. I watched one family be served a dish of something that was brilliantly green and got Lisa to ask the waiter over for clarification. Within minutes we too had a platter of fried *pimientos de padrón*. These small fat chillies, mildly hot, were sensational. They originate in the Galician town of Padrón, where apparently they are celebrated at fiestas twice a year. They still had the distinctive bitterness of green pepper but also a rich ripeness that counteracted the bitterness. Good olive oil and a sprinkling of salt were the only additions. I loved this dish. The waiter said that eating the *pimientos de padrón* is always a bit of a game. Some will be more *picante* than others and you can never tell which one will be surprising. (Later that year I grew my own and every one of them was fiery hot.)

Another morning started at La Boqueria, Barcelona's famous covered market. Every stall was exquisitely laid out – strawberries alongside cherries, pink-blushed apricots next to rosy peaches, sensational long black figs alongside green figs and miniature pears, and so on.

The cod stalls were fascinating to one who only ever sees the fish chunked and heavily salted or dried flat like a flap of cardboard. Here cooks can choose what piece of fish they want (the thicker the piece the more expensive). Cod was sold fully soaked, semi-soaked, finely chopped for *esqueixada*, already mixed as a salad or cooked and sold as a puree with potatoes. All manner of shellfish snapped and wriggled on the stalls, including the unbelievable *percebes*, or gooseneck barnacles, which resemble the scaly toes and toenails of some prehistoric lizard. *Percebes* are prised from sheer rock faces by daredevil fishermen who risk their lives as they hack at them in the short moments between the crashing waves that threaten to sweep them from the rocks. Understandably, they are very expensive.

Our holiday then moved to San Sebastián. Someone had recommended a beachside room at the lovely old Hotel Londres y de Inglaterra, a delightful choice. It was a very European resort – lots of elderly couples standing in the shallows and chatting, and soaking up the sun. The men had rolled their trousers up to their knees, the women had tucked their skirts into the legs of their knickers. Late in the evening a crowd gathered to watch the extraordinary sunset over the sea. The sun was a burning red ball hovering in a rose-pink sky. It slipped over the horizon, leaving streaks of brilliant light and a violet sky that slowly, slowly faded.

Our experience at Pedro Subijana's Akelarre in San Sebastián was exceptional. I had not yet become used to the foams and sleight of hand that we would encounter in every one of the restaurants we visited, but here I found the cleverness convincing and the flavours absolutely delicious.

First came a small red twisted bonbon, alongside it one scarlet and one gold nasturtium petal and one small square resembling a caramel. The bonbon wrapper was sweet red pepper skin (maybe made with agar-agar?) and inside was a smooth cheese filling, of the Pyrenean Ossau Iraty variety. The 'caramel' was a soft fondant of salted cod that wobbled in the mouth. The nasturtiums added a note of pepper. The dish was a deconstructed interpretation of the popular Basque dish of red *piquillo* peppers stuffed with a puree of salted codfish.

Then came oysters on an artichoke and oyster puree with a white spume of sea froth on top, which was in fact a sorbet of oyster juice. It tasted just like a mouthful of the Atlantic: cold, foamy and marvellously refreshing.

Next there were baby broad beans and peas under a mint 'snow', which was a frozen confection and tasted not only of garden mint but of menthol. I thought it unnecessary. But the baby broad beans were all double-peeled and not one of them was as big as my littlest fingernail! The warm salad was dressed with hazelnut oil. I did send a thought to the kitchen worker who would have spent more than an hour on the broad beans in my bowl alone, and there were many such bowls being served. Chef Pedro later told me there were twenty in his kitchen team. Two of them must have been on broad beans full-time!

Roasted milk-fed lamb under a potato 'cloud' came next. This potato confection was clear and shiny as perspex. It was crisp and full of potato flavour, while the lamb with flowering thyme was buttery and meltingly soft. And we ordered the 'Akelarre' gin and tonic for dessert, a jelly made from tonic water with its bubbles intact, a smooth gin sorbet scattered with crushed juniper berries, and thin slivers of candied Meyer lemon peel.

We had other dishes at other restaurants. Plenty of froth and foam. Plenty of smooth-as-silk sorbets of surprising character. Plenty of dehydrated, crumbled and painted-on flavours. The movement has inspired other chefs, in Scandinavia, United States and as far away as Australia. Some chefs have done a *stage* in Spain in one of the temples of the new gastronomy, again just as I had experienced so many years ago during the rise of *nouvelle cuisine*.

A few years later, in 2010, my close friends Angela and Duffy Clemens organised a weekend away in the Victorian town of Dunkeld beneath towering Mt Sturgeon in the Grampians National Park. Here I experienced again the new gastronomy, this time with an Australian accent. Maggie and Colin Beer drove from the Barossa, Dee Nolan and her husband, John Southgate, drove from Naracoorte, where they have a farm and produce the beautiful Nolan's Road organic extra virgin olive oil, and my friend Laine Sutton and I made up the party.

Dan Hunter is the talented chef of the Royal Mail Hotel Dunkeld and has spent time at renowned restaurant Mugaritz, another of the leading lights of the Spanish gastronomic revolution. We all descended on the Royal Mail Hotel on Friday night for the regular weekly gourmet gala dinner, all ten courses of it, matched with extraordinary wines. It was a marathon meal and there was much to reflect upon. Our unanimous opinion was that probably once a year was sufficient for a meal like this; there were so many extraordinary preparations and flavours and the procession of intricate dishes stretched the mind as well as the tastebuds.

One dish was titled 'egg yolk, toasted rye, legumes, yeast'. I remember crunch and a naked yolk and nothing more. Was this where we had toasted buckwheat, which was delicious? Better luck remembering the stronger tastes of 'eel, beef tendon, kohlrabi, potato'. Maggie, Angela and I all loved the heavily smoked eel and the sticky tendon, but many around the table could not handle the tendon and found the eel too strong.

Towards the end came 'fresh and dried berries, beetroot, black olive, rose', a luscious crimson and rose-pink combination that reminded me of the rich colours of velvet and silk. I remain unconvinced by dried powder of dehydrated anything. The texture in the mouth is unpleasant, reminding me of chewing chalk. But the dehydrated rose petals (brushed with egg white, we were told, before the drying) were exquisitely perfumed and crisp.

The theme of surprise and incredulity at the creations produced by some of today's most skilful chefs continued during the 2010 Masterclass weekend that is a highlight of the annual Melbourne Food & Wine Festival. Although I now feel quite detached from this world I am still fascinated to notice how technology has changed kitchen practice and facilitated astonishing techniques. It does seem as if nowadays magic does operate in some kitchens.

Peter Gilmore from Sydney's Quay restaurant demonstrated a delectable dish of butter-poached shaved squid on a garlic custard with a garnish of cooked radish and violets dribbled with a squid consommé. And then a chunk of Suffolk lamb, painted with rendered lamb fat and poached in a bag in a thermostatically controlled water bath, finally glazed with reduced lamb jus and served on a puree of celeriac. Both dishes were brilliantly successful.

I had a flashback to a dish I cooked for the Australian Tourism Commission in New York, San Francisco and Los Angeles in 1992, of a trimmed loin of lamb, poached in lamb broth (no thermostatically controlled water bath available in those days), served with a garlic custard and a silky puree of Jerusalem artichokes, broad beans and crisp parsnip wafers. And of the sixty parfait-stuffed and glazed quail presented almost hidden among a row of baby lettuces and violets that I prepared for a meeting of the Wine and Food Society of Australia many years before that.

This 'new cooking' is so profoundly different that I have to be careful not to react simply to its 'otherness'. It causes me to reflect on the resistance of many in the early eighties to what were perceived as the shortcomings of *nouvelle cuisine*. We heard stories of large white plates and small quantities of food, of greedy diners needing to top up with hamburgers after a meal, of outlandish combinations, of copyist cooks who became adept at reproducing exactly the photographed dishes in the chefs' cookbooks that came thick and fast. And yet there were genuine masters of *nouvelle cuisine*. When one tasted this food there was the surprise of the new but also unmistakeably delicious food that satisfied the appetite as well as the eyes.

Inevitably I find myself musing on the globalisation of restaurant food, how restaurants of a certain level do seem to feature similar dishes wherever you find yourself.

My overwhelming reaction to the latest generation of clever chefs is goodwill and benevolence. Mostly I do not want to know how their interesting effects are contrived. I just want to enjoy them. However, age does give you some degree of context and hindsight. My reaction to the new techniques being used now is certainly influenced by the generation gap.

I do get quiet pleasure, I even preen a bit, whenever I hear something being hailed as extraordinary or unique or never-seen-before, when I know it was part of my own repertoire a lifetime ago as far as the current commentators are concerned. They were not yet born or at school during the heyday of Stephanie's Restaurant. I do find it extraordinary that I have lived and worked through an entire generation.

Technology leaps ahead and brings with it possibilities not previously dreamt of. But just because one can make a smooth sorbet of bacon or duck fat, what purpose does it serve in the dish? I am irritated by dishes shown in a Spanish magazine: 'Gazpacho water soup with marinated thrush', or 'Escabeche of turtledove with cod and low-temperature egg', and wonder if this is really food anyone wants to eat. Are textures of hot and cold ever satisfactory on the same plate? (Well, yes, I answer myself. What about a dollop of cream on an old-fashioned hot apple pie; salsa verde on a poached chicken; horseradish on roast beef?) What if the cold melts into an unappetising mess on the plate? Does a smear of something colourful painted on a plate ever offer a complementary flavour, as does a spoonful of sauce? Does dry dust of anything offer pleasure to the palate? How often does a classic dish once deconstructed yield the same pleasure and texture as the original?

One of the alumni of Stephanie's Restaurant, Annie Smithers, has cooked at her own highly regarded bistro in the Victorian country town of Kyneton since 2005. Her food has always been precise, beautifully flavoured, fresh, and inspired by classical techniques and fine produce. She went on a whirlwind European eating marathon in 2010 and in a column detailed her experiences eating at Noma in Denmark, in 2011 judged top restaurant in the world by the San Pellegrino guide.

I emailed Annie, telling her I was struggling to find a 'balanced viewpoint on all of these minuscule mouthfuls of dust, dirt, foam, crunch, breakfast cereal that I am being offered'. She agreed and said she disliked that the dishes 'arrive at such breakneck speed it is impossible to analyse them or even fully appreciate the technical brilliance and unusual foodstuffs'.

And I do get irritated when a waiter describes eight or more flavours to be identified in one dish, but the dish is gone in one or two bites. 'Now where was that smoked tree bark?' I wonder at such moments. For me there need to be fewer dishes, so that I can think about the flavours, and there ought to be another bite or two to reinforce or reveal more, especially if you are offered a matching wine.

Our own cooking on the second night at that Dunkeld holiday was much more conventional. I had brought rainforest finger limes from my prolific bush so I could squeeze the tiny pearls onto freshly opened oysters alongside a platter of sea urchin roe on tiny toasts. Maggie roasted two of her daughter's delicious chickens accompanied by generous quantities of vegetables gathered from Dee Nolan's local organic vegetable supplier, and then I offered my favourite queen of nuts cake, served with glazed figs that I had been dipping in and out of syrup and drying on racks for nearly a week.

About this new gastronomy I remain an agnostic rather than an atheist. I love it when my suspicion is overcome by a culinary triumph. Fortunately I have never had any ambition to be a restaurant critic. And I can imagine that if you are a restaurant critic, the frequency with which you experience 'same as' dishes might very easily prejudice you in favour of the truly different. I do wonder what these chefs eat for pleasure, though. Hard to believe they go home and rustle up 'Salsify and truffle with milk skin and rape seed oil'.

22

Cupcake Memories

My Seventieth Year and What Comes Next

When I was in my twenties and before I was first married my expectations were that I would carefully select Mr Right and live happily ever after. My friends and I would sometimes discuss the attributes each of us felt were non-negotiable. I seem to recall that being a good dancer was high on my list – I was very young! Even after one divorce I still hoped for 'happy ever after'. And after the second, when I was emotionally bruised, secretly I hoped there would still be time and opportunity to find a partner who would love me. It was not to be. Given my acute lack of ease in large social groups, my inability to engage in small talk, my impatience with humbug and much frivolity, I am rarely the life of the party. I am also somewhat deaf.

I have been partially deaf for more than twenty years. After having had my hearing checked the diagnosis was a damaged hearing nerve that could not be repaired. I decided to deal with it properly after I had spent many years chastising Maurice for not 'speaking up'; he had the low male voice that is still the most challenging for me. I had always found it frustrating that my father often refused to wear his hearing aids and then complained that everyone mumbled.

I was determined not to be like that. Wearing hearing aids has been an excellent move. The only things that remain a challenge are those very low male voices, the phone sometimes, and very crowded loud places.

Because of the need to strain to hear at parties I found them exhausting and rarely rewarding. It is difficult to have conversations when every sentence has to be repeated and all around people are communicating with shrieks, nods and raucous laughter. I usually left such gatherings early and went home to read a book.

Twenty years on from my divorce with Maurice I can say that it is companionship I miss, and a shared interest in delicious and exciting food. I miss the might-have-been weekend explorations of fascinating country towns, or travelling to enjoy a festival, or spontaneous meals out, or carefully planned overseas travels. And I miss being touched. The long-ago sexual adventures seem, well, long ago. These days even the brush of the hand of my hairdresser or my physiotherapist, or a greeting kiss from a male friend, or a casual arm around a shoulder is comforting. It would have been great to have been able to share the highs and lows of all of those years with someone who thought I was special. Couples do not always appreciate the loneliness of the single friend.

There are some compensations. I do not have to make allowances for another's annoying habits. I do not have to justify my actions to anyone. I have learnt to be comfortable in my own company and generous in the way I invite my friends to share things with me.

My friends weave in and out of my life story. I could never have coped, could never have kept on going, without their support, their loyalty and most importantly their laughter. All of them have cared for and loved my children at some time. We have been through a lot together: births, deaths, broken hearts, marriages, divorces, serious illnesses, offspring troubles, financial hurdles. The ties are very strong. Giving up has never been an option for any of us; an extreme work ethic goes with this pre-Baby Boomer generation. I cook for my friends as often as possible. We read the same books. We tend to see the same movies. We share political views and are more or less engaged with current affairs and world issues. We have similar social values. We have no time for humbug, greed or manipulation. We all have a shared sense of humour and laugh a lot. I am certain my friends make allowances for my exaggeration and sweeping statements. We really like each other and are never bored in each other's company. It is a delightful bonus that our children have grown up as not only interesting and warm individuals but they also like one another, so that gatherings at Christmastime happily blend the generations. I am the only dedicated foodie but I have definitely influenced them all.

Here and there I see women who are fearful of being left alone, who have over the years baulked at doing things they see as 'male responsibilities'. This is not an option when you live alone. And I am unsure how I would cope with a mate who was ageing faster than me. My impatience could be a problem, I believe.

I have created spaces I enjoy living in. My daily pleasures are often aesthetic: the turquoise cover of the feather-filled couch in my study, where I take my occasional afternoon naps; the art that surrounds me. There is Purallena, the painted wood carving of a peasant woman holding loaves of bread in her gathered apron that I found in a tiny shop on a street in Andalucia; the coarse hand-woven rug from Poland with naïve wildflowers; the carved wooden goanna from Arnhem Land; and a coiled pandanus basket also from Arnhem Land in which I store my special cards.

My kitchen is just as I want it to be, with beautiful pots and special utensils displayed to be easily accessible and to please the eye. The walls are a rich butter-yellow, the benches are smooth-as-silk

Carrara marble, the windows look onto the garden. I am all for a bit of romance when choosing tools for the kitchen but I also insist on functionality. In 2004 I visited one of the last artisan copper saucepan makers in the tiny hamlet of Le Beaucet in the south-west of France and watched, fascinated, as he turned a smooth disc of copper into a bowl. I bought a traditional unlined copper jam pan with thick riveted brass handles and wide sloping sides. It is beautiful to look at, and as it now sits on my stove half-full of seething cumquats in syrup, its wide sides permitting a rolling boil without any boil-over, I am pleased with my cumbersome purchase all over again. The house is fragrant with the incomparable scent of cumquat marmalade in the making. One kilo of fruit has yielded three litres of fabulous marmalade.

Coming home on an autumn afternoon I am delighted anew by the glowing terracotta paving stones, lit by a low western sun. In the background is a weeping branch of crimson- and gold-splashed crabapple, still holding leaves that are now turning gold.

Every room in my house has special treasures, collected over a lifetime, and I never take them for granted. I look into each painting with pleasure most days. I have a particular interest in the still-life genre and colour is very important to me. Today I have a vase with pink-striped Asian lilies mixed with golden-orange tulips and the colours are so exciting. Last week it was cream stocks, green tulips and white lilies with butter-yellow throats. Solitude helps in this sort of peaceful appreciation. My weekdays are often filled with meetings where we air issues involving the Kitchen Garden Foundation that seem to be far from solutions. I arrive home feeling prickly with tension as well as just plain tired. Within a few minutes of being enveloped in my castle, I am restored.

Robert Dessaix wrote about the comfort of the ordinary in *Twilight of Love*. This idea struck a chord with me. It is probably why I am so attracted to still-life painting, with its glimpses into the intimacies of everyday life, why I enjoy taking public transport and listening in, why I find fascination in the view from close up and am less captivated by the long view or the unknown or the abstract. I feel comfortable surrounded by the well worn, the familiar and the much-loved, be it a chair, a painting or even a soft cardigan that probably ought to be abandoned.

I do love my garden. It is not huge although it seemed large enough all through the drought when I was hand-watering with my carefully calculated tank water. It has a metre-wide vegetable border each side of the front path, a remarkable lemon tree, a fenceline of roses with salvia, foxgloves and a summer burst of liliums. At the rear I have my crabapple trees, more roses, a stunning hedge of daphne beside the swimming pool and three fruit crates on castors for more edibles. At one narrow end of the pool is another hedge of rosemary, underplanted with Parma violets and studded with scarlet roses, and at its far boundary a wall of climbing roses and hydrangeas. I try for a mix of prettiness and being able to step outside most evenings and pick a selection of this and that for my dinner. Such a wonderful feeling.

In the springtime I can see the almond tree in blossom through my study window. Last night I served a lemon cake to friends with a bowl of sliced citrus. I bought the blood oranges at the farmers' market, but the lemons and tangelos came from my trees. The window box in my kitchen is fragrant with blue hyacinth. The pink daphne is in full fragrant flower. And the broad beans are also full of flowers. In my tiny hothouse I have the first tomato seedlings. The remarkable snow peas just go on and on. With such a small space, I find it better to plant snow peas than regular peas as the yield is so much better. Having said that, I do love my purple-podded peas and the flowers are a stunning violet. I planted a few more peas, this time a variety that has yellow pods (but the peas inside are still spring-green).

The summer garden is of course the most prolific. Zucchini 'Romanesco' is a favourite. The leaves are quite hairy and prickly and the fruit is pale green, ridged and very delicious. Last spring I planted an heirloom pumpkin called 'Potimarron' that just about took over the entire paved courtyard. It has become difficult to find space for a table and chair! They are intertwined with a climbing rose and have even started embracing one of my crabapple trees. The pumpkins, now a deep orange and gourd-shaped, taste rather like a chestnut. Purple beans are pleading to be picked, as are many eggplants and sweet peppers. Baby corn have brown tassels so they are ready for plucking. In the front beds are plenty of tender salad greens. Most of the tomatoes have not yet filled out but I did pick two green zebra and one anonymous deep-red one. The extraordinary yellow pole beans have reached the top of their stakes and are just starting to flower. I surprise myself with my excitement and satisfaction as I inspect my crops.

In 2009 I published the *Kitchen Garden Companion* reflecting my preoccupation with encouraging everyone to grow some of their own food. My own garden expands by the month as I find yet another spot to plant something edible. As with *The Cook's Companion* this newer work aims at reducing anxiety, offering accurate and accessible advice without emphasising the too-technical that can discourage newly enthusiastic gardeners. If I can do it, so can you, is really my message. I was thrilled when this book was published in the United Kingdom in an edition with adjusted growing information to make it applicable for the northern hemisphere.

Interviewers often ask if I still cook with enthusiasm. I find this a surprising question. My entire adult life has been intertwined with delicious fresh food. Why would I stop now? If I have had no time to shop for meat or fish I am quite content with a dinner of chargrilled eggplant and sweet peppers with a spoonful of my own pesto, some fresh goat's cheese, a handful of yellow beans and some soft salad leaves, or scrambled eggs on toast. In testing a dish for a special luncheon recently I was thrilled with a grass-green parsley and celeriac soup I made with tiny gnocchetti with saffron and fromage blanc. And what can be better than freshly dug waxy potatoes with your own just-pulled carrots?

I have a tradition of holding a big Boxing Day lunch party at my house, which dates from my restaurant years. We always worked on Christmas Day so it made sense to gather with friends and family the following day. The weather is almost always sunny, children play in the pool, and adults relax and catch up on each other's news. The food is always a focus. Initially it featured rather special leftovers from the restaurant; these days it is an annual cook-up that I find enjoyable and is a chance to check that my cookery skills for parties of thirty are still intact. Of course guests also bring delicious offerings.

Just as much as ever I find these days that my leisure time is precious. I listen to music, mostly jazz, I read or go to the movies. And I travel to exciting places for short breaks and longer holidays, both within Australia and further afield, usually with friends or sometimes with a group that shares my interest in landscape, art and good food.

An example of my favourite kind of weekend with friends was a trip at the beginning of springtime to Beechworth in Victoria with Helen and her husband, Bruce Lagay. My spirits always soar at the beauty of the countryside: brilliant green paddocks, the wattles golden and the new growth on the gumtrees a silvery plum colour. Here and there was a wild prunus; its dainty white blossom on dark wood offers a delightful note among the grey gums. Dinner was at Provenance, where Michael Ryan is the chef. The dish of the night for me was 'Confit artichokes, cured tuna, blood orange, olives and pangrattato', but I also enjoyed his 'Butter sauteed cauliflower, cauliflower puree, mustard sabayon, polenta shortbread crumbs, brown butter jelly'. And last but certainly not least was the delicious strawberry and yoghurt sorbet as part of the strawberry and rhubarb finale. It is such a pleasure to visit the countryside and eat food of such quality. It was not always so.

Another special recent outing was a weekend shared with Maggie and Colin Beer. We were guests of Alla and Alan Wolf-Tasker at their delightful country hotel and restaurant, Lake House, in the Melbourne spa resort of Daylesford. Lake House is lovely at all times of the year, but autumn and early winter are particularly special. We experienced the last of the falling leaves and the early morning mist over the lake, and enjoyed the stinging and bracing clean, cold air that necessitated scarves and layers for a morning walk around the lake, where we met ducks, geese and a purple-chested moorhen. The Daylesford Book Barn at the lake's edge is a treasure house for those interested in fossicking among secondhand books. Both Maggie and I felt we could spend a whole day there, pausing to be reinvigorated with coffee or even soup, also on offer at this remarkable small business.

I bought copies of the Fifth and Sixth *Victorian Readers*, the essential texts for all children of our era. Both books are anthologies of extracts from well-known works. As I picked up these well-worn little books, they felt so familiar. When I opened and read the tables of contents I was amazed at the memories that flooded back. The Sixth *Victorian Reader* opens with the Dorothea Mackellar poem 'My Country'. I can hear the class intoning it in unison. In the Fifth *Victorian Reader* there is Henry Lawson's *The Drover's Wife*, poems by Walter de la Mare and John Shaw Nielson that I have not thought about for more than fifty years but from which I now realise I can still recite lines.

Also on the shelves were two titles from the Billabong series in the original Ward Lock edition that I used to own and treasure in my early teens. I have never forgiven my mother, and am still mystified at her motives, for disposing of my collection of childhood books when I was a young adult travelling overseas. With my books also went my earliest creative efforts – a 'book' set in some fictitious boarding school with full-page drawings by Judith from down the road.

Each year for the last ten years Jean and John Tinney and I have spent a fortnight together at the beach in late January. I get a dose of vicarious grandparent pleasure as Jean's grandchildren join us for a few days. And all of our children drop in and out. Jean and I walk each morning. Sometimes Jean retells the story of a book we have both read and enjoyed but I can no longer recall. Even if I have loved the book I often don't remember it, but if Jean has read it, the story is safe. I am enthralled all over again. No wonder her grandchildren enjoy listening to her tell stories! Both Jean and John love words and can drive me crazy with their shared pedantry, but whenever I stop reacting, I always learn something new.

Sometimes we just enjoy the beach before the sun is high. I love its endless sweep, the slow creaming swell and the slap and suck of the waves. Sandworms push up their casts, seaweed strands leave an intricate pattern in the sand. Sometimes there are sleek black-clad surfers paddling or skimming the waves. Sometimes we pass another walker, or a dog. It is a wonderful way to empty the mind and just be.

I do love books and although I now use Google for information or to confirm a fact, I will never abandon my authoritative works, especially those where there is a significant 'voice' that adds to the pleasure. I read the newspaper online but am still seduced many mornings by the crispness of the paper copy. It is rare that I miss the evening news broadcast and often remember Dad at such times. It was always a sacred hour; we always knew never to telephone our parents between seven and eight p.m. until the *ABC News* and the *7.30 Report* were over. But I do read.

If I have a trip coming up I try to read something that will fill in a few basic facts but also communicate important atmosphere. Before a recent food tour of Sicily I reread *Midnight in Sicily* by Peter Robb, a terrifying account of mafia activity and its consequences. For a bit more about the food and the atmosphere I reread the lovely book by Mary Taylor Simeti *On Persephone's Island*. The maker of spleen sandwiches in Cefalu (ricotta, spleen and juice, lemon and grated matured ricotta – evil-looking and black) was one of the first to refuse to pay the *pizzo*, the payback to the Mafia. Our guide said he still has a bodyguard.

For another perspective on Sicilian history I loaded *The Leopard* by Giuseppe di Lampedusa onto my iPad for reading on the plane. Somehow I had never read this classic story before, and after the Sicilian holiday I remembered the line 'bougainvillea cascaded over the gates like swags of episcopal silk'. And it did too.

Still in Sicily was an adventure involving a long drive into the Madonie Mountains to visit three shepherds and watch them making their ricotta and *caciocavalla* cheese, the milk heated in copper cauldrons set into a permanent fireplace stoked with wood. On the way I saw my first cork oaks, which are stripped every nine years, leaving the raw trunks bright, bright red.

I had a marvellous trip to Mexico with my friend Frances Laurino, former principal of Collingwood College. We wanted to see the Mayan ruins of Palenque and Chichen Itza, but I also wanted to visit the Frida Kahlo Museum at Coyoacan. For a long time I had been intrigued by stories of Frida Kahlo and her relationship with Diego Rivera.

In preparation I had been reading the prize-winning novel *The Lacuna* by Barbara Kingsolver, which I loved. There is a lot of food in this book: chicken escabeche, sweet potatoes mashed with pine-apple, tomato and watercress salad, all mixed up with the politics of revolution and the history of Mexico.

I loved reading the lyrical descriptions of Frida, 'dressed like an Indian bride', always in frilled long skirts, ruffled blouses, her lustrous hair braided with ribbons, and always proudly defiant in spite of her constant pain.

I will never forget Frida's house. Inside and outside the walls were deep blue. The floors were butter-yellow, the doorframes deep green. The rooms were furnished with terracotta cooking pots and small terracotta ornaments, the beds were made up with embroi-dered covers and pillows and here and there were rush-bottomed chairs. And there was a small painted seat that had been made for a three-year old Frida. Paintings by both Frida and Diego hung on the walls. Scattered here and there were Frida-decorated corsets, needed to support her damaged body, and hanging papier-mâché skeletons. Death, fertility and pain were themes evident in this museum. In Frida's studio were brushes, paints, pastels, and an old wheelchair.

My strongest response to Frida and Diego's house was evoked by the colours. I cannot imagine living in a house that is painted white with minimalist furniture. Travelling often leaves me with brilliantly coloured memories, which linger when the details of the historical sights have faded.

Still in Mexico City we visited the Mercado de Jamaica. I watched men and women speedily slicing away the prickles from cactus pads, using a sloping piece of timber (like an old-fashioned washboard) as a chopping board. I wonder if the pads of the prickly pear bushes that are used in Australia by some farmers as effective stock fences, or that grow wild on our river banks, can be prepared and eaten in this way. In Sicily, while I have been served sorbet or granita made from the fruit of the prickly pear and the sliced fruit frequently appeared on the breakfast buffet, I never see the pads being used. It is always so intriguing when one culture uses an ingredient so differently.

Despite these marvellous trips and all the activity associated with being the founder and figurehead of the Stephanie Alexander Kitchen Garden Foundation there are many mornings I wake filled with dread. Dread of what? Rarely is there a definite reason – rather a vague sense of unease, of not wanting to face whatever the day will bring, an awareness of solitude, an unspecified feeling of inadequacy. Also I hurt in various parts of my body these days. My doctor friend Duffy says that if you don't hurt somewhere you're probably dead. Remembering his remark is enough to make me smile and roll out of bed and into the shower. The warm water can be relied upon to chase away the dread for the moment.

Objectively there are increasing signs of advancing decrepitude (My friend Jean Tinney, a researcher into ageing, doesn't like the word but that is what it feels like.) There is considerable wear and tear on my joints. I aim for two gym sessions and one Pilates session every week to delay the decline. My stretched tendons over one hip are similar to a worn-out patch of a pair of jeans, says my physiotherapist. I am still holding together but only just. One result is an inability to stand on one leg (which put paid to my hopes of learning the tango). Walking for more than half an hour becomes painful and I experience some pain going up and down steep steps. (The Great Wall of China in 2002 was a challenge!) The worst pain I experience is after a long session at the computer. I have to crank my body upright and hobble a few steps before smooth movement returns. All of this is, no doubt, the result of thirty-plus years of standing at a bench, chopping, and heaving boxes containing twenty kilos of ducks from the floor to the bench without asking for help. Note to young cooks: think of your back.

I was always secretly pleased with my smooth skin, although I hated the fact it was white and freckled. In my youth I could never tolerate the sun on my face. It would give me a headache very quickly so I sat with my head in the shade and allowed the rest of my body to fry, blister, peel and freckle, hoping for a never-to-be-achieved tan. But now my face is developing creases and the less said about my neck the better.

In writing my story I am surprised by how often I have pursued such ambitious projects. For such a timid creature I have bold and extravagant visions. They range from the ridiculous (to start a duck farm with one lover) to the foolhardy (to start a restaurant without any experience or money, and then do it all over again a few years later!). In my teenage years, without skill or patience, I ruined many a gorgeous piece of crushed velvet, shot silk or heavy lace, convinced I could make elaborate and stunning party frocks for myself. They never worked. I was impatient, refusing to read the instructions properly, and the dresses either fell apart after one wear or were consigned to the rag bag, half-made.

From the earliest days of Stephanie's Restaurant in Brunswick Street I wanted to establish a memorable personal style. Inspired by Liberty's of London the first tablecloths were a sprigged floral cotton, whereas every other smart restaurant had starched white cloths. After a year or so of nightly washing, these pretty but unserviceable cloths fell apart and I insisted that the replacements should be imported from Liberty's. Once Stephanie's moved to grander premises I decided on hand-embroidered white cotton tablecloths from China (with intricate cut-out floral borders that inevitably broke under a commercial iron) and as part of the upstairs renovation in

1989, I set my heart on a hand-loomed carpet of heritage design from Scotland at six times the price of a perfectly usable carpet. Other extravagances included hand-blown glass bowls for the salt, balloon wine glasses, exquisite platters and tureens, and more.

One surprise is that along the way I managed to convince others to support these decisions – well, not the duck farm.

Post-restaurants I have more good days than bad days. I do feel a bit like Pollyanna: I am *glad* I am alive and healthy, *glad* I have something to give back. I do know I have done with the performing; now I am eager to pass on what I know. I find it hard to forget or forgive the few occasions in my life when I have had to cope with calculated unkind behaviour. It is hard to forget but one thing I have learnt is that it is essential to push past hurt and disappointment. My mother always said that just when she thought she had wise counsel to pass on, her children did not want to know, but insisted on finding out for themselves and predictably making some of the same mistakes. In my case I need to ask my children's advice often as, like many other parents, I have been lapped by technology and have to be careful to keep my mind open to so many changes.

My standards for achievement are impossibly high – I am always wanting to raise the bar. And yet I downplay my actual achieve-ments – for what reason? I was named Victorian of the Year in 2010 and I told very few people. I suppose I felt that there were others more worthy of this honour than I. I was more pleased when my latest book, the *Kitchen Garden Companion*, won Best General Cookbook at the annual awards given at the prestigious International Association of Culinary Professionals in Portland, Oregon – a rare acknowledgement of Australian work in a field always dominated by American writers. It also won Best Food Book of the Year at the annual Australian Food Media Awards. And I did love reading that one of my literary heroes, Nigel Slater, voted *The Cook's Companion* one of his five favourite cookbooks.

I wonder if I would have pursued my vision of pleasurable food education for Australian children with such single-mindedness and such energy if I still had a husband or young children who needed more of my attention.

My two greatest achievements are my daughters. Lisa was my flower child. Born in the mid-sixties, an exotic and beautiful little girl, she has grown to be a beautiful woman, who has shown resolve and maturity in acknowledging and overcoming sadness and loss to achieve her present state of happiness and peace. She has a loving partner and is about to begin a new career as a freelance copywriter to add to her skills as a teacher and arts publicist.

She admits that being the daughter of parents with a public pro-file has not always been easy and can sap the confidence of even the most secure individual. But her easy warmth and friendly manner endear her to her friends and mine. She is a loving and sympathetic sister to Holly and has been delighted to connect warmly with her brother, Simon. She is a great eating and travelling companion but we both depend on Holly for help with directions. Although she resembles her father more than me we do sound alike. She is still fascinated by popular culture. She laughs just as her father did and he would have been very proud of her.

Holly's birth coincided with a period of relative relaxation for me and she could count on the full adoring attention of both parents and her big sister. Probably because of this Holly has grown to be confident and sunny-natured. She does look like me and has fol-lowed many of my interests. She has also inherited my prematurely grey hair (I was quite silver by the time I was in my mid-forties), fair skin and blue eyes. These days the colourists are much more skilled and Holly in her thirties is managing to delay the moment when she will have to admit defeat. She is tentatively starting to grow a little of her own food. She loves to travel, enjoys a good book, is a Francophile and writes well. Like me she likes to get in the last word. Also like me she radiates an air of 'I can do it' that can give the false impression of not needing anyone. And she has an amazing laugh.

I think that sometimes Holly might also wish that I did not have such a public profile but I can only shrug when this is mentioned and ask helplessly, 'Well what can I do about it?' But she also admits that now and then there has been a bit of enjoyable reflected glory.

She is a wonderful 'help desk' for any computer problem and an excellent teacher. There is no-one else I know who listens as carefully when I explain what it is that I do not understand and then will carefully and clearly talk me through the solution. She has many good friends but is still to meet her life partner. She is happily working in television as a trainee script writer, has three short films to her credit so far, with her skills as a trained book editor as a very useful back-up.

Perhaps it is best to finish with the story of the Big Seventieth Birthday. There were two celebrations. First came a cocktail party organised by the foundation a few days before the big day, when more than forty colleagues gathered to wish me a happy birthday. I was presented with an extraordinary book of photographs, personal messages and memorabilia that brilliantly captured the past decade. So many highlights. So many events. So many marvellous people.

On Anna Dollard's page is a note I wrote to her on 9 January 2001. It sums me up pretty well:

Morning Anna, Welcome back! Two projects this year. One, I really want to look into trialling some sort of gardening and cooking scheme in a school. Two – I think I need a website.

Not sure what they are but everyone says I need one? Talk later. Back 12. (Leftovers in fridge – testing white zucchini.) Stephanie

Oh dear, I can be so direct, but as Nina Simone sings, my 'intentions are good'.

In preparation for the big birthday party I booked a massage and bought a new party dress. I intended to head off looking my best, feeling great, and looking forward to seeing so many friends.

The party was a triumph and ninety guests had a fabulous time. My daughters were magnificent and masterminded surprise after surprise, assisted by my friends Kate Doyle and Tony Tan. It was held at Rippon Lea, a wonderful mid-nineteenth century mansion converted into a delightful reception venue. The tables were decorated exquisitely by friend and foundation board member Prue Gill with old-fashioned roses gathered from gardens near and far; the table wreaths were created by the children from two of our schools; and there were bowls of loquats and lemons to represent my love of an edible garden. A mystery guest, performer Eddie Perfect, sang a song he composed just for me:

Everybody's Got to Eat
There you go, Mary Burchett, seems it was worth it back
    there at the start
The legacy flows from that kitchen in Rosebud where
    food was your art
There the table was laden with hot conversation and
    ideas to win
Politics blaring and people still there when the light
    flooded in
There were rabbit pies and clear blue skies and sea

And a childhood for her children there both idyllic and free
She said, 'Oh, everybody's got to eat.'

The late Mary's daughter sailed 'cross the water, left
    libraries behind
The maker of lists she just couldn't resist what was out
    there to find
She'd be battered and burnt but she'd march on till her
    self-named restaurant was found
Mary's passion and love amplified through her just as
    a microphone amplifies sound
Everything with a beginning, middle and end
She could work hard, play hard, barely sleep then do it all
    again
She said, 'Oh, everybody's got to eat.'

Constant creation the vast conversation of friends
Everything with a beginning a middle and end
Textures and flavours and wine bottle saviours and art
Everything with an ending a middle and start.

And it's so hard and it's so good
And it's so subtle and strong sat round the table
And it's so late and it's so long
And it's you notating the truth
The absolute proof
Writing down the pages
At every stage
She said, 'Oh, everybody's got to eat.'
And it's simple and complex as that
'Everybody's Got to Eat'

Stephanie Alexander, the cook's companion, the mother,
   the teacher, the echoing sound
Proof from above that if you're given love then you share
   it around.

Diana and I both confessed to feeling a bit teary at this point.

Holly trawled through many old images and video interviews to create a brilliant docu-drama; it included video messages from old friends such as Ursula Chamberlain (now Ursula Kalt) from my Tours days, who now lives in Florida; Lisa's cousin Ken Montague from Toronto; and Jamie Oliver from London. Lisa engaged her friend Ken Schroeder to appear with his twenty-piece big band, The Moovin' and Groovin' Orchestra. Lisa and Holly both helped with the research so that the clever Hotham Street Ladies could create one hundred tiny edible sculptures, each one topping a delicious cupcake made by friend and former alumni of Stephanie's, Nat Paull. The sculptures included tomatoes on toast, baby Lisa and baby Holly wrapped in their blankets, red shoes, the French boat, the Jamaican flag, Rosie the chocolate poodle, fresh asparagus, madeleines, the cover of *The Cook's Companion*, a chunk of cheese, a cook's knife, gumboots and more . . . A mix of very personal references (the French boat) and known facts (the covers of my books), and some that had most people guessing.

Andrew McConnell created the stunning food accompanied by lovely wines from Yabby Lake vineyard. My only request to Andrew had been to include crab and squab pigeon. The suckling pig course was a delicious surprise.

On my sixtieth birthday I remember making a solemn speech that mentioned loss and mourning for past youth. I don't feel like that ten years on: I accept the gulf between me and the young. Actually, it is sometimes a relief. But I am reminded of it most days as I cope more or less well with technology. The saddest change has been the gradual loss of flexibility and the creaks and aches in my back and hips.

However, I knew that once I heard music I would find that I could still dance! It was quite simply the best party I have ever been to. I danced and danced and was not even a tiny bit stiff the next morning.

As I write this on the first day of my seventy-first year I wonder with some trepidation as well as curiosity what the next decade will bring.

Good health, I hope. And the energy to continue to support efforts to ensure that every Australian child is able to experience a pleasurable food education. And more opportunities to enjoy special times, good food and special places with my amazing friends. Above all else is my commitment to my precious girls. Follow your dreams. I will be there to support you and I will cherish you as long as I live.

Acknowledgements

Once again I must thank my friend and publisher, Julie Gibbs, for her trust and belief in my work. From my first rather tentative beginnings she encouraged me to pursue this project and made sure that I had wonderful people to assist me. Sandy Webster helped with the first manuscript report and I valued the initial read-through by then Publishing Manager Ingrid Ohlsson. Editorial Project Manager Jane Morrow then came on board and we have worked together most enjoyably to improve and polish the manuscript. I am especially grateful to Jane for pushing me when necessary to dig deeper into my memory for more detail and another story. Both Nicola Young and Nicole Abadee also helped editorially. The elegant design is the work of Evi Oetomo and Daniel New and the production by Tracey Jarrett.

I am grateful for the careful and meticulous eye of my Personal Assistant, Katie Barnett, and for the read-through of the manuscript by my daughters and certain of my closest friends.

Writing my memoir has been a fascinating project. It has involved lots of cross-checking and a great deal of introspection. At the end of the day my life has been about family, food and friendship. My warmest thanks go to all of my friends and family, especially my two daughters. We must all gather around a table together soon.

Index

A Shared Table 319
Abbotsford Convent
  building 306
Abdulla, Ian 319
acacia fritters 192
Accademia Gallery, Venice
  248–9
ackee 104
Adrià, Ferran 324
Agaricus xanthodermus 34
Age, The 217, 231, 267
Akelarre restaurant
  326–7
Alawa Primary School
  311–12
Aldor, Christine 45
Alexander, Holly
  (daughter)
  at grandfather's death
    294
  at Stephanie's
    Restaurant 154, 196,
    201, 245, 288
  birth of 133–4
  childcare for 143,
    153–5, 164, 175–6
  current projects 348
  docu-drama by 351

education 175, 181,
  226, 230, 259, 262–3
food preferences 176,
  181, 218, 297, 302–3
friendships 201, 225–6,
  227
overseas travel 136–8,
  157, 233, 246–8, 285,
  295, 297, 303
relations with father
  156, 182, 238–9, 242,
  246, 258–9
resemblance to 106
Alexander, Margaret
  (mother-in-law) 128
Alexander, Maurice
  (husband)
  arguments with 129–30,
    163–4, 178–9, 187
  career 131, 134, 144–5
  marriage to 126–38
  overseas travel with
    136–8, 165–72, 194,
    200, 228
  relations with daughters
    129, 133–4, 155–6,
    246, 258
  romance with 126–30

separation from 237–43
Alexander, Robyn 136
Alexander, Stephanie *see
  also* cooking; education;
  health issues; Kitchen
  Garden Foundation;
  library work; sexual
  relationships;
  Stephanie's Restaurant
  early life 16, 31, 51
  education 18
  friendships 333–5
  journalism by 208,
    216–17
  marries Maurice
    Alexander 131–2
  marries 'Monty' 99–105,
    118–22
  overseas travel 69–86
  seventieth birthday party
    348–52
Alice Springs 320–3
Annie Smithers' Bistrot
  248
Arzak, Juan 324
Atkins, Ian 70, 92, 247
au pair work in Paris
  80–6

Au Trou Gascon restaurant 230
Australian cuisine 7–8
Australian Food Media Awards 346
Australian Gourmet 3, 206, 222
Australian House & Garden 3
Australian Labor Party 13–14, 24
Australian Security and Intelligence Organisation 30, 32
Australian Tourism Commission 249, 329

Backwell, David 184
Bali holiday 130–1
Ballarat, Victoria 11–12, 26
Banksia Park 33, 39–40, 134–5
Barry, Ange 314
Barwon Heads beach house 238
BBC, work for 86, 88
Beaulieu-Sur-Mer 137, 166
Beauvilliers restaurant 230
Beechworth, Victoria 316–18
'beef on a string' 180
Beer, Colin 211–12, 277, 280–1, 285, 296, 328, 340
Beer, Maggie
  advice from 286–7
  chicken dishes 332
  cooking school with 183, 284–5
  first meetings with 211–12
  speech by 291
  television appearances 314
  travels with 277–8, 280, 296, 328, 332, 340–1

Beer, Saskia 314
Bell, Emily (grandmother) 9, 21, 271
Bell, John (grandfather) 9, 20–1
Bell, Mary Elizabeth (mother)
  childcare provided by 176
  cooking by 34, 41–6
  disposes of books 341
  early life 9–11
  financial support from 173–4
  gardening interests 28
  health issues 21–2
  houses owned by 26–9, 32–3, 219
  legacy of 4
  marries Winston Burchett 14–15
  on childraising 356
  overseas travel 36–7, 279–80
  relations with 49–51, 101
  writings by 1, 3–4, 219, 222
Bennelong restaurant 150
Bennett, Shannon 320
Berowra Waters Inn 150, 161, 184
Best Food Book awards 274, 346
Best General Cookbook award 346
Betty (mother's cousin) 10–11, 21, 265
Bilson, Gay 150, 160–1, 252
Bilson, Tony 117–18, 160–1
Bocuse, Paul 140
Bon Goût restaurant 161
Bonnici, Elena 184–5, 284, 289

Boothby, Brooke 135, 173
Boothby, Peter 135
Bowdern, Mark 183, 283, 287
Boxing Day lunches 339
Boyd, Arthur 52–3
Boyd, David 53
Boyd, Merric 53
Bradshaw, Betsy 155, 157, 230–1, 285
brandade 96
Bridge Road Café 281–3
Brillat-Savarin, Jean Anthelme 207–8
Britain, trips to *see also* London, trips to 75–6, 246–8, 298
Brown, Raylene 320, 322–3
Brunswick Street, Melbourne 143
Bryant, Simon 212
Burchett, Amy and Ben 219
Burchett, Caleb (great-grandfather) 14
Burchett, Caleb (nephew) 220
Burchett, Catherine 220
Burchett, Christopher (brother)
  early life 24, 38–9, 56–7, 214
  food choices 303
  in Northern Territory 199, 219–20, 235
  reaction to marriage plans 100–1
  recollections of Monty 106
Burchett, Clive (uncle) 12, 16, 39, 56, 135
Burchett, Diana (sister)
  at father's death 294
  at mother's death 220–1
  care of father 256–7

early life 17, 20, 22–4,
31, 36, 37, 50
food choices 303
helps with childcare
113–14
home duties 42
Home Economics
training 56
relations with 22, 50,
101, 148
Burchett, George
(grandfather) 18–19,
25–33, 37, 219
Burchett, Helen (cousin)
39
Burchett, James 14
Burchett, John (brother)
early life 21, 56–7
food choices 303
health issues 38
recollections of Monty
106
settles in Northern
Territory 219, 319
Burchett, Lillian 220
Burchett, Maria 219
Burchett, Molly (aunt)
39, 41
Burchett, Rainer 76, 78,
247
Burchett, Vessa (aunt) 78,
135
Burchett, Wilfred (uncle)
as journalist 19
early life 14
early meetings with 29–32
helps repair house 133
marries Erna Hammer
76–7
opposes Vietnam War
124
overseas travel 61, 69,
136–7
reports on A-bomb
attacks 264
writings by 219

Burchett, Winston (father)
childcare provided by
176
death of 294–5
designs house 14–15
early life 11–15
effect of wife's death on
221–2
family arguments 31
financial support from
117, 121–2, 130,
173–4, 246
health issues 26, 40–1,
222, 243, 256–8, 333
life of documented 2–3
love of books 5, 13, 36
marries Mary Bell 14–15
moves to Mornington
Peninsula 219
moves to Rosebud West
25
on Wilfred Burchett 32
overseas travels 14–15,
69
pride in family writings
219
relations with 23, 101
takes Canberra position
20
wine purchases 44–5
Work for Australia–
Refugee Council 77
Bush Food and Wild Food
Festival 320–3
'bushlava' 320

Café De La Mairie 297
Canals, Jack and Josie 159
caravan park 33, 39–41,
134–5
Carrier, Robert 203
Carved Angel restaurant
247
Castellani, Robert 184
Catholic Church, family
attitudes to 30

Cato family 177
Chaine Des Rôtisseurs
restaurant 179
Chamberlain, Ursula
95–9, 351
Chaney, Lisa 252
Changing 116
Chapel, Alain 140,
169–71
Cheese Club 282
Cheong Liew 209–10
Chester, Kathy see Wright,
Kathy Chester
Chez Panisse restaurant
250–1, 303–4
Chong, Elizabeth 44
Christian (lover) 74
Christianity, attitudes to
48–9
Claringbold, Cath 184
Clarke, Marcus 294
Claude's restaurant 149
Clemens, Angela 123–4,
148, 157, 183, 217, 281,
285, 296, 328
Clemens, Duffy 157, 285,
296, 328, 344
Colette 229–30
Collingwood College
304–6, 309–13
Cook and the Chef, The 212
cooking see also food,
interest in; seafood
at Les Frères Troisgros
191–4
at Mietta's restaurant
142
at Stephanie's Restaurant
145–6, 190
Boxing Day lunches 339
by mother 41–6
cuisine bourgeoise 157
early achievements 53–4
French 72, 82–4, 96–7
Jamaican 91–3, 104–5,
113–14

pub meals 128–9
Saturday afternoon
sessions 125
*Cooking & Travelling in
South-west France* 295–6
Cook's Companion, The
267–76, 287, 298, 346–7
Cooper, Sonia 183, 283
Corones, Anthony 209
Cousins, Jenny 150
cuisine bourgeoise 157
Cuisine Et Vins De France
160
cuisine gourmande 160
Cull, Sandy 271–2

Da Fiore, Venice 234
Dandenongs, holidays in
129
Dara, Dur-é 215
as employee 151–2,
159–60, 182
business partnership
with 240–2, 243,
245–6, 260, 263, 274
friendship with 215,
239–40
David, Elizabeth 41–2,
189, 205–6, 216, 247,
251–2
Desailly, Julian 150
Dessaix, Robert 336
di Lampedusa, Giuseppe
342
Disher, David 315
Dollard, Anna 282–3,
287–90, 296, 304–8,
319, 348
Dowd, Justin 184
Doyle, Kate 314, 349
Drakeford, Arthur 20
Dunkeld, Victoria 328
Dunstan, Don 209

*East Melbourne, 1837–
1977:* 174

East Melbourne, Burchett
family moves to 132
East Melbourne Group
174
East Melbourne Walkabout
174
Eating Out in Melbourne
140
Edible Schoolyard Project
303–4
education
Bachelor of Arts degree
107
Frankston High School
46–8
Red Hill school 46
Rosebud High School
47, 54–5
Rosebud Primary School
37
University of Melbourne
58–64, 67–8
elBulli restaurant 324
elderflowers 277–8
Eleven Deadly Sins, The
261–2
Eltham Barrel restaurant
156
English teaching work 94–8
Epicurean magazine 208,
216–17
Essendon, Victoria 16, 18
Evans, Len 161
Evans, William 183, 226,
233
'Everybody's Got to Eat'
349–51

Fanny's and Glo Glo's
restaurant 139
Feast of Pheasant 204–5
Fenwick Street house
130–2
Ferguson's Bakery 109
feuilletage 190–4
filet à la ficelle 180

fish *see* seafood
Fitzgerald, Ross 262
foie gras 170
fonds de veau 190–4
food *see also* cooking;
seafood
at university 65
Australian 198–200
children and 301–3
French 82, 96–7, 166
Jamaican 104–5,
113–14
journalism about 217
ongoing love of 338–9
specialist produce
158–60
suppliers 319
tripe 253–4
Fothergill, Craig 183
France
ambitions to live in 69
holidays in 136–7,
163–72, 228, 248,
259, 295–8
trips to Paris 80–5,
228–30, 297–8
working in 94–8, 102,
190–4
Frankston High School
46–8
*French Menu Cookbook,
The* 200
French Provincial Cooking
189
Friendship 293
Fringe Benefits Tax Act
244
Fulton, Margaret 42

gardening interests 337–8
Garzoni, Giovanna 278
Gault, Henri 140
Geelong Grammar School
56–7
Georges Blanc restaurant
230

Georgian House 45
Gertie (friend) 92–3
Gibb, Viva 183
Gibbs, Julie 270–1, 274, 277, 281, 282, 285, 295–6
Gill, Prue 349
Gilmore, Peter 329
Glenloth Game 159
Good, Joyce 52–3
Good, Malcolm 51–4, 108, 157, 216, 230–1, 285
Good, Malcolm Snr 52–3
Good, Tansy 143, 148, 149–50, 270
'Good Weekend' 217
Gourmand World Cookbook Awards 274, 296
Great Chefs' Dinners 190, 214
Great Depression 12–13
Greece, hitchhiking to 94–5
Green Pastures, The 63
'Greenslopes' house 26–8, 57
Grey, F. Millward 10
Gribble, Diana 269
Griffiths, Simon 284, 296
Guérard, Michel 140, 160
guinea fowl 170–2
Guy Savoy restaurant 230

Hall, Jerry 195–6
Hammer, Erna (aunt) 76–9, 86–7, 93, 102
Harney, Bill 235
Harold Mitchell Foundation 308
Hawthorn, Victoria 172–3, 177–8, 242
Hazan, Marcella and Victor 234
health issues
arthritis 185

broken arm 22–3
deafness 333–5
depression 114
dermatitis 112
pregnancies 92, 107, 109–10, 132–3
restaurant injuries 186
sunburn 23–4
Henderson, Fergus 298
Henley Beach, Victoria 9
Hewitson, Iain 195
Hitchin, Tony 216–17
Hodgson, Randolph 282
Holland, Louise 311
Home Beautiful magazine 208, 216
'Homeville' house 115–16, 125
Hong Kong Food Festival 202–4
Hosking, Richard 263–4
Hotel Londres y de Inglaterra 326
Hotham Street Ladies 351
Howqua River Camp 128–9
Hunter, Dan 328
Hyatt Hotel Group 204

Indigenous foods 319–23
Inn on the Park, London 205
International Association of Culinary Professionals 346
International Olive Council 254–5
Ireland 254
Italy
cookery school in 183, 277–8, 284–5
trips to 138, 228, 230–4, 277–9, 342

Jacobson, Howard 133
Jagger, Mick 195
Jamaica 103–6, 293–4

Jamaica House 106–12, 117–18, 121–2, 225
Jamin restaurant 230
Japan, trips to 10–11, 36–7, 263–5
John Downie crabapples 247–8
John Gardiner High School 175
Johnson, Matthew 275
Judith (friend) 33, 47, 341

Kahlo, Frida 342–3
Kalkardi Mignonnes 322
Kalt, Richard 97
Katherine Dunham Dancers 51
katsuobushi 264–5
Kennan, Jim 149
King, Truby 16
Kirby, Michael 149
Kitchen Garden Companion 278, 338, 346
Kitchen Garden Cooking with Kids 307–8
Kitchen Garden Foundation 246, 304–13
Kleinhenz, Christoph 183, 198, 231
Knox, Tony 141–2, 144, 195
Kosky, Lynne 307
Kristen (friend) 109, 111–12
Kyritsis, Janni 150–1, 159, 162–3, 183–4, 202, 210, 252, 270

La Boqueria 325
La Cuisine 229–30
La Physiologie Du Goût 207–8
La Pomme d'Or restaurant 118

INDEX

La Pyramide restaurant
167–8
Lacuna, The 343
Lagay, Bruce 226, 339
Lake House restaurant 340
L'Ambroisie restaurant 230
Latin restaurant,
Melbourne 66
Laurino, Frances 304–5,
342
Lawrence, Lorrie 290
Le Beaucet restaurant 336
Le Carré Des Feuillantes
restaurant 230
Le Grand Véfour
restaurant 229
Le Pont De L'Ouysse
restaurant 296
Le Pré Catelan restaurant
230
Leibler, Arnold Bloch 306
Les Frères Troisgros
restaurant 168–9,
191–4
Les Prés d'Eugénie
restaurant 230
Liberal Party of Australia
19
Liberty's of London 345
library work
as a profession 58
at Preston Technical
College 106–7
at Princes Hill
Secondary College
118, 122–3, 131, 134
by Winston Burchett 174
early involvement in 56
in London 86, 88
indexing and 275
Lightning Brothers 235
Lindsay, Geoff 184, 250,
270, 289
Little, Graham 127, 134,
136–7, 224, 261, 292–3,
295

Little, Jenny 127, 134,
136–8, 224, 275, 291,
292
Little, Jessica 224, 292
London, trips to 75–6, 86,
88–9, 205
Lortz, Peter 183, 284–5
Lous Landès restaurant
230
Lucas Carton restaurant
230
Lung Wah Restaurant,
Hong Kong 203–4
Lyn (college friend) 70,
115

Ma Gastronomie 168
Manfredi, Stefano 316–17
marsh samphire 199
Massoni, Leon 139
MasterChef Australia
313–14
McConnell, Andrew
317–18, 351
McLean, Valerie 283
McNeilly, Andrew 183
McPhee, Hilary 269
Meehan, Betty 209
Melbourne 6–7, 55, 65–6,
139–40, 158, 195
Melbourne Food & Wine
Festival 329
Menus for Food Lovers 267
Mercado de Jamaica 343
Messageries Maritimes
69–71
Mexico, trip to 342–3
MG Garage restaurant 150
Midnight in Sicily 342
Mietta's restaurant 141–2
Milburn, Ian 159, 199
Millau, Christian 140
Milligan, Tom 184, 186
Mionnay restaurant 169–71
molecular gastronomy
324

Molly (travelling
companion and
housemate) 93
shares apartment 79–80,
85, 89
travelling with 71–3,
75, 94–5
'Monsieur' (employer)
80–5
Montague, Ken 224, 293,
351
Montague, Lee 249
Montague, Lisa (daughter)
at grandfather's death
294
birth of 110
bridesmaid at second
wedding 131–2
business partnership
with 281
career 262, 308
current projects 347
documentary on Wilfred
Burchett 32
early life 50, 57, 111,
113–6, 118, 120–2,
182
education 124–5, 153,
155, 175–6
father's illness and death
214–16
food choices 181
marriage 293–4
overseas travel by 135–6,
157, 164, 224–5,
246–9, 285, 324–7
relations with father
135–6, 156
relations with stepfather
127–9, 238–9
Montague, Mervyn 103,
249
Montague, Rupert *see*
Monty
Montague, Simon 156,
214, 216, 293–4

Montague, Spurgeon 102, 293
Montague, Volney 102–3
Montague family 103
Monte Carona 277–9
Monty (husband)
    arrival in Australia with 106–19
    at family home 57
    first encounters with 89–93
    illness and death 213–16
    Lisa's relations with 124–5
    marriage to 99–105, 118–22
    new partner 156
Moran, Sean 253
Moulin de Mougins restaurant 167
'Mr Mulot' 297
Mugaritz restaurant 328
multiculinarism 209
Murray, Angus, Fiona and Virginia 227–8
Murray, Helen Pyke 8, 59–60, 64, 68, 116, 121, 132–3, 142–3, 148, 155, 157, 214–15, 225, 226, 228, 339
Murray, Jim 132–3, 157, 215, 225, 226, 228

Natoli, Basil 304–5
Neal's Yard Dairy 282
Nehru of India 3
New Book of Middle Eastern Cookery 206
New Caledonia, trips to 72, 157
'new gastronomy' 6–7, 324, 328–31
Newton-John, Olivia 63
Nieuwenhuysen Report 140

Nolan, Dee 328, 331
Noma restaurant 331
North Queensland holidays 226–7
Northcote house 132, 153
Northern Territory, trips to 16, 235–6
nouvelle cuisine 140–1, 146, 160, 324–7, 329–30

O'Donnell, Mietta 141–2, 144
Oldways Preservation Trust 254–5
Oliver, Jamie 311, 351
Oliver, Raymond 229–30
Olney, Richard 196, 200–1
Olympic Games, Melbourne 55
On Persephone's Island 342
Ossie (friend) 94, 101
'Other Half, The' 1
Oxford Food Symposiums 207, 254

Pallett, Steven 150, 184
Paris, trips to 80–5, 228–30, 297–8
Parish of St Elizabeth, Jamaica 103
Pasteleria Escribá 325
Patey, Julie 183
Patrick, Jan 47, 54
Patsy (travelling companion) 71–2, 75
Paull, Nat 351
pearl oyster meat 199
Pellegrini's restaurant, Melbourne 66
Penguin Books 271–5, 298
Penny (niece) 256
Perfect, Eddie 349–51
Perry, Neil 289–90

Peter (boyfriend) 54, 63–5, 68
Pheasant Farm restaurant 211, 287
Phillips, Franz 63
pigeons, twice-cooked 203–4
Pignolet, Damien 149, 153, 222–3, 238
Pignolet, Josephine Carroll 149, 222–3, 238
pimientos de padrón 325
Pizzaiola family 143
Pizzey, Caroline 272
Place des Vosges 84
Point, Fernand 167–8
pommes maxim 193
Poowong, Victoria 11, 14
Port Olimpic 325
Portobello Road markets 93
Potts, Michael 184
Poverty Lunch 253
Pralus, Monsieur 193–4
prickly pear 343–4
Prince Edward Island 262–3
Princes Hill Primary School 155
Princes Hill Secondary College 118, 121, 122, 131, 134, 143, 175
Priscilla (college friend) 70
Prix La Mazille 296
Provenance restaurant 339–40
Pyke, Helen see Murray, Helen Pyke

Quay restaurant 329
Queen Victoria Market, Melbourne 6–7, 158
Quinn, Simone 185, 270

Recipes My Mother Gave Me 45–6

Red Hill, school at 46
Reid, Margaret 17–20, 23
Reid, Preston 256
Reid, Robert 17–18
religion, family attitudes
    to 48–9
restaurants *see names of*
    restaurants
Richmond, Katy 62
Richmond Hill Café &
    Larder 281–3, 301,
    308–9
Riemer, Nicole 184
rillettes 96
Rippon Lea, Victoria 349
Rivera, Diego 342–3
Robb, Peter 342
Robinson, Robert 177
Roden, Claudia 206, 252
Rogalsky, Adriana 195
Rogalsky, Tony 195
Romaneix, Daniel 200, 218
Roper, Myra 61, 68
Rosa (dishwasher) 185–6
Rose (friend) 113–14
Rosebud, Victoria 24–6,
    37, 47, 54–5, 132
Rosie (dog) 258–9, 299,
    351
Rothbury Estate 161, 190,
    214
Roxon, Sally 184
Roy (friend) 97
Royal Mail Hotel Dunkeld
    328
Rush, Geoffrey 210
Ryan, Michael 340

salade de roquette 170–2
Salade Tahitienne 73
Salvation Army Daycare
    Centre, Northcote 143,
    153–4
San Pellegrino Restaurant
    Guide 331
San Sebastián, Spain 326

Santich, Barbara 253
saumon a l'oseille 168–9
Schneider, Faye 139, 144,
    195
Schneider, Hermann 55,
    139, 144, 158, 163, 195
School of Fine Arts, North
    Adelaide 10
Schroeder, Ken 351
seafood
    catching and preparing
        fish 33
    in France 184, 191–2,
        194–5
    in Spain 325–6
    in Vietnam 265–6
    'jellied seascape' 210
    marrons 199
    seafood 'rock pool'
        202–3
    supplies of 159
Searle, Phillip 209–10
Sedlak, Erich and Magda
    77
Sedlak, Eva 78, 89–92
Sessions, Bob 271
seventieth birthday party
    348–52
Sexton, Regina 254
sexual relationships *see*
    also Alexander, Maurice;
    Monty 64–5, 73–5,
    84–6, 334
Shared Table, A 319
Shing, Gabrielle 184
Shipperbottom, Mr 254
Sicily, trip to 342
Simeti, Mary Taylor 342
Sistine Chapel 233
Slater, Nigel 347
Smark, Peter 140
Smith, John 183, 242
Smith, Yvonne 241
Smithers, Annie 184, 201,
    248, 270, 331
snail farming 200–1

'Snips, Snails and Tails'
    evening 210–11
Society Restaurant,
    Melbourne 65–6
soufflé à la suissesse 200
Southgate, John 328
Spain, trips to 324–7
St John restaurant 298
Staley, Blyth and Gloria
    139, 195
State Library of Victoria
    36, 288
Stein, Rick 247
Stephanie Alexander and
    Maggie Beer's Tuscan
    Cookbook 285
Stephanie Alexander
    Kitchen Garden project
    see Kitchen Garden
    Foundation
Stephanie's Australia 199,
    235, 249–50
Stephanie's Feasts and
    Stories 251, 267–8
Stephanie's Journal 257,
    285–6, 290
Stephanie's Menus for Food
    Lovers 218–19, 221–2
Stephanie's Restaurant
    absences from 283
    awards for 206
    cooking for 202–3
    crises at 152–3, 198
    decision to close 285–91
    financial difficulties
        239–40, 244
    heritage constraints 245
    in the eighties 188–90,
        194–8
    material from archived
        288
    menus from 218–19,
        260–1
    moves to Hawthorn
        174–6, 177–9
    openings 142–54

34 ,3 42–45–

operating 187, 345–6
ownership changes 243–4, 274
recipes from 270
renovations 172, 245
suppliers for 318–19
Stephanie's Seasons 206, 249–50, 268
Stroschien, Brian 183
Studd, Will 281, 296
Subijana, Pedro 326–7
Sue-Ellen (staffer) 186
surveillantes 96
Sutton, Laine 328
Symons, Michael 207, 209
Symposium of Australian Gastronomy 207–11, 246, 252–3, 316–18
Szava, Anna 322

Tahiti 72–3
Tahitien 69–71
Taillevent restaurant 230
Tan, Tony 265–6, 349
Tansy's restaurant 150
Tasting Australia 324
tea ceremony 265
teaching children 3
The... *see under second word*, e.g. *Cook's Companion, The*
Thompson, Peter 3
Through My Kitchen Door 45–6
Tinney, Catherine 115, 225, 259
Tinney, Jean Watters
  first meetings with 59–61
  friendship with 157
  helps with childcare 115, 157
  Lisa stays with 225
  marries John Tinney 64, 92
  Paris apartment 222, 228
  research into ageing 344

return to Australia 115
return to Europe 121
travels with 68, 99, 100, 102, 229, 341
Tinney, John 64, 92, 94, 99, 100, 102, 115, 157, 171, 213, 222, 225, 228, 231–2, 341
Tinney, Michael 115
Tolarno French Bistro 139
Tom (boyfriend) 65, 70
Tony (major-domo) 284–5
Topsy Restaurant, Melbourne 66
'Towards a sensual food life' 246
Tripe de Luxe Restaurant and Tea Room 254
Troisgros, Jean 140, 190, 192–3
Troisgros, Olympe 194
Troisgros, Pierre 140, 192–4
Troisgros restaurant 168–9
Tunisia, trip to 255
Turner, Hilary 46
Turner, Mary 46
Twilight of Love 336
Two Faces restaurant 139, 144

Ullmann, Liv 116
University of Melbourne 58–64, 67–8

Vergé, Roger 140, 167
Victoria Street Melbourne 159
Victorian of the Year Award 346
Victorian Readers 340–1
Vietnam, trip to 265–6
Vietnam War protests 124
Vigano family 141
Vincent, Ange 321
Vlassopoulos, Jim and Melita 117, 225, 230–1

Voice magazine 226
Votavova, Irena 201
Vue de Monde restaurant 320

Waitrose Food Illustrated 274
Walnut Tree restaurant 247
Wane, Brian 183, 283
Wardaman people 235
Waters, Alice 250–1, 303–4
Watson, Barrington and Gloria 103–4
Watters, Jean *see* Tinney, Jean Watters
Westgarth Primary School 311, 313
Whiting Caprice restaurant 139
Whole Beast, The: Nose to Tail Eating 298
William Angliss College 150
Wilson, Jeff 184, 283
Wine and Food Society of Australia 161, 329
Wolf-Tasker, Alla and Alan 340
World Food Media Awards 274
World War II 16–17
Worrell, Frank 100
Wright, Bruce 157, 213
Wright, Kathy Chester 60–1, 68, 130, 157, 213, 224–5

Yabby Lake vineyard 351
Yarrunga, Victoria 305
Yves (lover) 74

Zanetti, Mara and Maurizio 234
Zuni restaurant 250